Contents

Acknowledgements

One of the effects of the changing conditions of teachers' work in recent years is that it has become even more difficult for them to accommodate research in their schools. Teachers' voices are being silenced in this respect at a time when it is even more imperative that they be heard. I am especially grateful, therefore, to the teachers who took part in the research on which this book is based. I would particularly like to thank Dave Howard, Patricia Berkeley, Susan Humphries, Susan Rowe, Gillian King, Gill Winterson and Peter J. Woods. They have given generously of their time and hospitality while working in difficult circumstances. I hope they gain some professional satisfaction and reward from the final product.

I have benefited from many discussions with my colleagues on the 'Creative Teaching' research team: Bob Jeffrey, Peter Wenham and Geoff Troman. Peter did the fieldwork for, and co-authored, Chapter 5. Many people have commented on parts of the book in one form or another, as conference paper, journal article or draft paper, some of them anonymously. My thanks to all of them, and particularly to Jennifer Nias, Andy Hargreaves, Martyn Hammersley, and Andrew Pollard; also to Shona Mullen, of the Open University Press, for some important points on the final manuscript. I have received valuable secretarial services from Sheila Gilks, Yvonne Wooster, Jan Giddings and Aileen Cousins. As ever, Kath has provided me with indispensable moral support.

Chapters 2, 3, 4, 5 and 6 draw on articles previously published, and I am grateful to the editors and publishers for permission to use them here. They are:

CREATIVE TEACHERS IN PRIMARY SCHOOLS

Peter Woods

Open University Press
Buckingham · Philadelphia

Aug 95

To Rebecca, with love
Wishing you a self-fulfilling career in teaching

Open University Press
Celtic Court
22 Ballmoor
Buckingham
MK18 1XW

First Published 1995

A catalogue record of this book is available from the British Library

ISBN   0 335 19313 7 (pb)   0 335 19314 5 (hb)

Library of Congress Cataloging-in-Publication Data
Woods, Peter.
    Creative teachers in primary schools : strategies and adaptations
  / Peter Woods.
        p.   cm.
    Includes bibliographical references and indexes.
    ISBN 0-335-19314-5. — ISBN 0-335-19313 7 (pbk.)
    1. Elementary school teaching—Great Britain.   2. Elementary
  school teachers—Great Britain.   I. Title.
  LA633.W66   1995
  372.11'02—dc20   94–23036
                                                          CIP

Typeset by Dorwyn Ltd, Rowlands Castle, Hants
Printed in Great Britain by Biddles Ltd, Guildford and King's Lynn

'Teachers under siege: Resistance and appropriation in English primary schools', *Anthropology and Education Quarterly*, 25, 3, 1994 (Chapters 2 and 3).
'The charisma of the critical other: Enhancing the role of the teacher', *Teaching and Teacher Education*, 9, 5/6, 1993, pp. 545–557 (Chapter 4).
'Teaching, and researching the teaching of, a history project: An experiment in collaboration', *The Curriculum Journal*, 5, 2, 1994, pp. 133–161 (Chapter 5).
'Managing marginality: Teacher development through grounded life history', *British Educational Research Journal*, 19, 5, 1993, pp. 447–465 (Chapter 6).

Part of the research for this book was conducted with the aid of a grant from the ESRC, Award No. R000 23 3194. I am grateful to the ESRC for its support.

Preface

This book is the product of the third phase of my research in the broad area of 'creative teaching'. During many years of observing teachers at work, I have been aware of a special quality which seems to pervade their best work, to inspire teaching and learning, to maximize learning opportunities, and to cope with difficulties. It enables them to devise 'coping' and 'survival strategies', to adapt to the curriculum, and to manage the conflict in the teacher role. In the first phase, my research in primary schools impressed upon me the extent to which a particular quality informs the actual pedagogy of primary school teachers. I characterized the quality as 'creative teaching'. Its nature, manifestations, effectiveness and attendant conditions were considered in Woods (1990a).

This led me, in the second phase, to consider critical cases of this kind of work. This involved researching a number of outstanding events in primary schools. Analysis of these led to the concept of the 'critical event' (Woods, 1993a). In contrast to routine processes and gradual cumulation of learning, critical events bring radical change in both pupils and teachers. The conditions favourable to their development include a supportive school ethos, certain resources such as time and finance, and critical agents. They also require some flexibility within the curriculum and scope within teachers' working conditions, and I speculated on the chances of critical events and other forms of creative teaching continuing in the National Curriculum, instituted in 1988. I concluded that, at that time, the National Curriculum appeared to be a mixture of opportunity and constraint in that respect.

The third phase, therefore, has focused on creative teaching in the National Curriculum. The aim has been to test and fill out the concept of creative teaching in a wider range of schools, and with teachers working in markedly different circumstances than before 1988. The research has taken two broad directions. One concerns classroom teaching, and the ways in which primary teachers construct atmosphere, employ tone and mood to good effect, and establish common knowledge. Research continues in this area and, it is planned, will be the subject of a future book. The second direction has been about a concern that is prior to classroom teaching, but which is, none the less, closely bound up with it: how teachers create the conditions for their kind of teaching. For creative teachers, the general conditions established by the 1988 Education Reform Act and other attendant legislation seemed markedly unfavourable. The danger is expressed by one primary school head, who deplored the 'straitjacket of the National Curriculum', and the 'dead hand of excessive accountability' which, in his experience, was 'driving creativity out of classrooms' (Harries, 1994). Teachers have also generally had a bad press in recent years, particularly over so-called 'progressive' teaching methods and their alleged responsibility for the supposed 'decline in educational standards'. Despite the difficulties of definition and proof in these areas, the general and strong belief in government circles has been that what is required in education is less freedom of choice and opportunities for creativity, and more prescription and direction. Teacher morale generally is said to be low (Pollard, 1992; Campbell, 1993).

Inevitably, many teachers find it hard to cope with such radical change, and especially with the continuous adjustments to that change that have been a feature of government policy since 1988, and that have added to the general overload, pressure and sense of chaos. But how are particularly creative teachers coping with these problems? How are their perspectives affected by the changes, and what strategies have they devised? Are they finding successful ways of handling them, ways that not only permit them to survive, but also to advance their own interests and aims? If so, might teachers generally learn from their experiences?

These teachers are not opposed to all the reforms. The situation appears to be still one of opportunity and constraint, with a measure of flexibility to negotiate a way between them. Adaptations show a range, from resistance to things teachers are absolutely against to professional enrichment through the National Curriculum. Personal responses also vary on a similar scale, from frustration and despair at one end to achievement and enhancement at the other. I shall examine the nature of these and reasons for the differences. A predominant theme throughout the book is the focus on the teacher's self, and the various ways in which these teachers have sought to determine its constitution and expression within their own conception of professionalism, in the face of the biggest onslaught upon it in their experience. In the main, these are success stories, but they are successful in terms of the teacher's self, which does not always result in gains for the educational system. The teacher featuring in Chapter 6, for example, chose to enhance his self by leaving teaching. Also, whatever success teachers enjoy in establishing conditions favourable to them is always precarious, sustained only by continuing resolution and struggle for what they believe in. Sometimes even that is not enough.

1

Introduction: adapting to intensification

Creative teachers

Who are creative teachers? What distinguishes them? Aren't all teachers creative? Quite the reverse, according to Willard Waller (1932, p. 431), who argued that teaching deadened the intellect, led to a 'reduction of personality', and made teachers unbending, uncreative creatures of routine. His text on *The Sociology of Teaching*, written in 1932, still represents the reality for many. Eggleston (1992, p. 43), for example, in strongly advising students to read it, describes it as 'probably still the wisest book ever written about life in classrooms'. It is a depressing view, and one that has been strongly challenged in some circles as being partial, unsubstantiated and outmoded (see, for example, Jackson, 1992).

I also have found, contrary to Waller's grim picture, that some teachers in English primary schools at any rate seem to have certain creative qualities in abundance. Previous study of their practice (Woods, 1990a) led to the identification of four major components: innovation, ownership, control and relevance. Innovation may extend the boundaries of the conventional. It can result from a new combination of known factors, or from the introduction of a new factor. It may be planned or serendipitous. There are broad aims certainly, but some learning outcomes are unpredictable. The process is as important as the product, being to do with the generation of ideas, which, in interaction with others, then breed more.

The innovation belongs to the teacher concerned. It may be the teacher's own idea, or it may be an adaptation, perhaps in new circumstances, of someone else's idea. It might be generated by an individual alone, or more commonly as a result of collaboration with others. Some novel aspect of the process is produced by the teacher concerned. The teacher has a certain autonomy here, and control of the processes involved. Nias (1989, p. 99) illustrates the personal satisfaction of teachers who reported, 'You're the one who is making it happen at first hand'. However, teachers' efforts need to be attuned to the values of the society in which they take place, and to their pupils' cultures. In other words, they need to be relevant. Teachers can be extremely innovative, but if such innovation is not relevant, they may have the morality of their teaching questioned, or be perceived as self-indulgent. The 'conformity' implied here is a very broad one, applies to no one ideological or political approach, and covers a wide range of views within a democratic society.

Creative teachers need choice, and the power to make it. This applies to their own capabilities and dispositions which empower them through self-knowledge (Powell and Solity, 1990) and qualify them as 'reflective practitioners' (Schön, 1983). As such they are able to see alternatives and to achieve analytical distance from their professional role, continuously evaluating their own performance. Even so, they must still have total practical involvement. Power to make choice also applies to the situation in which they work, and on opportunities being available for them to exercise their personal choice. They are inevitably constrained by systems and structures externally determined and imposed, but creative teachers can, to some extent, affect the situations in which they work, applying their talents to changing or modifying the circumstances and increasing the range of opportunities. They cannot do this without a large measure of commitment to the values they espouse, and strong motivation, and indeed, on occasions, inspiration, in seeing them implemented. Creative teachers seem guided by particular theories of pedagogy and of learning that cut across vague, all-embracing, bipolar concepts such as 'traditionalism' and 'progressivism'. They have holistic perceptions – of the pupil, of learning, and of the curriculum. They are concerned with the affective as well as the cognitive – 'body and mind, feelings and intellect' (Rogers, 1983, p. 141). The pupil is considered as the whole child, and knowledge is indivisible. These teachers are skilled at handling and turning to good use the tensions and dilemmas that pervade primary school life (Nias, 1989). They have a fund of knowledge – of subject-matter, pedagogy and pupils – on which to draw, and a disposition to experiment in finding the optimum means to advance toward their aims. They possess the ability and flair to formulate and act upon hunches, to 'play with ideas', but within a disciplined framework. They have adaptability and flexibility to cope with ever-changing sets of circumstances.

Creative teaching promotes creative learning, that is learning governed by the same principles. There is innovation – pupils are changed in some way, often radically. Christian Schiller (1979), a champion of creative teaching and learning, observed that the most remarkable experience of his working life had been 'to witness the appearance of children's powers which, when I began, we did not know to exist' (1979, p. 78). In this mode, pupils have control over their own learning processes, and ownership of the knowledge produced, which is relevant to their concerns. I have given examples of such teaching that takes place in the everyday world of the primary school in Woods (1990a), and of exceptional educational events in Woods (1993a). I am continuing to explore the nature of creative learning (see, for example, Woods, 1994). The situation has since been radically affected by the National Curriculum, introduced in 1988. In some respects the National Curriculum seemed to require creativity in teaching and learning (see Woods, 1993a; Fryer and Collings, 1993). In other respects, it seemed to inhibit and discourage such approaches, particularly inasmuch as they reflect what has come to be known as 'intensification'. Recent developments in education have given Waller a new lease of life.

Intensification

The opposite of creative teaching is teaching in which teachers have little or no choice but to carry out the dictates of others. In this mode, they are technicians rather than professionals (Schön, 1983). The argument is that they have become deprofessionalized and deskilled as their work has become increasingly intensified. This is a world-wide development affecting all professionals. The theory of intensification (Apple, 1986; 1988) derives from Larson's (1980) discussion of the proletarianization of educated labour. The argument is that as advanced capitalist economies seek to maintain and promote efficiency, so the sphere of work narrows, high-level tasks become routinized and there is more subservience to the bureaucratic whole. At the chalk-face there is more for teachers to do, including a proliferation of administrative and assessment tasks. There is less time to do it in, less time for reskilling and for leisure and sociability, and there are few opportunities for creative work. There is a diversification of responsibility, notably with a high level of specification and direction, and a separation of conceptualization in long-term planning and policy-making (others) and of execution (teachers). There is a reduction in quality of service as corners are cut to cover the ground. The economic depression of the late 1980s and early 1990s brought on crises of accumulation and legitimation which gave an emphatic boost to these developments (Apple, 1988). Technical control processes impinged further upon the curriculum. Centralization, standardization and rationalization became the norm in policy circles. By 1992, there were some areas in the USA where 'it has been mandated that teachers must teach *only* that material which is in the approved text book' (Apple and Jungck, 1992, p. 20).

It is not difficult to find evidence from research done on the effects of the National Curriculum for England and Wales in primary schools to support the intensification thesis. What for some was 'a dream at conception' turned into a 'nightmare at delivery' (Campbell, 1993). It is clear that there has been massive work overload, a loss of spontaneity and an increase in stress, that the sense of 'fun' and caring human relationships has receded in some classrooms, that quantification has replaced qualitative evaluation, that bureaucracy has burgeoned, that some teachers feel that they have lost autonomy and control in the curriculum, that accountability has become a matter of threat (Campbell and Neill, 1990; Winkley, 1990; Acker, 1990; Campbell *et al.*, 1991b; Pollard, 1991; Osborn and Broadfoot, 1992a; Pollard, 1994; Osborn *et al.*, 1994; Pollard *et al.*, 1994). Teachers fear further intrusion into pedagogy (see, for example, Drummond, 1991; Dadds, 1992). Some argue that the way teachers think and feel has also been exploited. They have been caught in the 'trap of conscientiousness' (Campbell *et al.*, 1991a), doing their best to meet the prescribed targets but compromising the quality of learning and their own health. Their inability to meet them all aggravates the 'guilt syndrome' (Hargreaves and Tucker, 1991). If they do manage to meet them and celebrate their accomplishment, this may only be 'misrecognized professionalism' (Densmore, 1987; Apple, 1988). That is to say that teachers may feel more professional through mastering the range of technical criteria and tests accompanying the changes, whereas in reality this skill is yet another example of 'the administrative colonization of teachers' time and space' (Hargreaves, 1990, p. 318).

However, this is only one side of the picture. Pollard (1992; see also Pollard *et al.*, 1994) concluded that, in general, teachers in primary schools accepted the broad terms of the National Curriculum, and were seeking to implement it. The most striking feature of teachers' responses was their acceptance of it. Campbell *et al.*, (1991b, p. 7), in their study of infant school teachers, observed that, though there were serious sources of dissatisfaction, 'our evidence suggests that the imposed change of the National Curriculum, far from de-skilling and de-professionalizing the teachers, was, on the contrary, seen by them as extending their skills and increasing their professionalism'. Campbell *et al.*, (1991a, p. 31) concluded that primary school teachers' hearts and minds had been won over to the principle of the National Curriculum, and that the main issue was now one of manageability.

Manageability, however, was a huge problem, undermining potential support, raising a large number of specific concerns, such as oppressive workloads, increased bureaucracy, the pace of change, and uncertainty about how long a change would last before being modified. There were issues of spontaneity, autonomy, enjoyment, pupil–teacher relations and stress. The new system of assessment was a major problem. In short, the pressures of implementation were in danger of expunging the potentially creative and liberating principles. These findings have been broadly reflected in the Primary Assessment, Curriculum and Experience (PACE) research covering both infant and junior schools (Key Stage 1 and Key Stage 2 in National Curriculum parlance). For example, Osborn *et al.*, (1994) found that, though about 20 per cent of teachers actually felt empowered by the changes, the majority of teachers perceived the impact of the changes on their work and role to be mostly negative, and that by 1993 a growing number of teachers were beginning to feel deskilled. Many of them

> talked of a loss of freedom and creativity in their teaching, of feeling increasingly like 'a machine for delivering a prescribed curriculum', as well as the loss of a career structure, and of doing a valued and worthwhile job (p. 4).

The teachers in the research upon which the present book is based were not dissimilar. A group of 12 teachers from five primary schools in one local authority area selected on the 'creativity' criteria discussed above were consulted. As in the Campbell *et al.*, (1991a) research, these teachers on the whole welcomed the 'structure' and the 'framework' of the National Curriculum, and its 'broadening'. It had encouraged collaborative planning, and targets had sharpened the focus of their work. On the other hand, criticisms were voiced that it was 'an imposition from above', and 'someone else's agenda'; of the greatly increased workload, often – the really exasperating point – for little or no educational gain that they could see. This was especially the case with the new requirements for assessment and recording. Unreasonable as it may be, they did get sudden attacks of anxiety about 'whether we are putting into effect all the legal requirements', and one teacher's 'nightmare is that someone will come into my classroom and tell me I'm doing it wrong . . . We don't need someone breathing over our shoulder, and if anybody is going to do that it ought to be their head'.

Their creativity, they felt, had certainly been affected. There was a compulsion to follow the programme planned and a loss of spontaneity. The most frequent and most regretted aspect of this was the increasing difficulty they were experiencing in finding time to respond to children's initiatives. One teacher commented: 'I've stuck to my plans more rigidly than I have done in the past. It certainly has cut down opportunities for taking an idea and developing it.' His teaching was 'alongside the National Curriculum, not alongside the children now'. All felt very strongly the pressure of time, and the mismatch between demands and their capabilities with existing resources. They felt under enormous pressure 'to get things done', but there was 'always more you can do'. Work had expanded throughout the break and rest moments of the day and deep into their own private time. They felt that, because of the pressures, their teaching methods had been adversely affected. They felt a compulsion 'to cover the ground', and 'not to waste a second'. One teacher reported: 'I find myself clock-watching and thinking, "That's 20 minutes of science time gone!".' Some hinted that they had been forced to adopt more formal teaching approaches. Creativity, according to one, was being diverted:

> There is a kind of creativity in having to select material from a whole list which is not of our making, and having to respond to other people's ideas far more than ever in the past, and that's demanding a kind of creativity which is fairly new to us. Equally there is a sense in which the National Curriculum has rather killed off any sense of creativity, because suddenly there's a prescription that has to be followed.

However, some teachers drew a distinction between government requirements, on the one hand, and classroom strategies and learning methods, on the other. They could use their professional expertise and discretions with the latter. One said that she saw 'professional salvation' in this. Confidence appeared to be a key factor behind the teachers' varying responses. Classroom observation suggested that the most confident teachers were also those who felt less constraint from the National Curriculum, and who felt that 'you can do creatively what you are required to do'. This did not involve sacrificing one's beliefs. One remarked: 'I have arrived at a philosophy of what I feel young children need, and I feel I would not be doing right by my beliefs and my teaching professionalism if I let that go because of the Orders.'

Strategical adaptation

Teacher reactions will be considered in more detail throughout the book. The brief extracts above give the flavour of some responses from the research. They are not unlike others reported among wider samples in other research, and they might be taken to support in some measure the intensification thesis. However, by 1993, some of the teachers in Osborn *et al.*'s (1994) research who had up till then felt they were being deskilled, were 'gaining the confidence to interpret and actively mediate the National Curriculum in ways which suited their own particular ends' (p. 5). They were finding sufficient flexibility to sustain their own programmes through strategical adaptation. Teachers have a record of considerable success in this field. As Troman (1993) points out, centrally devised curriculum development initiatives of the 1960s and 1970s were implemented in schools in different ways than those intended (see also

Murphy and Torrance, 1987). The National Curriculum is a different matter, having the force of law and being part of a body of legislation seeking to change the whole system, with policing mechanisms in place. Even so, there are signs of a similar process occurring. As Ball and Bowe (1992), Osborn and Broadfoot (1992a) and Vulliamy and Webb (1993) have observed, new policies and orders have to be mediated through teachers. 'The ways in which teachers translate new initiatives into practice are dependent upon their prior beliefs and practices' (Vulliamy and Webb, 1993, p. 21). Ball and Bowe (1992, p. 100) suggest that the 1988 Education Reform Act is in one sense 'a micro-political resource for teachers, LEAs and parents to interpret, re-interpret and apply to their particular social contexts'. They see policy not as a 'legislative moment', but as a 'continuing process of engagement, interpretation, and on occasions, struggle'. Similarly, Penney and Evans (1991, p. 4) see educational practice as a 'relational activity' wherein

the actions of individuals not only act upon, and help shape, create, and/or re-create the social and organizational contexts in which they are located, but are also shaped by those contexts and the political, social and cultural influences and constraints which are found within them'

Acker (1990) points out that the teacher creativity going into these adaptations might be seen by some as only occurring in the service of prescribed objectives. This, possibly, aids 'misrecognition'. 'Teachers' creative responses might then be seen as resistances or exploitation of the contradictions inherent in the prescriptions' (p. 6), but Acker is 'loath to discuss their perceptions as false consciousness' (see also Hargreaves, 1992). Their skill 'feels real to them and looks real to me' (p. 270). Acker's (1990, p. 271) head teacher commented: 'If we believe in the things that we've stood for for the last twenty years, we've got to hang in there.' Elsewhere, Hargreaves (1992) has found points for and against the intensification thesis in his study of 'preparation time' in Toronto schools. Certainly teachers' workloads and directed time had increased dramatically. However, he also found that, in some instances, the provision of preparation time provided room for reflection, improved the quality of teachers' planning, and led to a certain amount of *dis*intensification. This does not disconfirm the intensification thesis, but it does suggest that it cannot account for the whole range and complexity of reactions.

Some have noted a range of adaptations to the National Curriculum. Muschamp *et al.*, (1992, p. 9) found a continuum of responses, from acceptance, through adaptation, to rejection of parts of the curriculum. Osborn and Broadfoot (1992a; see also Pollard *et al.*, 1994) have noted that teachers' possible options appear to be: co-operation with the proposed reforms; retreatism; resistance; and incorporation. Most of the teachers in their study appeared to be 'incorporating', that is, 'feeling that they will accept the changes, but will not allow anything considered really important to be lost' (p. 148). Osborn and Broadfoot recognize that these may be only interim responses. They may be part of what Turner (1974) calls the liminal phase of transitions, a state of being 'betwixt and between', where those involved in change might experiment with a number of modes of adaptation before settling into a more permanent response. The concern of this book, however, is the responses of creative teachers, as defined by the criteria above. These criteria combine with a number of other factors, including personal values, experience, biography, career point, school culture and ethos, leadership, local circumstances, to produce a range of adaptations. The book is structured around this range.

Modes of adaptation

This focus yields a slightly different classification from Osborn and Broadfoot. There are five major categories. The first is *resistance*. Some teachers are resisting some elements in the changes to the extent that this becomes the prevailing mode with them. In one urban, multiethnic lower school, where they feel the issues that concern them and the needs of their children have been left out of account in a monocultural, monolingual National Curriculum, they have developed a discourse of resistance. Strong commitment to the cause of their children fuels a mood of fight and struggle. As a result, they have grown closer together in collaboration, and, in their efforts to help teachers 'regain the high ground', seek to articulate a whole-school perspective on the National Curriculum which embodies their cherished beliefs (Chapter 2).

The second category is *appropriation*. Resistance shades into appropriation, which is similar to Osborn and Broadfoot's 'incorporation'. Teachers seek to generate their own forms of power, to take over the National Curriculum and appropriate it to their own concerns through processes of recognition, identification, engagement and making alliances. They make it work for them. This is Hargreaves's 'colonization' in reverse. The school featuring here also identifies with a strong cause, that of the environment, and has achieved international acclaim for the development of its school grounds. This provides a basis for integrating the subject-centred curriculum, and also sustains a distinctive ethos which is a major source of their strength (Chapter 3).

The third category is *resourcing*. Primary school teachers have always made great use of 'others' in their teaching. The teacher's role might be changing radically in ways that some see as diminishing, but the use of others shows one way in which the teacher's role can be enhanced. The data for Chapter 4 is derived from the critical events research, but current research suggests that the practice still features strongly among creative teachers' work (see, for example, Jeffrey, 1994). Critical others challenge the taken-for-granted, introduce novelty, present new role models for teachers and students. They inspire and motivate, and help generate collaborative forms of work. They contribute to the authenticity of teachers' work by providing verisimilitude, contributing to the integrity of knowledge, fostering information and communication skills, and by validating teachers' and pupils' work as genuine endeavours within their discipline (Chapter 4).

The fourth category is *enrichment*. One of the 'creative teaching' research team, acting as 'critical other', joined with a teacher to test the possibilities for creative teaching within the National Curriculum. They taught the prescribed subject 'ancient Greece' to Year 2/3 children. The teacher had concerns about the orders, since they were 'very much dictated from above', seemed to challenge her autonomy, and to preclude the 'wide-ranging topics' she was used to. However, the project, as it unfolded, came to offer considerable creative possibilities, arousing great interest, excitement and motivation among children and teachers alike, stimulating them to high levels of endeavour. Achievement was related to specified attainment targets in the National Curriculum. The project covered the required ground, and did more, with the panache of a critical event (Woods, 1993a). The role of the researcher was critical. He took part in the planning and the teaching, provided specialist knowledge, secured resources. The collaboration made the teacher a 'bit more adventurous', gave her a 'whole lot of extra insight' and rekindled her enthusiasm. The collaboration had distinctive properties, being based on mutual aims, power-sharing, role-blending, and personal qualities. This case study showed that there were some areas in the National Curriculum where, given due resources, teachers' professionalism could be enriched, and their pupils' learning enhanced in radical ways. This is not to overlook the fact that history is one of the more prominent sites of struggle, or that, without the services of the critical other, the topic might have been experienced as restrictive.

The fifth category is *re-routeing*. In Osborn and Broadfoot's (1992a) scheme, 'retreatism' involves 'submitting to the imposed changes without any change in professional ideology', leading to stress and anxiety. This can be alleviated in a number of ways, including leaving the job. Since there is evidence that the most committed teachers are those most prone to stress, mainly through their reluctance to compromise (Woods, 1990a), schools may be losing some of their most dedicated teachers. There was one such in our research. However, for him this was a positive act of removal or redirection, rather than an act of retreat involving little choice in the face of superior hostile forces. To understand this fully, the teacher went into his life history, and particularly his early childhood. It was necessary to see how his self had come into being, developed, resisted attack, been mortified, survived, and at times prospered. His philosophy of teaching was rooted in these childhood experiences, which he saw as starkly divided between the alienating world of formal schooling and a natural world of real learning. Critical incidents and degradation ceremonies marked those occasions when the two came into conflict. The sense of marginality that resulted has stayed with him throughout life, though it had its moments of exquisite pleasure as well as intense pain. In managing his marginality, he has cultivated private places and a reference group of significant others who have supported and developed his preferred beliefs. But success in teaching has been his main support. This, as he defines it, has now been taken away from him by the changes, and the only way open to him to manage his marginality is to leave the system, in so doing finding new opportunities for lifelong ambitions. Triumphant in terms of self, his departure, and no doubt that of many others like him, is a sad loss to teaching.

It may be that these are predominant modes in some schools and with some teachers, as here. Elsewhere, a combination might be experienced. The National Curriculum is still a site of struggle, with changing fortunes as the battle continues. Teachers have to adapt to a changing scenario.

Self-determination

Ball and Bowe (1992, p. 112), in noting different responses to the changes from secondary schools and departments, suggest that they reflect different capacities (the experience and skills of the staff in responding to change), contingencies (staffing, students, resources), commitment (firmly held and well-established views), and history (i.e. of curriculum change). Those strong in these factors, they feel, have a better basis for autonomy and adaptation in line with previous practice. The schools of our research were generally of this kind. Apart from Peter (Chapter 6), and, late in the research, Dave (Chapter 7), they showed none of the symptoms of low morale among teachers that have been widely reported (see, for example, Pollard, 1992; Campbell, 1993). On the contrary, there were many expressions of enthusiasm for and dedication to teaching, and optimism for the future. Even in the schools characterized by struggle (Chapters 2 and 3), their mood, at the time, was one of defiance that sharpened and celebrated their convictions. It was a struggle they had to win. There was no thought of losing.

Clearly organizational culture, or 'institutional bias' (Pollard, 1985), and its history, is a key factor. However, running through these adaptations, and through the factors identified by Ball and Bowe, at an individual level is another pervasive factor to do with 'self'. Nias (1989) has noted the centrality of self among primary school teachers, how their teacher role is part of their substantial self (Ball, 1972), and how they suffer a form of bereavement if it is denied expression (Nias, 1991). Of course, they may 'personally' or 'situationally' adjust (Becker, 1964; Lacey, 1977), that is, change their beliefs and values to accord with requirements. Or they may 'strategically comply', that is, go along with changes while entertaining reservations about them. The level of commitment among our sample of teachers, however, ruled these out as options. They all, somehow or other, fall within Lacey's (1977) third mode of 'strategic redefinition', working in some way or other to change the situation in line with their values. Where a stark choice is presented, as in Peter's case, between situation and values, he chose to change the former rather than modify the latter, so preservation of self is still the major concern. In Chapter 7, I discuss some of the ways in which self-determination is manifested throughout the range of adaptations.

In essence, then, this book's focus is on the meeting point of intensification and self, and the coping strategies devised by teachers to manage the difficulties and dilemmas thrown up by the conjunction in line with their own interests. The notion of coping strategies combines structure and agency, system and individual, constraints and creativity. The new legislation provides a 'natural experiment' for research in this area, and the focus on creative teachers optimizes the chances of finding out more about the nature of teachers' creative inputs into such strategies. As Hargreaves (1984, p. 66) argues,

> coping with society in its institutionally mediated forms as a set of ongoing and perplexing 'problems' provides teachers with the important yet frequently taken-for-granted challenge to devise and enact, creatively and constructively, a set of teaching strategies which will make life bearable, possible and even rewarding as an educational practitioner.

However, as Pollard (1982, p. 28) points out, in Hargreaves's model the 'meaningful creativity of actors is acknowledged . . . but its importance tends to be diminished by the emphasis on constraint'. Pollard argues that we need to know what conception of 'self' teachers hold, and what purposes or goals they attribute to their actions. He also suggests that if we consider teacher 'interests-at-hand', they permit us to see how they 'become articulated as a result of structural constraints and dilemmas impinging on actors within micro contexts, but in so doing they reflect, and are primarily the product of, the particular self-conceptions and self-presentations which such circumstances threaten' (Pollard, 1982, p. 31). A note of caution must be inserted here. While the book concentrates on the agency/creativity side of coping strategies and adaptations, structure and intensification may seem diminished in power and influence, and give rise to an unwarranted optimism. However, it is an argument of the book that successful coping requires a clear view of such matters, otherwise the coping, like Densmore's professionalism, is likely to be 'misrecognized'. The result, I hope, is a reasonable optimism, grounded both empirically and theoretically.

The book aims to make a contribution to this theoretical debate, but is also geared to policy and practice. My own teaching and research careers have given me the conviction that creative teaching and learning are among the highest of educational accomplishments, and that they are increasingly under threat in the advance of intensification. If we can monitor and disseminate news of some success stories in coping with the National Curriculum and other changes we might help boost confidence more widely, and aid appropriation that preserves and promotes teachers' cherished values. The research asked, therefore, how far such teaching is promoted or constrained by the new educational provision. What factors and conditions secure its continuance? What strategies are deployed by teachers successful in continuing to promote such work? How closely does it accord with new requirements, and how vigorously are they underpinned by firm educational principles? Halpin (1990, p. 31) calls for 'the development of an archive of case studies of attempts by progressive schools and teachers to sustain their existing priorities in the light of, and despite, the requirements of the [Education Reform] Act' 1988 (which established the National Curriculum); and says that 'such work, properly disseminated, could illuminate curriculum strategy'. This book is a contribution to such an archive.

Research methods

Qualitative methods were used with schools and teachers judged particularly 'creative' by the criteria mentioned earlier. I have had a long association with most of these through the 'critical events' research (Chapters 3, 4 and 6). The headteacher of the school in Chapter 2 approached me requesting inclusion in the research, while the school in Chapter 5 was one selected in the third 'creative teaching', phase of the research. Detailed case studies were then carried out in these schools. This is not, therefore, a representative sample, either of teachers or even of creative teachers. It is an opportunity sample which demonstrates possible courses of action for teachers rather than generalities or typicalities among the profession as a whole, though the theory generated might be claimed to have general application (Glaser and Strauss, 1967).

Data collection was accomplished through school and classroom observation, interviews, study of documents, film and life history (Woods, 1986). These are discussed further as they apply to individual chapters.

The multiplicity of methods facilitated implementation of the maxim 'fitness for purpose', and enhanced validity through 'triangulation'. The general aim was to accumulate rich data and to produce 'thick description' (Geertz, 1973). Denzin (1989, p. 83) records that this 'creates verisimilitude. It captures and records the voices of lived experience . . . It contextualizes experience . . . It goes beyond mere fact and surface appearances. It presents details, context, emotion, and the webs of social relationships that join persons to one another'. The research then sought to generate theory from the data using the comparative method advocated by Glaser and Strauss (1967).

A particular feature of the research was the nature and extent of the collaboration in research – and teaching in the case of Chapter 5 – of the teachers concerned. This continues the joint work begun in Woods (1993a) – see also Woods and Pollard (1988). We have been working together in collecting data, in making analyses, and in presenting the work. These teachers were very articulate, but felt denied of opportunities to have their voices heard. In some ways I saw myself as a medium through which they could express their views, offering certain theoretical frameworks to which they might relate. Successive drafts were then discussed between us, ironing out any errors of detail and interrogating the analysis. The collaboration was not consensual on either side, but was conducted in a spirit of constructive criticism. I was mindful of the usual tests of validity in qualitative research, while the teachers were most concerned to 'get things right'.

2

Resisting through collaboration: a whole-school perspective on the National Curriculum

Resistance

Given the problems over the implementation of the National Curriculum, active resistance among teachers might have been anticipated on a large scale. The total boycott of national assessment in 1993 was the main such response. Collective resistance of this kind, however, has been rare, both on a national and regional basis. The weakening of the powers of the local education authorities has left schools isolated. What opposition there has been, therefore, has tended to come from individual schools or teachers, and has been selective. None of the heads interviewed in Croll and Abbott's (1993, p. 6) research 'could be classified as resisting or contesting change'. Osborn and Broadfoot (1992a, p. 149) found 'very little evidence of open resistance among teachers' (see also Muschamp *et al.*, 1992). Later, however, Osborn (1993, p. 20) noted some resistance in an inner-city school among teachers who were 'strongly child-centred in their approach', and who put 'children's needs' first. Vulliamy and Webb (1993) also believe 'that teachers' abilities creatively to interpret and resist policy directives . . . should not be underestimated'.

Much depends on how 'resistance' is defined, and to what it is applied. It is tempting to use the Collins definition of a Resistance movement: 'An illegal organization fighting for national liberty in a country under enemy occupation'. Perhaps that is a little extreme, though some teachers might feel in that position! I shall use it here to indicate active opposition to some significant part of requirements. It induces strong feelings, with a heartfelt desire to reverse the requirement. There is a marked tone, in consequence, of defiance, fight and struggle. The struggle is likely to be keen and lengthy – the school is unable to 'appropriate' or 'incorporate' the changes in question in any large measure for the moment. But it does have certain resources to keep it going. The resistance is not total, though it has substance and is not merely 'noise'. There may, equally, be strong support for other changes. But it is a prevailing mood, and the resistance is motivated by strong principles, which are consistent through both opposition and support.

This case study seeks to depict the character of such resistance in one school during 1992–3. Ensel Lower School[1] is situated in the inner suburbs of a town in the Midlands of England. It serves a largely working-class area, featuring terraced and semi-detached housing built in the first half of the twentieth century. At the time of the research, it had 135 pupils on roll, aged 4–9, 75 per cent of whom were of North Indian ethnic origin and whose mother tongue is Punjabi. There were eight teachers, including two 'Section 11' teachers.[2] They were a comparatively young and new staff, though the head, Dave, had had over 20 years' experience of teaching in primary schools.

What were they resisting? Not the idea of a National Curriculum as such, parts of which met with their approval, though, like most other teachers, they felt there was too much of it, it was subject to too rapid change, and it was inappropriately assessed (Pollard, 1992, pp. 111–112). Rather, it was more a matter of accessibility. The rationale for such a curriculum that they would support is one of 'entitlement', but in the National Curriculum they felt that some were more entitled than others. It was the demotion of the issues of equality, multiculturalism and bilingualism that concerned them: the monoculturalism and monolingualism of the National Curriculum; and the promotion of differentiation and centralism. Hardy and Veiler-Porter (1990) noted that ethnic minority children may be disadvantaged by the Education Reform Act (ERA) of 1988, since there was a lack of funding for schools to develop English as a second language. The Association of LEA Advisory Officers for Multicultural Education (ALAOME)

> looked in vain [in the Education Bill] for recognition that the starting point of many young children is communicative competence not in English (or Welsh) but in a language of one of the ethnic minority communities. Real access for such children is through a process of bilingual teaching in the early years' (in Haviland, 1988, p. 47).

There has been little change since. Burton and Weiner (1993) found 'little encouragement' within the Orders for English, mathematics and science for changes likely to lead to greater equality.

In the course of the research new Orders for English were issued, which emphasized, among other things, 'correct use of English'. For Ensel teachers 'this was totally inappropriate because it is not the language they would speak. They would use dialect.' The Orders were 'insulting to their children' (see Cox, 1993). They constituted 'an attack on culture'. In other ways this cause was being demoted. The number of officers directly involved in multiculturalism had been reduced, there was less in-service education, and there had been key changes in Section 11 provision. What courses there were were 'preoccupied with carrying out the National Curriculum. Your issues are not so important. So you're narrowing when you don't want to be'. Guiding principles in the changes are difference and competitiveness. As Elliott (1991, p. 146) has noted, the latter

> is promoted at every level of education . . . education is transformed into a consumer-oriented production process . . . In failing to recognize the internal values of education the ERA leaves little space for the development of those virtues which characterize the structure of social co-operation within any educative discourse'. Dave and his colleagues would agree. They are dedicated to a 'wider curriculum' which encompasses multiculturalism, and the personal and social development that that implies. To Dave, 'the National Curriculum is incredibly monocultural and monolingual, in a situation where we desperately need to widen it in terms of relevance and experience.

They consider the best teaching approach that ministers to their pupils' needs, as they see them, as being 'child-centred' – the very approach that has come under attack as attention has turned from curriculum to pedagogy. Some teaching under that label has come in for heavy criticism (Alexander, 1992; Alexander *et al.*, 1992), and 'Plowdenism' has been castigated in the press (see Wallace, 1993). Ensel teachers, according to Dave, felt very much under threat, and this was increased by the practicalities they were having to wrestle with.

> If you look at the programmes of study, there's a serious issue in the time factor for what we're required to do. It's a challenge to fit things together, and you do have to adapt your philosophy and your style, not always for the good.

Some have issued a call to arms. Drummond (1991, p. 120), for example, calls on primary teachers to 'promise each other "Not to Sell the Pass", not to see our child-centred principles nibbled away at, corrupted, abandoned'. The problem is that in some areas, the child-centred ideology had become a rather vacuous constraining norm (Alexander, 1992). There was a wide gap between ideology and practice. However, in other areas teachers felt it was having more success. But this success was not easy to demonstrate, and the practical application of the principles not easy to articulate. Drummond (1991, p. 120), therefore, argues that we must be

> clear about what it is we will stand for through thick and thin, being sure about which parts of our philosophy are not for sale. It is only this clarity, this principled understanding, that will sustain us in the tug-of-war between the requirements of the 1988 Act and the need to conserve our child-centred heritage.

Ensel teachers were in the process of doing this – a matter of identification and articulation. In the process, they were acting as professionals and opposing any tendencies to turn them into rational technocrats 'administering prescribed treatment in the light of the prescribed product specifications' (Elliott, 1991, p. 152). Resistance to this aspect, according to Dave, 'comes out of every pore. We feel extremely strongly about deskilling.' They acted as reflective practitioners seeking to incorporate the National Curriculum into their own broader concerns. They were at a stage, according to Dave, 'where we feel we've got to do something about it, but we're not sure how we do it. We're at the beginning. We have the vision, but we're not sure how to get there.' Part of the rationale for the research was to aid them in this quest – to encourage them to articulate their beliefs and to co-ordinate the response.

Who did the resisting? Degree and target seemed to differ among the staff according to how long they had been teaching, and specifically to whether they had been trained in the National Curriculum. The head, Dave, and the language co-ordinator, Susan, both of whom had been longer in post than their colleagues, were perhaps more critical. They placed the National Curriculum within a pre-1988 context of training and experience. Dave reported 'a tremendous increase in anxiety levels at first' among existing staff, which Susan said had 'increased since, owing to all the record-keeping, evidence to be filed away, but for very little purpose'. Penny and Vanessa, on the other hand, just recently out of college and trained in the National Curriculum were more optimistic and compliant, though after her first year Vanessa had changed her mind about some things. Getting up at 5.30 a.m. to write reports, having to move furniture to accommodate new classes for the new school year (because the caretaker said it was not in his contract), and a number of other 'extras' had taken the edge off her original idealism. This supports Dave's point that his staff were 'at different stages along the road', but that basically 'it was the same road'. Though at different career stages, and with different individual relationships with the National Curriculum, the staff were agreed on the central, underlying issues.

What form did the resistance take?

A discourse of resistance

'One thing we can do about it,' said Susan, 'is to talk about it'. The most obvious mode of resistance is discourse. The staff employed a kind of 'fighting talk'. During my visits to the school, and theirs to me, this was well to the fore. It was based on their strong commitment to a cause, which produced strong feelings, as it does generally among teachers of bilingual children (Savva, 1994). This is the moral dimension of teaching (Tom, 1984; Hargreaves, 1994). It stirs their passions, stiffens their resolve and determination, gives them a sense of urgency. This is not just a rational, cognitive matter. Something is wrong, and something needs to be done about it.

The National Curriculum was biting harder and harder, but it had stiffened their determination. It was 'not going to beat them'. 'When you really believe in something, you can't just sacrifice your own principles. You have to find a way'. One member of staff was not

> going to just give in because I feel so strongly about certain issues. I said to myself 'I'm going to divert the truth a little. I'm going to interpret it *this* way.' I'm going to keep elements of what I believe in, otherwise you just sell your soul really.

When the new English Orders came out,

> [there] was total resistance to these. The barricades have gone up. There's no way will we give in to those possible threats. We are going to continue the direction we want, come what may.

There is basic work to be done at an ideas level. Somehow the issues that concern them have to be 'brought back on the agenda', and they have to 'fight to regain the high ground'.

Ensel teachers remain optimistic. Dave says he has to be, 'because it's such a vital issue and at the moment the full forces have not been brought together to begin to combat some of these ideas'. He is concerned about the short term 'because of the tremendous pressures on teachers', but his staff remain quite buoyant. This has much to do with their individual qualities, but also

> the issue of bilingualism is something which actually keeps us fighting because it is an issue so glaringly not being addressed nationally or locally. You get to the stage where you start to raise the banner on the roof of the school . . . There is a genuine belief that there needs to be this battle of ideas, and a growing belief that we need to be fighting back.

There is, in other words, an extra ingredient here in this school, a commitment to a cause:

There's really something very concrete that we can grab on to and say, 'Look, this is ours and we've got to resolve this one', and so in that process you suck in all the other issues as well.

Collaboration

It might be argued that the need for whole-school planning to meet the demands of the National Curriculum has increased the need for teacher collaboration and co-ordination. However, the context of teachers' work, and particularly time and curriculum constraints, make this very difficult (Little, 1984). In these circumstances, there might be some 'bounded collaboration' which does 'not reach deep down to the grounds, the principles or the ethics of practice' (Hargreaves, 1989, p. 17) but which is concerned with more superficial *ad hoc* matters. There are worse dangers, it appears. Croll and Abbott (1993, p. 8) found the primary schools of their research 'shifted from an approach to managing change which placed strong emphasis on collegial and participatory approaches towards placing more emphasis on managerial and directed approaches'. In some circumstances, this managerial approach might appear as 'contrived collegiality', which is administratively regulated, compulsory, fixed in time and space, and other-directed (A. Hargreaves, 1991, pp. 54–55). In other words, the collegiality is organized for management, not for teacher empowerment. Osborn (1993, p. 13), however, noted that teachers were 'moving towards more collaboration in their professional work'. These authors are aware of the phenomenon of contrived collegiality, but still found that most of their teachers welcomed the new collaboration, and 'felt that it added a new dimension to their professionalism' (p. 14).

Clearly, collaboration is a complex issue and has many aspects. In broad terms, one might expect that in cultures marked by compliant and retreatist modes of adaptation, contrived collegiality might prevail. With resistance and appropriation, characterized by strong self-determination and accord on values, genuine collaboration of some kind might be more likely. The Ensel teachers, who are of the latter kind, were in the process of developing a 'culture of collaboration' – a 'set of norms about ways of behaving, perceiving and understanding underpinned by jointly held beliefs and values' (Nias *et al.*, 1992, p. 2). The central binding force, according to Dave, was the general appreciation among the staff of the 'need for the children to be educated within the context of a very firm and very great cultural knowledge'. There was a 'sense of feeling comfortable' about that basic point, though 'within that context there were many discussions, and some disagreements'. There was a strong accord among them, therefore, on basic values, on educational beliefs and on teaching approach. In some important respects, these were at variance with the values and thinking behind the 1988 Education Reform Act. The collaborative culture thus had a political purpose. It was their major resource, and possibly would gather strength from adversity. In this way it could have the opposite effect to that noted by Hargreaves (1989, p. 17) that, where curricula are heavily prescribed, 'teachers are left with little to collaborate about'.

For the moment, however, the Ensel staff felt somewhat beleaguered. One of the reasons why the high ground had been lost, according to Dave, was that their beliefs had not been well articulated, not even 'thought through'. The changes had been 'an enormous challenge to their ideas. They have to be reviewed as part of the resistance. You have to fathom out what is compatible to the National Curriculum, and what not'. Susan said, 'You have to bend and twist all ways', and 'You need to have some good defence, really'. It has to be noted that, while the democratic participatory management style at the school was good for this in one way – in promoting discussion and reflection – 'it creates its own needs in the context of the sheer number of decisions which have to be made in the present climate . . . It's a very slow process.' In their conversations with me, however, over a two-year period of association with the school, they did articulate those beliefs and illustrated their practical applications. There was considerable agreement among them, suggesting that the collaboration was strong at the basic and most important level – that of ideas. To some degree, the 'thinking through' and 'articulation' was going on *in* the research. What follows, therefore, is a contribution to that process as well as a commentary upon it.

A whole-school perspective

Since teachers' accounts complemented each other to a considerable extent, their story can justly be considered a 'whole-school perspective'. The term 'perspective' indicates an amalgamation of beliefs and practices. The Ensel perspective does not arise from seeking to apply a set of abstract principles, as for example, in the 'child-centred ideology'. Sharp and Green (1975, p. 86) considered that this contained 'powerful and evocative sentiment', but that 'its implications for curriculum practice are vague, imprecise and therefore problematic'. Its practical defects have been effectively exposed by Alexander (1992). These teachers would almost certainly consider themselves child-centred, but it is the hard-edged application within their own situation that is of concern to them. Their discussions, therefore, are not 'the type of act of communication' which represents 'a ritual of commitment and will be rhetorical rather than express intricate meanings about how a child learns or the teacher operates' (Sharp and Green, 1975, p. 170). Rather, their perspective develops from their particular situation, and the problems and constraints that confront them (Berlak and Berlak, 1981). Theory is applied to these in a practical way, informing their solutions and adaptations. Personal biography and professional experience also influence the perspective. In this way, Ensel teachers retain a sense of control over their own endeavours, are creative in their resolution of problems, are principled as far as is practically possible, and reflective and realistic in their appraisal of their accomplishments. I consider the perspective from their views on curriculum, learning and teaching.

The curriculum

There was considerable support for the National Curriculum in certain respects, especially among those recently trained into it. For Patricia, in her second year as a teacher of Year 1 children, 'it doesn't pose too much of a problem', and there is something to be said for children 'dealing with the same subject areas, the same patterns of learning' across England and Wales. Penny (a mature entrant, in her second year) felt that it had

> been drawn up in the main by people who know a lot about their subject areas . . . I can't see that there's anything wrong in what we're being asked to do. In fact, we're being asked to expand what we give to the children, but it's how we do it that counts.

Vanessa (a mature entrant, in her first year) said: 'I like to think I'm teaching through it rather than just teaching it – I can use it. There are some very good, very useful schemes of work.' The only area that bothered her was history which 'shook me. I feel much of the other areas are actually looking at processes of learning within them, but history, I've got to do "the invaders of England", etc.' Susan (in her fifth year of teaching) agreed that it helped to provide a framework, for example, in technology and science, 'the programmes are set to help them and suggest ways in . . . That is good because you can't have children missing out on whole chunks of scientific discovery.'

There was general agreement, as among teachers elsewhere, that there was too much ground to cover in the National Curriculum. This both diluted the content and squeezed other things out. Penny spoke of 'the sheer amount of it' and pointed out that

> things like harvest festival and Diwali are really important to the children, and it's not always easy to tie National Curriculum science, geography, history into it. It's difficult at Level 2 where they've actually got to start questioning and say whether things are really true or myth. You've got to keep that separate from your Diwali, and we'll have to keep it separate at Christmas.

Dave also mentioned the problem of needing to draw in the external events to make the National Curriculum more meaningful: 'How do we use it to embrace and deepen what we're actually doing within the National Curriculum at that particular time?' This is part of a 'wider curriculum' that is very much to the fore in a school like Ensel, but which has no place in the National Curriculum.

Patricia also said:

> There is too much. We need to stand up and say 'Hey, hang on a minute, this has got to stop, we can't keep taking on all this stuff'. We have to work within what there is, but it's incredibly difficult. We do need to be fighting back and saying 'Come on, this isn't appropriate for the children, far from it'.

Susan felt so much of the National Curriculum was

> very restrictive and prescriptive – you've got to cover this this week, and this next week, and you've got to jump around and it's not flexible at all . . . It's impossible to actually cover all the areas of the National Curriculum very well, and feel that you're succeeding with it. It's saying to me 'You've got to do this topic at this time of year and this topic at that time'. It doesn't leave much room for creativity.

Margaret (Section 11) amplified this point:

> We did a little session on disasters at the beginning because of the famine in Africa, the floods in Pakistan – and although that week's finished, the children still want to talk about Africa. You may have to say 'Right, we've finished with Africa', because they may not be achieving a tremendous amount more in the attainment target, which is so counter-productive when you've sparked them off. You could be doing so much in actual understanding, in discussion, in talking and listening, in increasing their vocabulary, because every time it's a new subject there's always new words coming in.

Susan pointed out that there were a number of 'weighty issues they should be discussing and tearing apart and arguing about'. For example, they wanted to consider how they could convert into classroom practice the theory in language that they all believed in, but 'we're finding it very, very difficult to achieve this . . . it's all going by the wayside a little bit'. The humanities especially – history and geography – she saw as 'very worrying':

> I don't see the relevance of a lot of that for our children, I really don't. It's very white and Eurocentric, and that's not good at all. It's got to be far more flexible, so you can take from it what is relevant to your particular children, what's going to give them some sort of stake. This is about people that have got no relevance to them.

In new Orders for English that came out during the research (1993), there was 'less opportunity for speaking and listening, which is bad for our kids'. Margaret felt the National Curriculum was almost *anti*-multicultural. Patricia thought 'the problem is when you're dealing with children who have special needs or particular problems'. She also thought:

It's so content-based and there's so much to get through that we're forgetting the basics of what children need at this age. They're still developing physically, emotionally, socially – there's so many other skills that are not fitted in with the National Curriculum.

Rashida, a Section 11 teacher, also regretted that

there was a lot about the academic side of it, but they don't really consider the social things, the social problems . . . We spend a lot of time just going over things. We have to cover this, we have to cover that . . . Also, there was insufficient time to practise really essential activities, like reading.

There was a feeling that they were going through a transitional period. Margaret said people were

more comfortable than they were two years ago. There was a tre- mendous amount of fear and panic. You were getting new sets of things almost weekly and it was really depressing. You felt con- stantly under threat that you were going to be found out that you didn't know what to do.

On the other hand, it was not clear how long the transition was going to take. Susan has been 'trying to adapt to it for four years – and I'm still adapting!'. Riley (1992, p. 2) notes the next step, and a greater challenge than absorbing the subject Statutory Orders, is to 'incorporate the National Curriculum into primary philosophy, with holistic learning at its heart'. How do Ensel teachers view learning?

View of learning

Autonomy, ownership, empowerment
It is the *process* of learning that is important here. As Vanessa put it:

You're not looking at what's going to come out at the end because you're looking at how the children are and are developing. It's what's happening inside the child that is important.

Dave also

believes very much that it's about processes rather than about knowledge as such. It's about learning to learn, which is something very different from the kind of highly structured imparting approach.

This is not to say that Ensel learning does not take place within a structure. Some simplistic understandings of child-centredness have children pursuing more independent courses. This is not the 'Ensel way', regardless of the National Curriculum. Dave pointed to the 'real books' debate, and how misconceptions arose about the approach from those instances where 'books have been thrown at the children in a way which isn't sensitive to their needs at those particular times'. The structure is the child's own point of learning. 'Real books' are a tool to build on that, and are of little use outside that structure; and, of course, the level of books introduced at certain points of the child's development is linked to views about levels of complexity and about rates of progression (see Campbell, 1992).

There was consequently much talk of 'starting from where the children are', and 'moving them on from where they've already started'. This requires deep pre-knowledge of the child. To this end, Dave stressed the importance of 'creating a system whereby we have very, very close contact with home and with parents', involving home visits and parent interviews. The indications are that children are 'developing tremendous language skills before they come into school . . . On that basis alone, we need to tap into that. The parents have created that relationship, helped create that knowledge, so they're a major resource.'

The school has a home visiting system, with the two Section 11 teachers (one of them bilingual) making frequent visits; a pre-school visiting system; and an open school policy for parents. Dave is keen for parents to develop a sense of 'ownership', building up their confidence to come into the school, breaking down 'the barrier at the doors' and 'building bridges'. This was necessary, since 'Asian families treat teachers with much more respect than white English, and regard schools as the professionals' province'. They have, therefore, been given a 'parents' room' within the school, somewhere in the school that is theirs, and that they can use on their own terms, take 'their friends and their family', and where they will not be challenged in educational terms. Rashida, female and Punjabi-speaking, plays a key role in this policy, since 'in her country, ladies don't talk to men', but through her 'they have good contacts'. The policy has had some success and some parents are 'actually helping in the classroom now'.

This, therefore, is a policy of partnership between teacher, child and parent. Parents have

> tremendous knowledge and skills related to their children's development at the pre-school stage . . . What we need is to use those skills and knowledge to life in school which is appropriate to the

children's needs and to where they are culturally and socially . . .
without that part of the equation I think we're on a losing wicket!

The aim is ownership of knowledge (Vygotsky, 1962) and autonomy.
Rashida, for example, argued that

we should make [children] more independent. If they have word
knowledge, can read and write, they can go and research themselves. They can find out a lot more than we can tell them . . .

Rashida seeks the empowerment of Freire's (1970, p. 20) conscientização,
which 'enrols [people] in the search for self-affirmation'.

How do we know when ownership has been achieved? Tests are applied similar to those used in assessing children's needs. Dave mentioned
a number of measures. First, 'a much more detailed knowledge of the
children through observation of free-flow play or other processes they're
getting involved in in the classroom'. Then, 'through very close observation, assessing their knowledge through hands-on experience, concrete
experience – a very practical basis'. Third, 'resourcing their needs based
on those detailed observations, and facilitating ownership of those resources by the children in terms of the way they use them'. You also talk
to children as an 'equal language user; sometimes use appropriate recording systems'. The quality of interaction between teacher and child and
between children is critical. The tactic is to 'tune in to what the child is
doing and drawing into that on the child's terms, through what their
perception is of what they're doing'.

Collaboration, co-operation, negotiation

There is a firm belief in the value of co-operative work among pupils
(Vygotsky, 1978; Edwards and Mercer, 1987). Dave is aware of the criticisms of some group work (Galton and Williamson, 1992), but he has no
doubt of the value of children working together and 'actually beginning
to solve particular problems together'. He gave examples of shared writing, where they can pool ideas and share problems such as transcriptional
ones. He described an instance from his own experience of two boys
building a bridge out of waste material in two sessions, one with him
present, one on their own. Dave said: 'the quality was actually much
greater in terms of what they were getting out of it when they were
working together without me'.

Dave gave another example of two boys, one whose mother tongue
was Punjabi, one Arabic, who got together to make a card for Diwali.
They got the message down in Punjabi, then tackled it in Arabic:

The boy who could speak Punjabi spelt out the letters for the other
boy and he wrote it down in Arabic, but he wrote it down literally
letter by letter in Arabic, but in the English direction. He said, 'Well,

the next step is to turn it round the right way'. Here is an environment where two children are working together and creating – because to me it *was* creating – a situation where they're beginning to use language in a real way and beginning to understand how it's working. That, to me, is part of this 'ownership' process.

Vanessa pointed out that she wants to know each child (a requirement in promoting autonomous learning and ownership of knowledge), and that, with 26 children, their experiences are so varied that it is a difficult task for her on her own. So she is

using the children themselves as well – the idea of collaborative group work – basically friendship groups, with children with similar backgrounds and interests.

Already, after only five weeks, she has

evidence of children who are now doing those things much more freely. When they first came into the classroom they would only talk to me. Now you can see that if they're not sure about something they'll talk to each other, and in the last instance then they come to me.

She is trying to break down the idea that 'the teacher is the one with all the knowledge', and to help them see 'they can work with each other and through each other'.

The basis of Margaret's work as a Section 11 teacher is to promote interaction among children. She mentioned one boy who began three terms earlier 'without a single word of English', but who was now

brilliant, largely because he's a very social child. So it's not a case of saying Section 11 [staff] were wonderful with this child – they weren't. He desperately wanted to be able to talk to his peers. The teacher is incidental almost . . . I honestly think that when it comes to a second language they learn far more from each other than they do from us. They might learn from us that 'Is a horse brown?' is correct rather than 'Does a horse be brown?' but they'll have been learning about the horse from their friends.

The creative spark, in other words, and the central meaning come from the children, with the teacher acting as refiner, corrector, editor, consolidator.

Margaret works with small groups, and children 'quickly overcome [the] shyness' that they feel in a whole-class situation:

Once they understand they can speak in Punjabi and the others will explain to them and help them in their own language as well as in English, they feel less isolated. Once they realize they can communicate, it seems to overcome an enormous barrier in the shyness angle.

Sometimes, she might have planned a lesson, and

> it goes off entirely at a tangent. Because that tangent is actually quite useful and valuable, we let it go. In the language field, whatever you're doing, whether it's maths, geography or whatever, the main thing is to get them talking, listening, understanding. So it's almost as if the geography is a secondary element.

She gave an example of some boys in reception who were 'terribly into World Wrestling'. She had to admit to

> actually hating it, but they get so excited about it and so want to tell you about it that it's a shame to stop them talking . . . The whole group are off, even the ones who are normally sitting there and are very quiet, because it's their culture, their thing. They really do take off, and they're the ones doing the work. If one makes a mistake, others will correct him.

Occasionally one or more white children will join such a group because of interest in the topic, and they will both be 'a useful resource for the work you are doing in that group . . . and themselves learn acceptance and tolerance'.

Confidence and motivation

The children cannot have complete freedom. They cannot, for example, decide 'that they are going to do this or that'. The onus is on the teacher to make whatever is offered within the National Curriculum 'something that they can then take over and own, and want to then develop. It's harder in some areas for some children than in other areas and for other children'. Autonomy and ownership are clearly principles to guide action rather than to be realized in practice across the board. Too many factors bear on the aim, including children's presenting behaviour. They must 'want to learn', but motivation is socially and culturally conditioned. It has much to do with confidence – the children's feeling that they are in natural (as opposed to alien) surroundings, within a supportive culture; that they can rely on others (teachers, peers, parents) to safeguard their interests and promote their concerns, and that they can trust them; that they can express themselves freely, without fear of ridicule or punishment; intuitively, that they can achieve certain things that lie within their fields of interest; and that they can apply maximum effort and energies freely.

There are two major problems affecting the confidence of Ensel pupils. Firstly, the fact that 75 per cent of them arrive with little knowledge of English. Following Wiles (1985), the school sees bilingualism as a considerable potential resource, but, for a time at least, there is much groundwork to be done in equipping children with communicative competence to meet the demands of the National Curriculum. The culture of the school may be vastly different from that of their home, increasing the problem of 'culture clash' generally experienced by pupils starting school. Language is central to forging the relationships that overcome such conflict and cultivate a sense of belonging.

Susan said that most children arrived able to speak some English but that they lacked confidence, and 'a lot were afraid to speak their mother-tongue'. Susan wanted to promote both, and tried to encourage them to explain things to each other in Punjabi, for if 'they're struggling for vocabulary, struggling to express themselves in English, then that will put them back'. In general the children came in with quite a positive attitude about school, as it was highly valued in the community. But that was vitiated by the feeling among parents that 'the school's got the ultimate answer and they don't really want to take much part in learning themselves', and the language difficulty. In general, 'it doesn't take long before they feel happy that it's absolutely fine to speak in Punjabi'. The real problems rest, perhaps, with the real minorities in the school, such as the girl who had just arrived from Pakistan, with no English. She responded to the teacher, 'trying to make sense of what was going on around her', but on this occasion her peers let her down, 'mimicking her accent and laughing at her'.

The second factor derives from the school's preferred approach. As Dave puts it:

> You're presenting a culture within the classroom that is encouraging children to take risks and to be confident in doing that, be confident in getting things wrong, and to feel confident about understanding that things are wrong or inappropriate in those particular circumstances. Now that is a big and important culture to create . . .

Dave likened the process to building vertically in a play situation:

> Part of the development of their knowledge is to put the final block on which they know is going to make the model fall down. Letting that happen and then rebuilding is very important in the scheme of building up that kind of confidence as individuals.

They need to have the confidence to take things to the limit.

Penny also thought that confidence was

> one of the absolute keys, because it is really damaged often before you even get them. They feel they can't do anything, whereas they've got to feel that there's an awful lot they can do. We have to teach them this, rather than what they can't do.

View of teaching methods

The pedagogical approach displayed four major factors: relationships; naturalism; scaffolding; and balance. I shall consider each in turn.

Relationships

The cultivation of relationships and the quality of interaction between teacher and pupils is of central concern. The quality derives from knowledge of one's children gained from their observation and from knowledge of what they are doing. To Dave, that is the key,

> because if one is attempting to have an equal relationship, what you're actually doing is interacting with the child, actively exploring ideas together.

The emotional link is important here because the interaction

> comes out of a security with the teacher. Very often you are exploring with an individual child their perceptions of ideas, and a lot of that kind of interaction has to be based on trust. You have to establish this with parents as well. It's not a process of taking over a role, it's a process of complementing it. This can be quite difficult in the early stages when parents can become very worried about that aspect.

As a reception teacher, relationships are the first item on Susan's agenda:

> I don't try to teach a, b, c, etc. on the first day of school. We play. I get on the floor with them. We do things together and try and find out what their interests are. I talk to them about that and encourage that. I want them to know that I am interested in them and I want to know about them first.

Patricia is 'quite pleased with the rapport' that she feels she has gained with her children:

> They seem quite happy and settled and we have lots of times when we're talking and just have some nice times together. This is good, because quite often you have days when you're shouting at them. It's nice to have those times when you can have a bit of a laugh, and they want to come and show you things.

Naturalism

There is an emphasis on real contexts and purposes within the child's scheme of relevances. This aids motivation as well as understanding. Finer attention to form, such as spelling, grammar and punctuation, follows once the point of the exercise has been grasped. Dave feels this makes for a qualitatively superior experience. In relation to language, for example, he says:

> You're going for the richness of language, you're going for the opportunities to use language in different ways in quick succession – language for different audiences, language for different purposes, and actually using language in a variety of ways.

Patricia likes to give her children choices. She has a writing table for 'emergent writing', wants them to 'have a go' regardless of spellings in the first instance:

I try to set up an environment where there's opportunity for them to go and try something out, go and have a look at something that might be new to them, and play with it, discover, find out about it, talk about it, and then try and focus in on aspects that I feel are important or that they have brought to me.

Just as children learn best through naturalistic processes, so the most meaningful assessment is made in context, and in line with teaching philosophy. The behaviourism of national assessment is contrary to Ensel ideals. Vanessa thinks

It's irrelevant and does an injustice to children, especially in a school like this where we're developing collaborative learning. I don't have any ability groups, the children work in all different sort of groups. We don't have A, B and Cs and grades. Then suddenly at SAT [Standard Assessment Tasks] time, you're putting children into a situation where they have to work on their own, and not only that, they mustn't look at other people or talk to them.

Some children will be disadvantaged, for example,

the child who is having difficulty with his writing, but his ability to tell you things is quite advanced, and his number is quite advanced, but his pen to paper stuff is difficult . . . Again, the children who are bilingual who could explain to you in their mother-tongue are not allowed to.

The oral aspects, such a strong feature of many of these children's culture, are not given any weight. It is a system aligned to a monocultural, white, middle-class society. Vanessa's preferred mode of assessment is to 'go from the other way'. Assessment is crucial because you have to know how children are learning, but you can't say

this is where this child ought to be at a certain time because it depends where it started from. It depends what experience the child has had, and it also depends on the fact that we don't all keep working at the same level at the same time. You can have a child who doesn't move for a few weeks, and then suddenly goes leaps and bounds. You have to have continuous assessment to know how the children are doing, and what you need to provide them with to help them move on.

Vanessa refers here to the somewhat outmoded notion of 'stages of de-velopment' associated with Piaget (see Donaldson, 1978), which, among other things, can have unfortunate 'labelling' consequences. She gives an example of her continuous, naturalistic, diagnostic assessment:

I'm going to look at how they are talking in groups, explaining their ideas and thinking. So I've set up situations, designing Diwali cards at the moment, with groups of five or six children. They make the card and then we talk about it. I'm challenging sometimes, saying 'What do you mean? How do you think you're going to do that?' The children then come back to me and talk and listen to each other, and sometimes I'll say things like, 'Oh! I'm just listening, I'm just listening you know, ask somebody else' – that sort of thing. So in that situation I can assess how they're using their language. It may be nothing to do with the Diwali card in the end, but how they're able to relate to others in the group, express their ideas, what role they take . . .

Patricia also considers that the Standard Assessment Tasks are biased, because 'we're testing children on really their knowledge of English'. She prefers

more of a practical assessment, by actually watching, observing children, what they're doing with a particular task. You could also just let them draw pictures to explain something, or have people in who can speak in their own language.

Susan also talks of 'testing in context'. She does group her children by ability for certain things. She would

introduce vocabulary to each of these groups from the reading they're doing, and would let them use that vocabulary to re-create new sentences, write something or make their own book. Then I would ask them in isolation, once they've used it in context, I would hold the word and play a lotto game maybe with it to see if they can read that word. I would want to keep a check on their understanding with 4- to 5-year-olds. Later on I think the National Curriculum testing would be fine if it was more to do with ordinary happenings in the classroom, rather than having to do a piece of reading about going swimming to some leisure centre type place, which lots of them may have no experience of. If children could write their own stories from their own imagination and you could look at them, bearing in mind spelling and handwriting . . . so in context and from their experience and their interest, rather than you enforcing something upon them . . . And it should be diagnostic, not just putting a tick somewhere. It's got to mean a lot more than that because it's got to be of use to you, the child and the next teachers. It's got to tell them where they're at, what their problems are and how to help, and what their strengths are. Pure statistics I don't really believe.

Penny supported the idea of national assessment in that 'it's really making you look closely and see whether children really do understand', but the volume made it so time-consuming and superficial.

It's easy to teach and do a tick list saying 'They all know that', but to really assess is much, much harder. In some ways it's easier to pick up from odd children . . . Today, for example, one child drew cylinders, cuboids, all the shapes that we've been learning. I'd actually assessed him, but if he'd been a child I hadn't assessed, it would have been ideal. I could say, 'Right! That child knows that because he's come to me with that.' That shows the child's really internalized it, knows it and is using it. But of course with a whole class of children for every assessment you've got to do, that's impossible.

Scaffolding

Ensel teachers referred to the popular constructivist idea of 'scaffolding' (Edwards and Mercer, 1987; Maybin *et al.*, 1992). In general terms, the teacher is an enabler and facilitator, aiding children to learn how to learn. She does this in a variety of ways. Sometimes she provides the idea or spark that starts them off and/or carries them along. Patricia explained that in mathematics, for example,

they can pick up an idea and take it off and use it, but quite often you've got to give the maths ideas to them first. One boy made a robot, and then I suggested that he saw who was taller or shorter than the robot, which he did for our class. Then I suggested he went to another class. He's actually owning that, because I'm not saying 'You can do this and that', but I'm putting the germ of an idea there. If he wants to he'll pick that up and develop it into a fully-fledged flower.

Vanessa describes how the teacher encourages the flower to blossom, while also bearing in mind the question of correct form, such as spelling and punctuation:

A child in my class who as yet cannot write his name legibly and is 8 years old, has real difficulty with the mechanics of writing. I've not focused on his writing but focused on his storying. He has produced a book – a wonderful book, a beautiful story – that the children in the class are now using. Now because I believe in the scaffolding, me providing the supports for him to develop, he was able to come to me a week ago and say 'I've got a story, I want to write'. He knew because of all the things he'd heard from me and what I was saying about not worrying about spelling or what it looked like, he could read it back, that he could come and in the end he said it to me and I put it straight onto the computer. So the spelling is mine, the structure, the content, the grammar, everything else, is his. He did a lot of work then – cutting it up, organizing it, and making it into a story, into a book for the class to read. Now I feel that if I hadn't been the sort of person who believed in 'this was what he wanted to do and I could provide the structure for him', I may well have focused on 'Oh, no, you can't write a story yet because your letters aren't being made properly, let's get your letters right first', which I think is obstructive.

I asked Vanessa if there were a danger that because of the management difficulties involved, there may be some children in this classroom who don't actually get round to putting this into words, who don't really learn to write and to spell.

Oh, but they do! What all of the children in the class are now doing is this. When they're writing, they're writing entirely on their own straight into draft. At first they would come to me and ask for me to put a word down that they knew they couldn't spell, and that was the first thing that struck me. They knew what words they hadn't got right so were very well aware. I've said, 'Well, you have a go at it, think about it, say it over, think about s. . . sounds and things you can . . .' – you know, good old phonics coming in – and if you're not sure, put what you think it is and if you can't think of anything, put a line and then we'll come back to it'. So they then come back to me when they've finished the piece of work and they tell me which words they're not happy with. They'll circle them or whatever and we'll talk over sounds again and then they'll write them in – the look, cover, write, check method – and what I've found is that in the early days some children were still just sitting at the table and were a bit shaky and a bit worried if they'd got to write on their own. But now there's nobody in the class who's not writing so I can see what words and the 'thens' and 'thats' and 'thes' that they've got, but having a go at 'comfortable' and putting a 'c' and an 'm' and 'f' and a 'b' in the middle, it's very good. So it's side by side, these things have to be developed side by side because I want the children to be able to construct stories. It doesn't mean that I'm not interested in their handwriting or their spelling. It's bringing the two along, but it's making them responsible for it and the realization that they are their best critics, they know, and they want to do it properly. I haven't got anybody there that doesn't want to do it very well, in 26 very different pupils, and they know that they can come to me at a certain time so we're building the two things up together.

Penny also uses what they call a 'side-by-side' strategy:

You've got to give them the skills, because if they haven't got them, then you're not allowing them to develop. So we have a sort of skills thing underlying – we do learn to form our letters correctly, we do learn to do joined-up handwriting, we do learn instant recall of number bonds, and the nitty-gritty skills bit. But whenever possible, I try to totally free them from having to produce work which is correct. So when they're writing, for example, spelling doesn't come into it . . . They're resisting like mad, they're still wanting correct spellings, but we're trying to encourage them to put whatever they can on paper, because it's the content on paper that is the important bit.

The basic, low-level task of spelling is thus given creative energy to blend in with the constructive nature of the exercise. Patricia explained how children built up the pattern of sounds within a word. She likes children to engage in 'emergent writing', where they are encouraged to 'have a go at mark making of any sort':

It's making them think, which to me is far better than having children copy sentences that you've written. I think there's a place for [copying], but I think they make more progress where they have to actually think about the sounds in the words they are saying, they're not copying it where they don't have to think.

Margaret encourages children to negotiate among themselves, to co-operate in the production and testing of ideas. Then she will co-ordinate their efforts:

They negotiated the story between themselves, then gave me the finished version. I wrote it down. We then read it through, . . . altered it, added things, took things out . . . They'll say, 'Oh, you forgot this bit!' 'So where do you want me to put that?' 'We want to put it here and this is what we want to say.' So we'll end up with a hotch-potch of a story *they* have negotiated and I have actually written . . . Sometimes, the very little ones will start off with a picture. You'll ask: 'What is it, would you like to write about it?' (I use puppets quite a lot with the little ones.) And they might say, 'Yes, the spider is climbing up a tree'. So you'll write 'The spider is climbing up a tree'. Perhaps they'll go over it, perhaps they'll go under it, perhaps they'll colour it. Very often they choose how they're going to change your writing into their writing. It's their words . . .

As they progress,

> some of them will write their own completely, so perhaps you and/
> or other children will go through it with them afterwards and help
> them to edit it. Sometimes they'll edit it totally on their own.

To draw children out, Margaret will at times play the learner:

> You get instances where they're stumbling about in a description,
> where they don't actually have the words to say what it is, so then
> you can bring in others, 'What do you think he means? I don't know
> what he's talking about!' I find this playing dumb helps a lot and
> you get the others to explain to you. Often they give you the words.
> If not, you can try some, and 'Yes! Yes!' they all grab the word.

Margaret is a member of the group, therefore, and

> usually the stupid one they're having to explain things to . . . Then
> they all focus on telling you, and perhaps they'll disagree, 'No,
> that's not right, that's not what happened', and they'll be explaining
> rules and regulations and so on (for example, over the wrestling).

Margaret is a

> less than equal member, because I don't have the information that
> they have. It's a reversal of the teacher–pupil role, and it's very
> useful for them to be teaching you something.

When she took a course in Punjabi,

> I used to come back and run through what I'd learnt the day before
> with my groups, which they used to find hysterical, because I mis-
> pronounced everything. They would then take over and tell you
> where you were going wrong, and add words to it . . . They seemed
> to really find that quite stimulating.

Susan also used this tactic:

> They're always saying things to me, and they laugh because I can't
> understand them. I say 'Oh! You'd better tell me what that means,
> I'd love to know!' They try to teach me a word and they laugh when
> I say it wrong. I try every day and 'Oh! Have I got it right today?'
> They're ever so keen to give you a bit of vocabulary.

Margaret does not like it when one of the children becomes less than
equal:

> It's a power situation, isn't it? If you have power, then it's OK for
> you to give it away and then take it back, but if you haven't, it's very
> different.

Vanessa commented:

> There are individual people and you're not in a position of power.
> You could be, but that's not what you should be there for – not to
> put a curriculum over them and 'you will do this and you will do
> that', but to do them justice.

Dave pointed to another implication for teacher power. While trying to
inspire children and spark their creativity, one was hoping to bring together a number of different things so that the children made 'the right
noise'. However,

> they may not make the noise that you're expecting. It could be
> something else, which is a very uncomfortable thing to happen in a
> sense. It should be very exciting, but it can be very uncomfortable
> because it's challenging the teacher's power over the situation. What
> you're saying is that we're going in the direction of the children, and
> that needs courage because you're putting their ownership first.

Dave acknowledges that he has felt some discomfiture himself in these
situations, partly because there is a residual feeling of traditional teacher
culture, which, despite one's best intentions, engenders a feeling of caution about where it is leading, and partly because it may not be a direction
that is immediately related to the National Curriculum.

Margaret feels that, in spite of teachers' good intentions, with a lot of
them, including herself, there is still

> almost a Raj mentality that we actually really know best, and they
> oughtn't to be doing it that way, they ought to be doing it this way.
> It's one of these situations where it's done with the best possible
> motives and intentions, but it's meddling in a culture that's very
> strong.

Margaret has been experimenting with getting children to tell their stories
and using a tape recorder to record them, and developing the writing
from that. At the moment, though, they were 'all too intrigued with the
tape', but she would carry on.

Balance
Ensel pedagogy is balanced through orchestration, variety, managing
constraints, and structure.

Orchestration
This is the ability to combine potentially conflicting elements in the
teacher role harmoniously, such as cultivating emotional ties with the
children on the one hand, and keeping order on the other (Woods, 1990a).
Penny agrees that this is one of the key factors in getting the balance right:

There are times when you have to say: 'Right! You will sit down, and you *will* learn how to do this, you'll *have* to do this.' They find the balance difficult, because at times they're allowed, for example, to go and measure children throughout the school . . . They'll come up with this idea, and with things like data collection in maths, you give them the help to get them started on a simple data collection, let them see they can extend it and then when they ask to do it, support them in doing it. This is very idealistic compared to what has happened in my class this morning!

The problem here was

the children's behaviour . . . getting them all motivated at the same time. Some might be really keen and working really well, others, you've set them a task and they're not doing it.

It is easy to instruct a whole class all doing the same thing, but

the hardest thing is to have children working on their own initiatives, taking control. At the moment, you may not have found the key to the unmotivated children, so what they're doing may not be the standard you want them to do it to, or the quality, or the behaviour that you want. That's the dilemma – of having the two sorts of things in the classroom.

Variety
Ensel teachers use a variety of methods depending on the aims of the exercise and on constraints that may be operating:

I like to give the children a chance to have a choice in what they're doing, but there's times when I like to have a more formal approach, where I know exactly what they're doing . . . I could be working with the whole class, doing something that's actually recording, whether it be practising letters, or some form of number work. But then we have practical work as well where the children are reinforcing skills and discovering new things as well.

Variety is also important from the children's point of view:

If children are working the same way all the time, then that's not really helping them to develop. They need an opportunity to work as an individual, to collaborate with somebody else, work with new people, even go to a different classroom and work with other children. You need a range of situations to keep them interested and enthusiastic, and they're learning new skills from it.
  Sometimes if children get a very long and complicated sentence that they want to say, and writing it would be too much for them, in

that instance, I'll write it for them . . . I'd scribe it for them so that they've got it, that's their story and I can read it back to them . . . Also, for letter formation there's a place for actually sitting and practising, and quite formally learning how the letters are formed. If they haven't got the skill coming second nature to them then that's going to hold them back when they're writing . . . So there's a place for that, and a place for letting them have a go as well. I think the skills complement each other.

Managing constraints

Sometimes one is forced to use a variety of methods not through choice, but through constraints. Vanessa wants to enable 'the children to become as autonomous and independent as possible within the classroom environment', but was finding this difficult to put into practice. Some of her children 'had not been used to that kind of independence', so she was 'having to readjust and step back all the time – starting perhaps with smaller things that I had hoped to'. Already, in her first term, ideals are moving to meet practicalities.

Class size is the most immediate constraint operating against a philosophy that prioritizes the individual child. As Patricia explained, it was sometimes difficult to operate in her preferred manner because

> with 24 children it's very hard, however much you'd like to, unless you've got the number of adults there to work with little groups and be there when you're saying these important things, then they end up being off-task, because there's no one to draw them in, focus them, talk to them about it. It does become a bit chaotic sometimes, so quite often I have to work in a more formal way so really I'm just managing the children.

Last year Patricia had two nursery nurse students working in her class for three days a fortnight, and that made a

> big, big difference because they helped supervise children, simple things like just washing their hands for dinner . . . When you've got 20-odd children in the toilets and there's a riot going on, and then you're trying to settle a group in the classroom, you can't be in two places at once, and they're very lively children as well. You find sometimes you've got all these wonderful ideas about things that you want to do, but the reality of it . . . It is quite frustrating – you don't want to lose that enthusiasm, but sometimes it is a case of having to keep them down to make it manageable.

Susan emphasizes the realistic, practical approach of the staff, and their suspicion of abstract ideologies.

I don't try and create a completely autonomous environment simply because of the restrictions, the numbers of children, the environment that I'm working in, the lack of equipment to some extent . . .

She feels that

some people might even lose touch with what they actually believe in because they encounter so many problems along the way, and perhaps they have reinforcement from different areas – 'Well, no, the three Rs is the only way, haven't you found that out now?' – your confidence can be easily knocked.

This latter kind of strategic orientation has been called 'internalized adjustment' (Lacey, 1977), wherein the individual changes to meet the prevailing system. Ensel teachers practised a kind of 'strategic resistance', fighting for what they believed in, but with a firm grasp of practical realities, which at times forced them to compromise. Susan admits that

while we've been working here, a few of us have been grappling with problems of, say, teaching reading, for example. We know what we think we believe in, but whether we can actually achieve that by putting it into practice we're not sure, so we're very confused about that issue.

Structure
A fourth feature of balance is the way in which teachers organize the work and the children to serve a 'fitness-for-purpose' approach, and to avoid the excesses of some attempts at child-centred learning noted by Galton (1989), Alexander (1992) and others (such as long queues at the teacher's desk, low-level tasks, pupils frequently off-task). Vanessa explains how she tries to avoid this (though she 'hasn't got it right yet'):

If, for example, we've been looking at shapes, I'll identify a group of children that I want to work one-to-one with within that group. The rest of the class, we've developed things that are ongoing over a period of five weeks, some things that aren't, some things are just little investigations that I've put out. We have a checklist of jobs so children know that when they've completed one task and have got to a stage where they need help from me, they can move on to something else. So they are directing themselves within the direction that I have set up . . . Everything is available for them in the classroom, they select their own materials, they cut their own paper, it's all there. I don't lay it out for them, I don't set a table up . . . they go and choose and select for themselves.

This principle of choice within a guided framework is not easy for a teacher to 'bring off', especially where children have been more used to directed work.

Clearly some elements within this perspective are in line with the imposed changes. There is support for certain elements in the National Curriculum and, among some, of aspects of assessment. The constructivist approach to learning and the balance and fitness-for-purpose approach to teaching accord with the recommendations of the Discussion Paper by Alexander *et al.*, (1992). On the other hand, there is opposition to some elements within the National Curriculum, as well as its quantity, restrictedness and prescription; to not placing children's needs first; to not considering the whole child; to formal assessment and to unnecessary bureaucracy; to differentiation and competition as opposed to co-operation; to dwindling opportunities for creativity, open-endedness and 'real learning'. Ensel teachers are working to neutralize the effects of these elements in securing the practical application of a consistent philosophy.

Teacher professionalism

Ensel teachers thus know how they want to teach and are not going to be dictated to. They still feel in control of teaching processes, and are working to adapt the curriculum to their pupils' needs. They consequently strongly resist the notion that they are becoming deprofessionalized. Patricia said:

I certainly don't feel from a very personal level that I've been deskilled. The National Curriculum has to be delivered, yes, but the way that you do that, the way that you interpret those attainment targets, is a very personal and a very professional thing. Each teacher isn't going to teach the National Curriculum in the same way because we all have our own ideas about particular teaching styles, or particular ways of working with individual children. While we're all striving for the same end result, we're going to approach it in very, very different ways, whichever suits you as an individual, and whichever is best for the particular children in the class. I certainly wouldn't expect all my children to be working in the same way. I would be looking at their needs, and how best I can fit my teaching and the way I can work with them so that they're achieving those skills that they need as part of the National Curriculum. So, yes, you are looking back and researching and reflecting what worked, what didn't work, and going off in different angles and trying to bring in new ideas. I think there's still a place to be able to do that, but it is very difficult because there is so much National Curriculum.

Penny agrees:

> You deprofessionalize yourself – that's up to you. There's no reason
> for any teacher not to be a professional. It's what you do with the
> National Curriculum that counts.

Penny still feels that 'there is an awful lot of scope for the individual
teacher', though on the other hand, 'there's so much volume in the
National Curriculum that if you're going to teach thoroughly, you may
not get through it all'. This may be a temporary problem, and it certainly
doesn't outweigh the advantages. In fact, Penny feels there are now more
opportunities for *re*professionalization than dangers of *de*professionalization. She compares working in a previous school nine years ago, which
was a 'very good school', but 'not doing all the things that we're now
being asked to do with the children':

> There wasn't the – just the whole variety of things – it was much
> narrower. There was not nearly as much science obviously, but
> there wasn't the geography and the history. We weren't being asked
> to give the children all of this richness now that we are being asked
> to give them. So I think from that point of view it can be an enhance-
> ment to your professionalization because you've really got to find
> out a lot more about the whole of the curriculum and you're having
> to go to other professionals ideally. You're having to go to the his-
> tory co-ordinator, the science co-ordinator, to find out from them. So
> it's a learning process for us as well, whereas in the olden days you
> could have had my philosophy and you could have stuck on a
> relatively narrow curriculum albeit that it's a curriculum that has
> been child-orientated.

Here, Penny disputes whether there are any deprofessionalizing tendencies to resist.

Susan, however, draws attention to contrary tendencies:

> There are so many issues to take on board, and all the record
> keeping and the checking off of this attainment target, that attain-
> ment target, and the sort of testing side of it, SATs or whatever. At
> the end of the day where is the real time for the children? This is, I
> think, what concerns a lot of teachers. Once you were able to spend
> time after school making the classroom an inviting environment to
> display the children's work. To be honest, you struggle now for the
> time to actually do these things. Sometimes you go home and
> you've got things to tick off, and this evidence to produce and that
> evidence to produce, and you come in ill prepared for the next day
> because you haven't got the hours in the day. You're being
> stretched every which way, so many demands being made on you,

and I don't see the relevance of a lot of those demands either. I'm there for the children. Obviously some of these ideas and some of these new innovations are important but I think it's all become very top-heavy . . . Nobody reads it, this is the whole point – nobody reads it or is interested. And this is what worries me – I'm spending hours wasting . . . and I'd rather be doing things for the children, I'd rather be making an exciting place for them to be rather than getting a bit of paper, putting my glasses on and squinting at tiny, tiny bits of writing and ticking a few boxes. A waste of time, I get cross at that, you know . . . There's all these weighty issues that we should be discussing and tearing apart and arguing about. At the moment in this school we're trying to put together a discipline policy and we're trying to improve the language basis, more like the theory of what we believe in, more translatable into the classroom if you like, and we're finding it very, very difficult to actually achieve this because there are so many other things going on. It's all going by the wayside a little bit.

These teachers are very concerned about theory, and a 'close relationship between a knowledge of theory and research and actual practice'. Dave feels that, in order to regain 'the high ground', 'there has to be a very, very strong and very clear idea of why we're doing things, what educational pay-off it has for the children in the learning process'. The impulsion here, therefore, is to develop even further as a reflective practitioner (Schön, 1983) and as an 'extended professional' (Hoyle, 1980).

Penny illustrates this kind of thinking in her comments on a government-promoted Discussion Paper (Alexander *et al.*, 1992) aiming to promote debate in primary schools about pedagogy. The reflective practitioner is able to evaluate this document for itself, as well as its stipulated target. Penny, for example, criticized the document for generalizing on an inadequate base. It was 'so negative. They ought to be looking at why group work wasn't working, not damn the whole lot. What schools have they researched in?' Penny feels they should have looked in other places, where they might have found the practice they criticized working. She feels that much in the report is right (classroom instruction, for example, is important), but their sweeping claims are suspect. Another illustration of this is Penny's comment on the claim that 'the progress of primary pupils has been hampered by the influence of highly questionable dogmas', which has led to 'excessively complex classroom practices' (Alexander *et al.*, 1992, p. 1). Penny says:

It's not the dogmas that have been around a long while, it's the old-fashioned teaching . . . You have young probationary teachers who go out and within one year of being in the classroom, they either have the strength to carry on with their beliefs, or get sucked into the old ways of teaching . . . and therefore they carry it on. It's only very few teachers can actually get out there and change anything, so nothing's really changed.

The ORACLE studies support Penny's view inasmuch as 'progressive teaching . . . hardly exists in practice' (Galton *et al.*, 1980, p. 156) and 'didacticism still largely prevails' (Galton and Willcocks, 1981; see also Bennett, 1976).

Margaret also is optimistic in the long term, though for the moment

most teaching staff aren't fully conversant with things, principally because every time you think you've got it, they move the goal posts, and you're totally flummoxed again.

As with children and parents, it is a matter of confidence, which only comes gradually as ideas are put into practice and you begin to feel 'I can do it'. If the ground-rules are continually being altered, then you are continually being 'flung back to the beginning'. However, Margaret feels that this is a transitional stage, 'people are already feeling more comfortable than two years ago'. In the long term, issues like multiculturalism, currently squeezed, will return in force.

Once people have actually mastered what it is they have to do, then they'll start actually looking at it and think, 'Well, actually, we could do this'. If we did a project on housing, for example, you could bring in a lot of other things. A project on festivals would bring in a lot of multicultural issues, 'families' likewise. But there's almost a fear of the National Curriculum at the moment: 'How do I get it all in? And are they going to be able to read at the end of it?'

Whatever is happening to the teaching profession as a whole, Ensel, at the time of the research, had developed a strong local professionalism closely geared to the particular needs of the children at that school. The changes initiated by the 1988 Education Reform Act were strengthening their resolve, highlighting the issues and forcing them to consider ever more closely the bases of their beliefs and the efficacy of their methods. There are dangers in resistance. It is not an easy route to follow, especially for a school in isolation, and makes heavy demands on physical, mental and emotional reserves. For the moment, however, as long as Ensel teachers felt they had some room for manoeuvre – some scope to adapt the National Curriculum to local concerns, control of the teaching processes, hope for a reasonable and meaningful workload – resistance through collaboration was their chosen course. It might help promote their aims in unsuspected and radical ways. It might, in due course, develop into full 'appropriation', which I discuss in the following chapter.

Notes

1 Pseudonyms are used throughout this chapter.
2 Special funding arrangements were made under Section 11 of the 1966 Local Government Act for the educational needs of 'ethnic minority' children.

3

The creative use and defence of space: appropriation through the environment

The Coombes County Infant and Nursery School at Arborfield in Berkshire has acquired international recognition for the imaginative development of its school grounds, including a prestigious Jerwood Award in 1990. A 'Learning through Landscapes' report (Adams, 1990) records that 'an immense variety of environments have been established, using every available inch of space'. The head, Susan Humphries, sums up their policy:

> We see the outside of the school as a wealthy resource which can be drawn upon if we are prepared to plan its development. We wanted the outside environment to reflect the same degree of care and imagination which was given to other areas of the school.

I spent two days at Coombes in 1991. I was shown round the grounds, observed lessons and activities both inside and out, studied documents, and spoke with teachers, pupils and parents. I have maintained contact with the school and visited it several times since then. I was impressed and intrigued by the school's achievement and wanted to record it. In addition, I wanted to know how such a school, so used to success, coped with the National Curriculum and other changes, much of which ran counter to its philosophy. In the first part of this chapter, I consider the Coombes achievement and the factors behind it. I describe the planning and nature of the grounds, and examine the learning principles behind them. There are two groups of principles, connected with 'involvement' on the one hand, and 'holism' on the other, with the major theme of 'environmentalism' running through both. These lead to inspired teaching and learning. In the second part, I shall discuss how Coombes has 'appropriated' the National Curriculum within its own culture.

The Coombes ethos

The school grounds: a creative use of space

Coombes opened in 1971 on a small, flat, barren site seeded with rye grass and edged with chain-link boundaries, and depleted through the ravages of builders. Every year since then the school, under the guidance of Susan Humphries, has worked to develop the grounds into an area of beauty in its own right and a rich resource for learning and development. Through the years, teachers and children have worked together in producing 'a living time-line'. The grounds represent the history of the school. The layout is depicted in the figure opposite.

It is 'planted for teaching' in a systematic way, since they were keen from the beginning that 'the school should be set in a wood – its "kindergarten"'. Trees in the grounds represent all the common species of northern Europe. There is a profusion of spring-flowering bulbs, two wildflower meadows, sunflowers, pumpkins, herbs, fruit bushes, vegetable plots, a rock garden, four ponds, hedges, animal enclosures (for sheep and chickens), herbs, an ivy garden ('where the spiders live'), a minibeast sanctuary, a turf maze, compost heaps, a ditch, clay pit, earth mounds, orchard, nut orchard and many nooks and crannies. All this is teeming with life, including fungi, algae, mosses, butterflies, moths, birds and a variety of small mammals. A simple inventory, however, cannot do justice to the planning of the site. An all-weather concrete nature trail takes us round, bringing us close to the various features, through oak, larch, Norway spruce, black poplar, hazel, silver birch, hornbeam, etc., the trail wooded nearly all the way round, skirting the playground, bringing you near the ponds but keeping 'discrete boundaries' for safety purposes, and close to the animal pens. At points along the path 'time capsules' are buried – biscuit tins containing work by children and adults 'for future historians'.

Sue explained how she had 'extended' the small area allocated to the school by introducing a system of banking. When the school was first built, 'there was no back drive down – we made that ourselves; and the site was totally flat and everything was on straight planes'.

> The area doesn't alter but by the introduction of a few mounds and troughs you get a bigger area; and you get micro-climates, because if a stepped bank faces south or north . . . nature's very susceptible to the slightest change in either position as far as the wind reaches the plants, or the length of sunlight, amount of light or shadow.

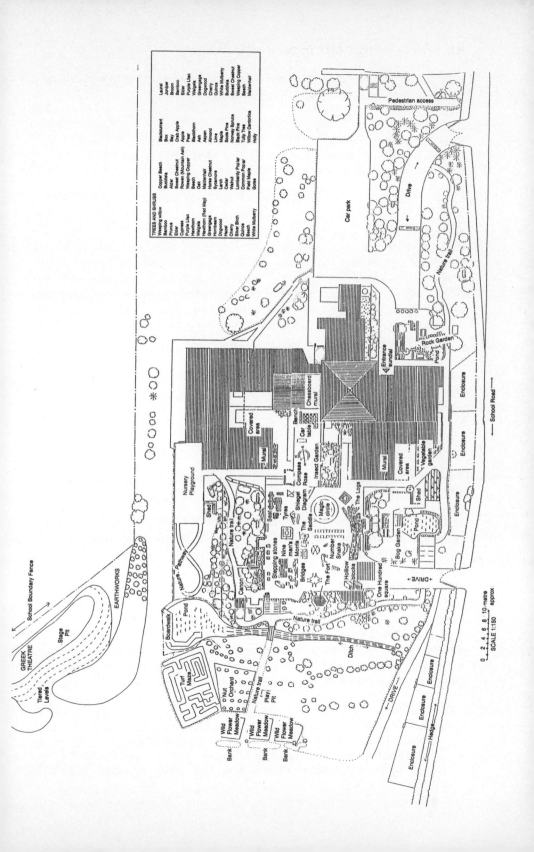

GREEK THEATRE

School Boundary Fence

Tiered Levels

Stage Pit

EARTHWORKS

Pedestrian access

Drive

Nature trail

Car park

TREES AND SHRUBS

Weeping willow
Bamboo
Prunus
Elder
Cypress
Purple Lilac
Hawthorn
Weigela
Hawthorn (Red May)
Grengage
Hornbeam
Dogwood
Hazel
Cherry
Silver Birch
Quince
Beech
White Mulberry

Copper Beech
Buddleia
Alder
Sweet Chestnut
Rowan (Mountain Ash)
Weeping Copper
Oak
Maidenhair
Horse Chestnut
Sycamore
Larch
Cedar
Walnut
Lombardy Poplar
Common Poplar
Field Maple
Gorse

Blackcurrant
Box
Bay
Crab Apple
Pear
Blackthorn
Ash
Aspen
Almond
Lime
Maple
Beech
Norway Spruce
Black Pine
Scots Pine
Tulip Tree
Willow Centoticus
Holly

Laurel
Juniper
Broom
Bamboo
Elder
Purple Lilac
Pear
Weigela
Greengage
Dogwood
Cherry
Quince
White Mulberry
Buddleia
Sweet Chestnut
Weeping Chestnut
Beech
Maidenhair

Entrance sundial

Rock Garden

Pond

Enclosure

School Road

Covered area

Mural

Chessboard mural

Bench

Car table

Insect Garden

Compass Rose

Mural

Covered area

Vegetable garden

Shed

Pond

Enclosure

Enclosure

Nursery Playground

Shed

Nature trail

Canon

Seat

Tyres

Stepping stones

Nine man's Morris

Shlegel Diagram

The Saddle

Magic circle

The Logs

Bog Garden

Bridges

The Fort

Number Snake

Hollow blocks

One Hundred square

DRIVE

Boardwalk

Pond

Nature trail

Ditch

DRIVE

Turf Maze

Nut
Orchard

Play Pit

Nature trail

Wild Flower Meadow

Wild Flower Meadow

Wild Flower Meadow

Bank

Bank

Bank

Enclosure

Enclosure

Enclosure

Enclosure

Hedge

0 2 4 6 8 10 metre
           approx.

SCALE 1:150

In this way she had created space in the narrow spit of land between the school and the road.

> You've got a *trompe-l'œil* effect. From the spot where we stand to the road is no distance, but in filling the middle ground you create a depth which isn't there at all. It's surprising how the arrangement of forms and a planting scheme create this powerful illusion.

She has some old photographs with the buildings on the other side of the road, and 'they surprise you because you realise how close everything is to you'.

Aconites, snowdrops, crocuses and narcissi flower before the trees are in leaf. They are set in natural drifts so you can see and smell them, avoiding the formal ranks of town parks. The aim is for a 'natural profusion of spring flowers to delight eyes and hearts'. On one side is 'a shelter-belt so the wind doesn't scour the playground'. There is even a 'secondary shelter-belt' behind. The playground was 'not very hospitable' to begin with, and 'the centre must be kept open because it's tarmac, can't be colonized easily' and the children need the space to play in all weathers. You can plant trees around the edges to

> provide constant contact with the plants and the smells and the changing forms all the time . . . The idea is to put children in a woodland setting where, around the hard edges of the playground, trees droop, drop leaves, shed blossom, produce apples . . . Plants in the gardens offer different smells to attract insects, birds and humans, and if you want to go on a ladybird safari or you want to do snail-racing, it's all available to you.

The school site has to be 'managed'. Coppicing and pollarding are regularly carried out on some of the trees. Coppicing involves cutting a tree back and induces 'throwing a lot of new spurs, providing very good cover for birds, and better nesting potential'. Pollarding removes the crown of a tree (preventing it growing too tall), and it then sends out new branches from the top of the stem. Willows were treated in this way, the cut branches then providing nourishing food for the sheep. A horticulturist friend of the school had demonstrated how to prune the fruit trees. Sue herself comes out with secateurs occasionally but to do several things, including 'to prevent the horse chestnuts coming through, and anything that is an alien, such as laburnum or sumac that come in with the leaf litter'.

The school explains its aims, strategies and central philosophy thus:

> Learning, play and dreaming have a unity which inspire each other. Adults tend to separate the parts, children do not . . . We help them stretch their intellectual powers by teaching out-of-doors and organ-

ising natural renewable resources in the same careful way as with organising an indoor classroom. Fruit trees bloom and fruit over pathways; maths diagrams cover the tarmac; old logs and low walls provide seating, and there are many places to hide and be silent . . . It is continually evolving . . . by adding new trees, new playground designs, different playground furniture – and by seasonal changes, daylight length, plant growth, and animal and insect activity. The hard spaces are framed by gardens and woodland areas and protected by them. All provide easy hand, eye, ear and nose contact and feed the intellectual, emotional and spiritual elements. Around the playground are boats, walls, logs, stepping stones, a tunnel, a bird wall, buildings (a castle, a look-out post, a cave, a play table, a house), all designed to excite the imagination and interest, and provide lots of dramatic play.

The playground is marked out with designs for games collected from around the world: Pong Hau Ki, a Schlegel diagram, Nine Man's Morris, Achi, Star, concentric circles, a number snake, a hundred square, a chess board (with pieces made by a parent), a logic track, a compass rose (a guide to the school's position). Whenever the weather permits, the children all eat out of doors, under the canopy of the trees. They bring out the tables and put them on the pathways. Occasionally they set up old carpets under the trees for the children to sit on.

Sue points to how things could have been improved, for example

the pinetum should have been extended by another five or six metres, so that there would have been nothing in this area except cone-producing trees. You could have gone from tree to tree, looked at the characteristics and noted the similarities and differences . . . Again, it would have been better to group silver birch together with the holly so that there was an aesthetic keynote there. You'd have grouped the species of oaks together so that you could move from tree to tree, showing children how they differed.

She hopes others learn from these points. The site is still developing. For example, she pointed to the trees lining the drive: 'Eventually these trees will arch. In three or four years they will join up, and give the sensation of an old country lane.'

Many schools, especially those inherited from the Victorian era, are rather grim, austere and sombre buildings, with a hard surface for play (if fortunate), and a field for games (if even more fortunate), the whole surrounded by a wall or fence signifying a strict boundary between the school and the outside world. Unsurprisingly, many pupils have experienced these as alien, imprisoning places from which they have been glad to escape at the end of the day back into the real, natural world (see, for example, Chapter 6). Coombes contrasts markedly with that kind of school, offering a resource which many might have assumed would be more 'naturally' available beyond the boundaries of institutional life. It also enriches not only the official side of school, but also the informal. Research among 7-year-olds has shown that playtime and dinner take up 28 per cent of the school day (Tizard *et al.*, 1988). The playground has wide educational significance. It is an arena, for example, for the transmission of cultural information, especially about gender (Grugeon, 1988; 1993). However, the quality of interaction might be variable, with bullying and fights prominent (Tizard *et al.*, 1988). Further, teachers seem to feel that the quality of children's interaction is declining (Blatchford, 1989). In some ways, then, it is not surprising that pressures in the National Curriculum have been leading to demands that playtime be reduced (Ashley, 1993). An alternative strategy is to make more provision for playtime. Research by Blatchford *et al.* (1990) showed that children themselves wanted, among other things, more permanent equipment, better game markings, 'green' additions and structural changes – items provided at Coombes. Thus children's informal interaction, as well as their formal education, stands to be enriched by these developments. Coombes would say playtime is not just worthwhile but essential.

Learning principles

Clearly this kind of development is strongly motivated by love of, and concern for, the environment, and the desire to give children a good start to becoming environmentally literate. It speaks to one of the major issues confronting the world today. It is one of the cross-curricular themes in the National Curriculum. But it is not only an issue and a theme. It is also a major resource for learning in general, equivalent to the indoor library. There are three major principles underpinning the teaching approach to the construction and use of the grounds: involvement, holism and inspiration. The first two produce the third. I shall consider each in turn.

Involvement
One of the school's handbooks affirms:

> Children will not easily be persuaded by adult talk, by reading books, or seeing slides or photos. Their energies and inclinations demand action – and where better than in their own school grounds. Education from the close-at-hand is what carries communication and power and provides the foundation stones and building blocks for the adults of the future.

Elsewhere is stated:

We learn by touching, smelling, hearing, seeing and responding emotionally and spiritually to stimuli. We can reinforce the experience by talking, reading and writing, but the starting points have to be direct, personal experiences . . . Our intention is to give predictor experiences, and to expedite and give learning to more abstract and symbolic thought through these concrete starting points . . . the spiral curriculum is based on these early starting points.

'Hands-on' activity is considered essential, and the grounds are designed to facilitate it. The 'all-weather' concrete path through the grounds was planned so that 'children will have contact with the wild flowers and with the fruit, without disturbing the very delicate under-storey'. Around the beds are 'herbs and pleasantly smelling things that you can pluck and pocket, because it's something that you might draw out later on when you need a little bit of nose and mouth comfort'. The children distribute handfuls of sunflower seeds in the gardens, and then farm them:

They can pull the sunflower out, take the seeds out of the head, pull it apart to see how it's constructed to get some idea about the detail . . . I know that lots of people don't like those ideas about picking, but we believe in giving children back their rights . . . Hands are the cutting edge of the mind, and if you don't put hands on, and have smell and taste and contact, then you cannot actually move forward or progress. It isn't any good bringing children out here with their hands behind their backs. They need to have hundreds of seeds in their hands to plant. The result should be prolific enough for children to harvest in quantity and investigate the whole plant.

New opportunities are appearing all the time. In the ditch, rushes are beginning to grow, and

When you're talking about rush torches, rush mats, or reading the traditional stories like *Cap o' Rushes*, there'll be the means in the school gardens to come out and access the plant itself. Books offer vicarious learning – for young children, the direct experience is crucial.

On the last day of the Easter term it is traditional for everybody to make their own 'bird nest' from materials which the birds use naturally.

So you pick apart two or three old nests and you look at books or slides. Then you go out and you identify moss, straw, twigs, dry grass, dead leaves. Then you put these things together and you try to make a nest. Of course, the easiest ones are those made of moss because they hold together so well.

Many different kinds of life abound. The habitat piles guarantee hibernating newts, and

> [there] are niches for different forms of life. If we shifted this lot now, I could absolutely guarantee we'd find five or six toads. That would be enough for a group to have a lesson. You'd have to come out and find them first, but it's absolutely dependable. They would be handled gently, placed in an aquarium, and brought indoors. They would have their lesson on living things, then bring them out later in the day and release them, so they return to their original habitat.

The children pond-dip throughout the year, finding newts, toads, frogs, water snails, insects, leeches, dragonflies and many other forms of life. There are some 'remarkable butterflies, caterpillars and moths . . . the minute you get a whole lot of wild flowers, you begin to get a lot of night-time activity with moths'. They had set moth traps, so that the children could study them, being sure to release them afterwards.

On the afternoon of the second day of my visit, the shepherd came in to wash the sheep. All of the school witnessed this, suitably clad in rubber boots and aprons. They joined in the hosing and washing. They felt their fleeces before and after. Sophie felt 'lots of bits when she rubbed them', Richard 'lots of dirt', Chris 'some twigs, and it was very scratchy'. After their shampoo they were 'nice and soft'. Others said, 'It stunk of dirty', 'I rinsed the sheep with a hosypipe'. Afterwards they wrote about and illustrated their experience. Alex (5 years old) wrote a page of emergent writing, but he read it to me with perfect sense. Apparently, it was his first attempt at writing. This was what he read:

> The water was warm and the sheep liked it. All the boys and girls thought it was good. They put in the bath took turns at squirting at the sheep with the hosypipe. The sheep was scared. The hose was too fast. So it just be brave and didn't scare it. It was nearly liked it – liked the bath, but not the hosypipe.

This seemed to me a brilliant attempt at a first story, which conveyed the basic details, the feelings involved (especially of the sheep), and some intelligent reasoning.

The dominant feature of the grounds is undoubtedly the trees. There are immediate rewards in terms of learning, and also a larger one. 'Growing a future wood is a most rewarding experience'. The school has a 'grow your own forest' idea, which involves all the children, and gives a sense of directly contributing to a small part of the planet. That very autumn they had planted some 30 trees, with each class group having six trees to plant. Sometimes they sowed seeds, pips or stones, but most trees were bought as whips or larger. 'That means you can get hands-on, and can help to dig the hole and all that sort of thing.' Children had been planting trees regularly for 20 years. Some years, a class might only have had a couple of trees to plant, but in other years 'every child in the school will plant a tree – that's the nicest thing'.

Having planted trees, you have the right to enjoy them. For example:

> We always pick our own Christmas tree and we cut it down cere-monially, stand around it, carry it in, and decorate it on that day with things the children have made. If you have the responsibility and the joy in planting, you are entitled to pick and harvest.

Ivy, holly and mistletoe are also grown and used in this way. The same applies to the fruit trees – apple, pear, quince, medlar, cherry, almond, hazel, chestnut, walnut and plum. Some fruits are eaten fresh, others are used to make jam, jelly and chutneys; the rest are taken home. In September, every child goes out and ceremonially picks an apple, goes in, rubs it, bites it, and eventually goes out again and plants the pips, which also connects with traditional tales such as those of Johnny Appleseed and William Tell. The crops help the teachers deal with vital concerns such as

> diet, methods of food preservation, experiments with salt, sugar and vinegar, the seed-to-seed cycle, patterns of weather and its effect, mildew and fungus, decay and death, symbiotic relationship, para-sites, soil structure, annual and seasonal patterns, food chains, our dependence as human beings on the soil in general.

In other ways, too, trees are a considerable resource. There are trees 'to climb, to work under, to swing on . . . Their shapes, textures and colours fill the mind as well as the skyline.' They play among them, eat under them. Branches overhang recreation spaces and become part of their re-creation.

They have planted trees around the playground and up to the school buildings,

> mitigating the effect of the prevailing east wind, giving colour and shape to their once naked boundary, and offering children eye, ear and nose contact with a range of living things. What the children view from the school windows and in the playground is a variety of pictures, changing throughout the year. It excites their interest, stim-ulates their curiosity, and feeds their intellect and imagination.

Above all, it's the *feel* that you get from it that counts.

The hands-on experience is taken through from the input of knowledge and sensation – the initial sowing of seeds, planting trees, handling leaves, etc. – to demonstrations of its output – the making of books, plays, bird-nests even, and the cooking and eating of food. There are some magnificent bound books on display, all made by teachers, with some help from parents. Some of these have wooden covers, painted illustrations and beautiful photographs. They provide both a record and a vivid means of reflection. Among them are 'The Coombes Potato Harvest', 'Coombes School's Stone Soup', 'Coombes School's Recipe Book', 'Porky and Brian' (about the school's pigs), 'Pumpkin Day', 'Making Pancakes', 'A Planter at Work: A Guide for Young Woodlanders', 'Megan the Sheep', 'Growing Food: The Seed to Seed Cycle', 'Cutting Down a Tree', 'A Bird's Eye View of the Coombes', and several stories. At the time of my visit there was a painting exhibition under the heading 'Our first trees are in blossom', with pictures of quince, cherry, pear, plum, apple and medlar.

This close contact with the grounds, the application of all their senses, and their involvement in its development and maintenance, gives the children, Susan feels, a sense of ownership. There are no complicated rules governing their use of the grounds. Susan was 'very deeply influenced by the view that "no one person owns land, or the past"'. During the summer and autumn they have days when the car park at the front of the school becomes the playground. The children are free to go into the wooded areas there. Compaction and wear problems prevent this happening every day, for you would have 'no herb layer left, and no regenerative system'. There was also a 'lot of fascinating caterpillar and insect life, like the hawk-moth, for example, which drops off trees and depends on a soft landing and an immediate burial to go through metamorphosis'. If it is compacted, then it can't go into its next stage, and 'that's been the tragedy of a number of wild areas where you let folks go anywhere'.

It is a freedom, therefore, which operates within rules emerging from the exigencies of natural preservation. It is the same natural laws that give the children their rights – rights with responsibility. A school pamphlet asserts that 'an imaginative, rich environment which meets all human needs is every child's right. By working with children, we're assisting them towards the future which is theirs'.

The range and variety of places for children to go, to observe, to play, talk, sit quietly on their own, adds a further dimension to children's learning and development.

> It gives the children a new feel and a sense of ownership about many of the places in the school, and they don't have to play only in the same spot. It's so tranquillizing for them. It isn't something that you can verbalize, but being surrounded by beautiful things in interesting form has a deep effect on the human psyche.

Holism
For the Froebelians, nature study is a means to understanding the unity of creation:

Country children grow up in an environment of farms and gardens where there is birth, life, death, life re-born year in, year out in a wealth of example . . . the whole seasonal rhythm of nature that mirrors the rhythm of life itself. This, in its wholeness, is not experienced by the city child. We cannot recreate it in the classroom, but we must seek whatever instance we can to illustrate this cycle of life . . . to develop an appreciation of the beauty, purposefulness and slow sureness of natural growth (Hutchinson, 1961, p. 1).

This emphasis on holism is a prominent feature at Coombes. The staff make no distinction between the learning environment inside and outside the school, and work to promote the universality of the learning experience.

The 'oneness' of life

In attaching learning to natural life, there is an aim of showing its roundedness, interconnectedness, patterns and rhythms. These are firm bases for learning. The whole grounds, for example,

are meant to be something of a botanical clock, so that the production of small groups of wild flowers like bluebells, snowdrops, lilies of the valley, come at dependable points in the year. So the botanical clock runs and re-runs, and gives you some idea in the two years that you're here of continuity and the annual cycle.

Projects in the grounds follow the cycle of the seasons, with festivals, special days, activities such as sowing, planting, picnicking, harvesting and dramatic events. Two years is a long time in the life of a child, but Sue brings other aids to inform understanding of these cycles, such as photographs, the making of books, and the showing of slides.

There were enough sunflowers that year for each child in the school to have one, and for use in maths, science and art work. Their growth rates were observed, and heads dissected to show their seed arrangement. They had a sunflower jungle in the school hall, and had a 'teddy bears' picnic' where they feasted on sunflower seeds, margarine made from sunflowers, and sunflower honey. Sharing and co-operation are important principles underlying these events.

The environmental aim is also prominent. Among these trees, Sue likes to think it gives you a feeling of 'being in a jungle' and 'the delicacy of the rain-forest':

If you can begin to glimpse something of the fragile nature of the planet and about how some resources are renewable, and that, in renewing them, there is an adventure and a beauty, and the tying of the human to the rhythms beyond a single life . . .

The centrality of the earth is emphasized:

> Crops such as rhubarb are harvested by the children, who then wash, chop and cook it and feast on it before they go home. This is an essential experience if you're to understand that all food comes from the soil and all matter ultimately returns there. Children pick blackcurrants, squash them, look at the colours, know that that's the basis for blackcurrant yoghurt, Ribena. It's tying you to origins, it's giving us literally food for thought.

Sue considers it vital that children be involved in growing and harvesting food crops. They grow peas, beans, onions, marrows, pumpkins, tomatoes, artichokes, potatoes. This activity is used in all curriculum areas. At harvesting, for example, children are involved in sorting, setting, counting, grading, weighing and estimating for mathematics. Social education as well as technology is a central feature in the cooking, eating and sharing of food, some of which takes place in an 'earth and sea festival' which is part of the celebration of the autumn harvest. Food not eaten or used at school may be taken home. Children thus witness at first hand the seed-to-seed cycle.

Processes are experienced from beginning to end. An example is when the sheep are sheared:

> We start a wool workshop immediately that day . . . felt-making is lovely. You can look at hats and other things, but you're also making thread and twisting fibres for strength and doing technical things with it. The children begin to understand that the raw fleece is the basis for carpets, blankets, clothes.

The school also has a textiles day, when the wool is fleeced, dyed, carded, spun or woven or knitted. The children also make simple spindles.

Every attempt is made to ensure that as little as possible is wasted at Coombes. The sheep are moved every three weeks, and 'in cropping the grass, they're actually helping the wild flower production'. When there is no grass to graze, coppicing and pollarding provide fodder for the sheep. The basic soil is clay. So they have dug a ditch and opened one end to give a clay bed. Children harvest the clay to resource their craft work. Seeds are returned to the ground. Thousands of tons of leaf litter swept from the roads by Wokingham District Council have been dumped at the school and used for landscaping. The leaves form compost heaps which decay to provide humus-rich forcing beds.

> Dead animals are buried, and later disinterred for study of their skeletons. If children or parents come across a road kill which is not in too bad a state, we encourage them to bring it into school. We then bury it and leave it for 18 months or so. Then the teacher will

exhume it. What we try to do is to match up a fresh carcass with an exhumed one. There are badgers, cats, foxes, etc., buried all over the grounds.

Integrating the curriculum
The holism that ties all the children to matters in hand through the mediation of the environment is reflected in the way the environment also serves as an integrating force on the curriculum. A school pamphlet declares:

> What we do outside at school feeds what happens inside and resources it, and vice versa. It has significance for every curriculum area, and in particular for language. The environmental work acts as a catalyst throughout the school.

Language is particularly important, the children being continuously involved in describing, explaining, questioning, experimenting and testing. They contribute their ideas to change, write about their experiences, sharing them with others. Flowers are used for mathematics, science, language and craft work. There are opportunities for historical and religious research. The system itself is the medieval one where everything flourishes with the 'weeds'. 'There's rosemary, and wode for dyes, and bay, all sorts of historical and medieval plants.' This year they made pot-pourri, herbal teas, jellies, etc., from the crops. Sue pointed to the lambs: 'How do you get across this metaphor of "feed my lambs", or "as the Father cares for his sheep" – the poetry of the Bible – unless you have direct experience at some point with these things?'

Through these means they try to give children 'connectors' with past traditions and age-old customs. They seek a positive valuing of the past, a link with their cultural and spiritual heritage to give meaning to the present. Sue argues that personal foundations are necessary for the appreciation of literature, art, music, religion, history, etc. Environmental work 'introduces and reinforces concepts of creation, care, order, love, families, birth and death, all of which may be ascribed to a supreme being'. A favourite quote is that of Sir Thomas Browne: 'If you want to know God, look around you. Nature is the art of God.'

Coombes is offering one way in which an overfull (Campbell *et al.*, 1991a), compartmentalized curriculum can be integrated. D. H. Hargreaves (1991) has raised questions about coherence and manageability in the National Curriculum. He distinguishes between content coherence (within and between subjects), and experiential coherence, that is, learning as it is experienced by pupils. He summarizes John Holt's (1964, p. 34) view of pupils standing 'amid a bomb-site of disconnected bricks and fragments'. Teachers are facing 'a massive task of curriculum co-ordination', and much of that is left largely to them. He fears that many teachers will render the task manageable by doing things in a mechanical way by ticking off checklists. Coombes offers a way of achieving coherence through bringing the curriculum to life. Through the environment, it is able to demonstrate the interrelatedness of subjects and their internal consistency, through methods that feature single subjects and through multidisciplinary topics. They break down the traditional boundaries between school and playground, and between school and the outside world. By regarding the grounds as a 'classroom' or 'library', and by promoting interaction among all these spheres, they contribute to a sense of unity. The world is the school, and the patterns, cycles, regularities and interdependability of natural forms of life present cohesive agencies for the curriculum. With the kind of environmental education envisaged by Wheatley (1992, p. 30), it is 'far more than just a combination of programmes of study extracted from science and geography. It also encompasses moral, cultural, spiritual, political, aesthetic and emotional dimensions. It touches on all aspects of our lives.'

Involvement and holism also find expression in the social life of the school. Where children are taught in a context which is 'very social, very involving, and democratically underpinned, it's likely to be absorbed and remembered and taken in as an owned part of what is being done to you'. Further, the social life of the school is

> the beginning of morality. That is what buoys it up emotionally. We come at that through increasing the social ambience in the school and people's awareness of each other. You create society in the microcosm in such a way that it isn't competitive, it's very much dwelling on the collaborative and the co-operative, and our responsibility to each other. It's the only defensible morality . . . The most important thing we could do is to provide an education for a high social IQ so that children can adapt and absorb, and know the really pertinent issues, the multicultural and multifaith issues, if we're to live in a world that doesn't see itself in such separate bits.

Inspiration and excitement
Motivation, stimulation, inspiration, confidence – are all generally regarded as highly significant factors in learning. The gardens provide an air of excitement around the school, a buzz, that engages all the senses and keeps them alert. The involvement and holism contribute to this. Another contributory feature is relevance. A school pamphlet draws attention to the value of natural experiments:

> Our study of minibeasts, our design and technological experiments (to move logs, make shelters, lift weights), our experiments with fire, earth, clay, water and sound, are part of the perfectly natural opportunities which arise from their outdoor setting. The populations of

plants, fungi, insects and animals are the necessary elements for classifying, counting and recording in a curriculum which needs to be relevant, interesting, and, above all, meaningful to children.

In fact, it brings the whole curriculum to life. For example:

> You come out in the autumn term and there are hundreds of pine cones. There's a remarkable amount of fungi, beautiful fly agaric, for example, elderberries . . . That's what makes your fairy stories and literature come to life.

Nature induces a sense of wonder. Sunflowers, for example, 'give you this ability to show how a single season's growth from a seed as big as your fingernail will outstrip you by three times, because they grow up to two metres tall or more'.

Egan (1992, p. 130) has identified 'transcendent human qualities' in trees, and suggested how they can stimulate 'romance, wonder and awe'. It is interesting that he should select the topic of 'trees' within the subject of science as one of his illustrations of the promotion of imagination in teaching and learning. Useful as his proposals might be, however, they do not seem to include the kind of hands-on experience that is *de rigueur* at Coombes, which arguably does even more to advance his aims in stimulating children's imaginations.

Sue believes that children need to be challenged, and to be given chances to take risks to stretch their mental and physical capabilities. The playground, for example, is meant not to be 'a prison exercise yard', but needs to be developed into 'a place of a thousand opportunities',

> to encourage fantasy play, good social behaviour, the expression of motor skills, big physical movement – jumping, leaping, hiding, hopping about. Many of our playgrounds aren't physically challenging enough.

She feels that an excess of caution has led to children being provided with a sterile setting, which is against their needs. They 'actually need risk', and, if it's not provided, they miss many opportunities for development. She cited the children of privileged backgrounds, who ski, ride, aquaplane, glide, etc., 'during the holidays and at school'. The teachers also needed an element of risk, and this contributed to the excitement:

> It's the atmosphere that's set in a room – when you walk into a classroom and you feel that buzz coming out from the children, a sort of subdued excitement, or not so subdued excitement, a certain vitality, which comes in part from the teacher being vulnerable to experiences . . . We're constantly putting ourselves at risk in front of the children, and some things can go disastrously wrong. It's necessary for children to see that.

Some conditions for success

Coombes has become a show school, with an international reputation. It has won awards, features regularly in the educational press, has been the subject of television programmes, has had books written about it and serves as a resource and model for others. It serves regularly as a site for field trips for other schools. In 1989 the school had 948 visitors, looking at issues such as environmental provision, and the way in which the science programme operates. The school is frequently contacted by people wanting information. It had been visited by educationalists, landscape architects, designers, environmentalists, ecologists, etc., from Finland, Sweden, the Netherlands, the USA, Japan, Nigeria, France, as well as the UK all in the same year. The staff have contributed to local and national in-service teacher courses, to international courses (in the USA, Australia and the Far East), and to national projects such as 'Learning through Landscapes'. What are the factors behind its success?

At the centre of operations is the 'critical agent' (Woods, 1993a), Sue Humphries, who had the vision, faith, values and beliefs to launch the project, the resolve and patience to sustain and develop it, and the personal skills to surround herself with and inspire like-minded people to contribute to the enterprise. In line with her philosophy, Sue's self was invested in the school, and I shall discuss this further in Chapter 7. Sue is supported by a staff of like-minded colleagues who share her vision and are equally enthusiastic. Some have written articles and books, and appeared on television. While Sue provides leadership, it is leadership by example. 'There is no line manager', she says. 'It's consensus politics here. If a teacher can see a fun way to deal with something, then they know they can go and do it.' There is no bland conformity among them. 'All our staff have got very different ideas about what should be done', said Sue. 'They don't always concur.' Consequently the group is very creative.

> If you're working in a very comradely way, other people's interests will work on you. If somebody says 'I really think we should do *The Water-Babies*', everybody's digesting this idea and thinking, 'Yes, but how?' She'll then go on and say, 'I see one of us as Tom, and here we all are, and there's the children doing the different features of the book', and breathing life into it and taking up the moral issues out of it. So you find yourself caught up in *The Water-Babies* out of one person's enthusiasm for it. If you're susceptible to each other you want to see your fellows succeed, and you want to see the idea come to fruition. There's been a lot of talk about 'ownership', but actually it means a certain determination to see an equal success in the teaching group for each member of staff.

The staff do agree, of course, on the basic values. A measure of difference on points of detail, and the freedom to express it, is regarded as healthy. There has developed at Coombes, therefore, a distinctive culture of collaboration (Nias, *et al.*, 1989) with its prominent characteristics of valuing individuals, interdependence, openness and trust (see also Pollard, 1985). Sue spoke of the ability to 'catch messages out of the ether', and being

> deeply aware of the culture that you represent, and constantly enlarging or modifying it, and the way that we beam back to each other what we stand for in very frank discussion. That's probably one of the reasons why our staff meetings meander about a bit, but we're very busy catching clues from each other about what our culture is . . .

Beyond the staff, they have developed a strong supportive community culture, which is all part of the Coombes ethos. Sue spoke of the 'tremendous support' they received from parents; 'if you organize it, you make the whole community part of the work'. An illustration of Sue's opportunism was given during the sheep-washing. Limara said: 'My mummy washes her own hair, and she used to be a hairdresser.' 'Aha!', said Sue, 'I have a bright idea . . . If we asked her to come in, would she give us a demonstration? I'll volunteer to have my hair done!' Thus are ideas generated to sustain the flow of interaction between school and community, and between schoolwork and everyday life. There were frequent 'displays of community affection which hasn't dwindled a bit', and a 'very impressive underground network which reaches out to people miles away and pulls them in to serve the school's traditions'.

Sue spoke of 'days of excitement, when it works for all of you – pupils, teachers, parents – as a kind of yeast'. There was an open door for parents to enter the school to observe or to assist. The school was a 'laboratory for anyone who steps over the door'. Especially if people feel that they want to do something, the more people develop a sense of ownership – an ownership action plan – we're all going to be better off for it'. This again, then, is promoting a sense of ownership, and involvement in process. The more it is theirs and the more they can enjoy what it has to offer, the more they will help promote and protect it. It is also another aspect of the holism that pervades the underlying philosophy, involving all who have links with the school in whatever role. On special days, when extra adult help was required, they turned out in force. But they were free to use and enjoy the grounds themselves. Sue has fond ideas of an 'open school' for use by the community in the evening, perhaps as a place for youngsters to go, but there was damage to the grounds in initial experiments.

Community Service Workers are another resource. Every day there is somebody from the courts serving an order, and on the whole this works well.

They go and work in the classrooms at times. It's therapeutic for them to be with young children, and it's nice for the children to have another adult model, and somebody younger than the teachers. That's how we get the labour done basically . . . for instance, I've got a couple of really tough lads at the moment. They've put the tables out on the pathways (i.e. for dinner), and they don't mind how much running out to the tables and back they do.

Some work at the school at weekends, under teacher supervision. Sue herself

might do eight Sundays on the trot, and then I'll work with a whole party of them, perhaps a dozen. We'll start at ten in the morning and finish at four in the afternoon. They'll do some biggish, labouring job that I can't manage, like mixing cement, digging holes, cutting turf, sometimes even playground painting.

Sue is a strong believer in the idea of community service. She said if she had not gone into teaching she would have entered the probation service.

Conclusion

The Coombes experience bears on issues of crucial current relevance. The first concerns the theory of learning and the teaching methods espoused by the staff. In its emphasis on involvement, activity, discovery, freedom, risk, child-meaningfulness, 'bringing the curriculum to life', imagination, holism, non-cognitive as well as cognitive processes, creativity, owner-ship, and so forth, it is in line with current constructivist approaches (Edwards and Mercer, 1987). These retain some of the elements of Plowdenesque child-centredness, but have the teacher in a stronger facil-itative role. Primary pedagogy is currently very much a subject of debate, as noted in earlier chapters. Within this debate, Coombes keeps strong faith with its beliefs, grounds its principles in practice, and produces results in excess of National Curriculum requirements (this is the subject of the next section). In other words, it shows how, given certain condi-tions, it can be done.

A distinctive feature is the constant generation of intellectual excite-ment. Many of their activities have the features of 'critical events' (Woods, 1993a). They show concern for the same kind of rhythm of learning, involving detailed planning, pupil and teacher creativity, and sometimes frenetic building-up to a 'celebration', or, as Sue described it, 'a day with a big kick in it'. Personal and social education figure promi-nently, together with the subjects of the National Curriculum, and teachers as well as pupils are changed and developed as a result of their experiences.

· The aim is learning that is more meaningful to pupils than purely academic exercises. So much learning in formal education is of the latter kind. Research on young pupils' perception of mathematics, for example, has shown that for many it was 'an activity . . . divorced from reality', and that this view 'starts for many pupils in primary school if not before' (Hunter *et al.*, 1993, p. 23). Where parents helped their children, 'unfortunately, by providing practice in routine rules and number facts they may actually have been strengthening the children's perception of mathematics as a formal exercise' (p. 23). The authors recommend that 'the links between the mathematics being taught and the child's life outside school need to be made explicit and established very early in the primary school years' (p. 25). The same point holds for other subjects. A wealth of research points to how knowledge becomes compartmentalized, particularly at secondary level; how groups of teachers struggle for status for their subject (Ball, 1982; Goodson, 1983), in the process differentiating from others; how that status can come to be associated with subject 'marketability' (Ball, 1981; Measor, 1984). These tendencies will inevitably be given a boost by the subject-centred National Curriculum, with its 'core', 'foundation' and 'other' categories. The Coombes experience offers a model for countering these trends (though not obliterating them), and for grounding knowledge in pupils' worlds.

Secondly, Coombes illustrates the importance of context for learning. This, of course, is a major point in constructivist literature (Donaldson, 1978; Bruner, 1983). Sociologists also have drawn attention to the significance of the nature and arrangement of space for learning, and for conceptions of knowledge. Different contexts tend to induce different forms of behaviour from both pupils and teacher (Stebbins, 1970). For example, the traditional organization of the classroom, with teacher on a raised podium with pupils facing in serried ranks leaves little scope for anything other than 'talk and chalk' (Edwards and Furlong, 1978), and sends clear messages about the unequal relationship of teacher and pupils. Westbury (1973) argues that 'chalk and talk' techniques are dictated by context rather than philosophical conviction, context in turn being determined by resources (see also Hargreaves, 1988). In other words, it is a 'coping strategy' (Hargreaves, 1978; Pollard, 1982).

Much of this research on space in schools was done in secondary schools. Primary schools appear to offer more variety. King (1978, p. 18), for example, found an infant school head advising: 'Make your room an exciting and stimulating place to live . . . a specially devised environment which allows the children to be individuals growing at a pace and in a way most suited to their individual capacities'. The contents of most rooms in his research reflected this aim. Coombes goes one better than this by applying this principle to its grounds. This provides a living classroom, with strong roots, continually evolving, which provides more of a link to children's own knowledge than an inside classroom, and a base for a holistic future, offering integration of curriculum and of self. It might be argued that by taking over the grounds in this way teachers appropriate for control purposes areas that used to be pupils' private places. However, it would appear in this instance that many more opportunities had been given for pupils to be private, and for them to fill that privacy how they wished. Furthermore, the 'arrangement of props', as it were, is guided by a grander design than teacher control, that is, environmental education in its broadest sense (see Wheatley, 1992).

How does a school like Coombes, with its highly distinctive ethos and strong sense of autonomy, adapt to the high level of prescription in the National Curriculum? In the next section, I portray this as appropriation.

Appropriating the National Curriculum

Introduction

The reforms instituted by the 1988 Education Reform Act represented a major challenge for Coombes. In particular, the subject-based nature of the curriculum, the high degree of specification, the behaviourism of the assessment, and the trend towards specialization in teaching, all militated against their philosophy.

The basis of the Coombes reaction to the reforms is one of appropriation. To appropriate is to take over, to use as one's own. In this case it implies that the school uses the National Curriculum to further its own ends, even though in some particulars its values seem diametrically opposed. This, of course, is not as simple as it sounds, and is not carried off without difficulty. However, in some respects the new requirements are well served by the Coombes approach, and they make full use of that ('engagement'). The well-established and internationally acclaimed ethos and achievements of the school give the staff a secure platform from which to view developments. They have to meet requirements, but do not do so slavishly. As reflective practitioners (Schön, 1983), they analyse the intensification for what it is, they do not become swamped or alienated by it ('recognition'). Comparing their responses with others' aids the identi-fication of their own values and beliefs, and sharpens and promotes the 'Coombes vision'. In their adaptation, they seek, and gain, the support of other key groups ('alliances'). In what follows I examine these key features of appropriation (recognition, identification, engagement and alliances). Through them it will be seen that what was feared as being potentially damaging, has, in some respects, strengthened; through confusion has come, in places, more clarification; and from despair has come new hope and stronger will. These comments were gathered largely from a recorded two-hour discussion with the whole staff in May 1993, supported by informal conversations and observation during the day (and by previous visits), documents on curriculum policy, articles written by members of the staff on general school policy, and notes on a recent 'focused visit' by two LEA inspectors. They were followed up by further discussions seven months later. My visits were part of a long-term study of the school, begun two years earlier.

Features of appropriation

Recognition

There is evidence of intensification (Apple, 1986) at Coombes. The school cannot avoid the pressures completely. Indeed, they are a considerable concern. However, it might be argued that the *recognition* of these is a form of appropriation. Teachers retain their reflective ability and are able to analyse the new developments for what they are. They recognize the threat of alienation that full compliance would imply. Their outlook is still governed by the old and continuing ideal, and they evaluate by its terms and criteria. They do this in spite of having been told 'not to criticize the materials for the first two years'.

Teaching the National Curriculum is 'impossible with a capital I', and 'it's very constraining in many ways as well'.

> It's just the enormity of it, and that's why you're dipping in all the time and just touching the surface of lots of things. It's the legal requirement as well, and that's what gives the biggest problem. That's when I get into my idealist mode and say, 'Well, if it carries on, I can't be a teacher', and I think lots of people consider that option.

This states the problem, but also asserts that there will be no change in the self, no loss of principle. Many of the school's activities would be justified in the National Curriculum, but there is no longer time in which to do them:

> What defeats us a bit is the vast amount of paperwork. You've only got a certain amount of time in the day.
> Our teaching time has been reduced because you spend so much of your time standing back observing and assessing that it must have reduced the time that you're actually teaching them or interacting with them.

Corners have been cut:

> When we did King Arthur, they all had a costume. There's no longer time to do that. You're lucky if you've time to make them a hat!

And other triumphant areas, while still triumphant, had been trimmed. Judy, for example,

> still runs a staggeringly good eisteddfod every year and does all sorts of lovely work, but once upon a time they'd all have been bards. We'd have had sheets, and made swords . . .

Other activities and projects had been lost altogether, such as the huge model towns they used to build, or acting out ceremonies at church. They had lost flexibility. It was 'a lot more difficult to say, "Today I'm going to do so-and-so because I want to and because I feel like doing it, and it'll be good fun . . ." ' This was not self-indulgence, nor did it happen often, but 'now and again it's so refreshing to just disregard everything and do something spontaneously' . . . 'on something that a child might have mentioned'. In curriculum terms, art and music have especially suffered. They still do much in this area in their classrooms, but there is no longer time to practise in the hall for concerts. 'There's too much going on for music.'

One of the most insidious effects of intensification is the misdirection of creative energy. Whereas before you would go home 'buzzing with ideas' to follow up for the next day,

> you're now spending so much of your energy on paperwork and form-filling, and the grind of it, and the feeling that you might be dropped in on at any minute, that you're exhausted. So much of our creative energy is being sapped, and that's a dreadful admission, but I think it's true.

On the other hand, you are required to go through processes that you know are unnecessary:

> You stop every now and then and think, 'What am I doing this for? I know that child can do it, I know that child understands it . . . without having formal assessment', but there is someone up the chain who comes in to look at your bits of evidence . . . That's sad, isn't it? I mean it's a game we play. We now think of what evidence we'll have at the end of it as opposed to thinking of the quality of the experience and the learning experience that would go on. You're now all the time thinking: 'Well, would it show that the child can do this, or do I need to adapt it in some way to show that the child can do it?'

Their main grievance, in common with many other primary teachers (see, for example, Pollard *et al.*, 1994), was with standardized national assessment. In the first run, in which Coombes pupils in general exceeded their standard levels, Sue felt 'we wasted three weeks – we all stood still'. They 'hated doing these tests' and it 'made their blood boil' because many of the tests were simply 'bad education'. They felt 'insulted' that they had 'no redress to analyse the tests and to come back and say "I'm sorry, this isn't working", or "this isn't suitable"'. Nor were they able to argue about other highly debatable aspects, such as 'the way the National Curriculum emphasizes early attainment of some specific skills like reading and writing'. These were all 'highly political attributes of a good education', and they were being 'forced through some hoops that don't sit very easily on us'.

These teachers clearly have a conception of education that they feel is superior to that embodied in what they were at the time being required to do in the National Curriculum, where the emphasis was on 'product and standardization of the product'. In some respects, the contrast was enhancing their vision. It aided their sense of identification and unity in quite a cathartic way.

Identification
'Identification', therefore, is the second appropriation strategy. Comparing teachers' own views and practices with others, and with those involved in the National Curriculum and assessment, brings the principles on which their practices rest to the forefront of their minds, forces them to articulate, and hence sharpens their beliefs.

There were examples of past glories:

> We spent an enormous amount of time setting up massive exhibitions of work from the children. We did scarecrows, where every child made a life-size scarecrow and set it in the school grounds.
>
> I've been on courses where I've been shocked with some head teachers and co-ordinators of technology . . . we were talking about the re-drafting of attainment targets, and 'food' is no longer in Key Stage 1 . . . but it's one of the things which they can have as a common shared experience . . . You think of all the history that you get from time-lining, different cooking equipment and so on . . . but they said: 'No. If it's not down in black and white, then we will not encourage our teachers to teach it because they've enough in the National Curriculum and that's how we'll leave it.' And that's a sad thing, isn't it? That people look at those documents and think: 'This is it!' If we're honest, we actually look at the programmes of study and we giggle, we laugh at some of the examples. We've said: 'Is this serious? Is this meant to be an example of teaching this part of the National Curriculum?' It's so limited, and there's so much more you could do.

Humour aids the appropriation here. It lightens the gravity and disperses the offence. It ridicules the opposition, while boosting one's own morale (Martineau, 1972).

Coombes teachers rely on their tacit knowledge, which has been so strongly validated in their experience, and which is brought out even more strongly by comparison with some others:

> Our instinct is to keep on doing what we believe in and give the children first-hand quality experience in depth. When I look at little bits of the curriculum . . . we go into some other schools and we see them trying to implement something like science or technology or history or geography from a worksheet. We know how it *can* be done, and it can be *real*, and they can experience it, and we know we're doing the right thing . . . every time we go out we see things, and some things we think, 'Oh, that's good, we'd like to take that on board', but we also come back reinforced in our beliefs . . . The science SATs, for example, were nonsensical: paper and pencil tests – that's not science!

They gave examples of 'meaningless' versus 'real' tests. One purported to test children's understanding of magnetism, giving them pictures of items and asking them to indicate by a tick or a cross whether they would be attracted by magnets or not. Some children were putting a cross by the metal spoon. In discussion later, they were saying it had to be the correct metal – it had to have iron in it. The child, in fact, knows more than the test requires, but would have had that answer marked wrong. Similarly, the flower that was portrayed on the test could have been a 'metal brooch, a real flower, a plastic flower – it could have been anything – but it isn't testing anything'.

The teachers were proud of their children's imaginative and creative responses to unimaginative questions, like one where a go-cart was shown on a slope, and they were asked, 'how would you make the go-cart slow down?' One child had a wall at the bottom, not for the cart to smash into, but just wide enough for the cart to go through while rubbing its wheels on the sides of the wall, thus slowing down. Another drew himself at the bottom and explained, 'I'm going to push it back up the slope'. Another felt you didn't have to do anything since it was near the bottom of the slope and would soon slow down when it reached the bottom. None of these reasonable scientific answers were supplying the 'pull' answer required. Another question on the 'sun in the sky' had no compass points, no time of day in the pictures – 'it was just nonsense'.

The teachers here contrast their emphasis on process and creative reasoning with the objective approach of the National Curriculum requiring single correct answers. As with the old IQ tests, the more creative the children, the more likely they were to get the test wrong, because they could see different answers as being correct for very good reasons. The teachers applaud the latter achievement as good thinking, and decry the former for its blinkered small-mindedness.

A further contrast is provided by some teachers in other schools, where it was felt 'there had been a dangerous amount of complying', to the extent that teachers were in danger of losing not only control, but also their minds. They had achieved technician status, operating others' directives without question. Similarly, some in-service courses on how to apply the tests had been 'quite slavish about it, dotting the i's and crossing the t's, and quite reverent about the stuff'.

One new recruit opined:

> Coming in from the outside and having been to many other schools over the last few months, I've found this a truly dynamic staffroom. Everywhere else I've been, staff are so down, they're moaning, they're complaining, they feel very threatened and under pressure. They're using all their energy in that direction instead of saying: 'OK, this is where we are, this is the situation, what can we do about it, how can we use this?' This is such a refreshing change coming here'.

Elsewhere, the staff identify the market-forces argument behind the government reforms. They had heard that certain schools were being 'targeted' to be 'failing schools', that is, schools that were not meeting the criteria:

> It doesn't have anything to do with quality, with what you're giving to the children as an education. It has to do with market forces, money, power . . . and that's not what education's about – it's about people, not commodities.

> . . . you're not turning out a can of baked beans. You're dealing with the life of a child. You cannot impose those business terms.

There has been anger, regret, sadness, but also humour, dynamism, analysis, resistance, triumph. They face the crisis creatively, seeking ways in which they can use it to further their own brand of education. They have lost some activities and opportunities, and are pressurized for what they see as unproductive ends. But their vision is all the sharper, by contrast with the new order and many others' reactions to it.

The distinctive climate engendered at Coombes has been assailed, but not broken, by the government's reforms. Validated by years of work and experience, acclaimed by others on an international scale, it exists on a stronger and wider educational dimension than the government's efforts. This knowledge is the keystone of teacher morale in the school, so threatened generally (Pollard, 1992, Campbell, 1993). At the end of one round of SATs, one staff member said:

> It's been depressing because I disagree so much with that, but I only have to listen to my colleagues speak and to actually be reminded of why we're here and how much we believe in that. That's why I'm

here, too, and as long as we keep hanging on to that and believing in what we do, then there's very much a future, and that's what we're all fighting for.

Coombes can rescue and inspire new recruits. A student teacher at the school, now coming to the end of her year's course said,

> On a purely personal level about this school, I started the PGCE in September very confident, very positive, very committed . . . but until I came here I was almost on the point of dropping out, because every other teaching experience had been amongst people that are so demoralized, they just couldn't see anything good about anything at all. It was just having to match tasks to the National Curriculum and follow it slavishly, patchwork. I thought, 'I can't do this, this isn't what I believe in'. Coming here has changed that because we've seen how it can work. This environment's given me back my faith and it's given me hope . . . I've found that the children are put first. I've seen the National Curriculum, which I saw as paperwork in college, actually come alive for me in ways that I never thought it could come alive. It's shown me lots of ideas that I've never heard anywhere else . . .

A fellow student agreed:

> We've seen that it can be done, after struggling through the winter months, not thinking that this is possible, to actually see it, and the children enjoying it, it's wonderful to find. We just wish our colleagues could have come along as well . . . The great proportion of people on our course have felt demoralized when they've been called out for teacher practice.

Another wished

> I'd had a school like this when I was their age because I hated school. It was boring, dull, all sit at a desk and 'this is the work we're going to do today'. To come here and see the children enjoying it so much, it's wonderful . . .

All the teachers, in one way or another, affirmed their dedication to Coombes and its values:

> I did an afternoon's supply when Sue fell on a sunflower seed, then I did a maternity leave for someone and I've been here ever since. It's a very, very special place, and there is no way I have any wish to be anywhere else.

Others repeated this sentiment in a round of reaffirmation of commitment. The school's distinctiveness was its major strength, but also, in current times, was seen by them as a potential weakness, since it was:

unconventional, which is a word often used of us, but is not seen as a strength in the present government's vocabulary. It's seen as something that goes against the grain, and therefore is a danger and a threat.

In the face of these dangers, however, the main thing was 'not to lose our integrity'. Fortunately, their main resource is permanent. There are times when they sound a bit 'doom and gloomish':

> but you've only got to take a deep breath and just step outside with the children and then you know exactly what it's all about. When you watch the children out there really experiencing and learning and developing all these concepts which are detailed in the National Curriculum, that's what it's all about . . . I can't wait till the SATs are over. This Friday we'll be having a drink to celebrate and then I think we'll get back to what it's all about – really teaching the children.

This research provided them with another opportunity for reflection:

> I think it's very important for us to hear what we believe from each other, and you're giving us an opportunity now to just think back to what we do stand for professionally . . . with our debating in this way, possibly nothing will come out of this for two or three weeks, but in fact we're all articulating what we believe to each other, and that takes you on a little stride. It's quite subtle actually . . .

The reflectivity of the staff is aided in other ways – for example, by the numbers and variety of visitors (about 1000 a year), and by the visits and travels of the staff themselves. With regard to the first, there is the kind of reinforcement that comes from the enthusiasm and gratitude of others, as in this letter of thanks from a delegation from a local borough council.

> What an inspiration you are to us all! . . . You would have been delighted if you could have heard the comments . . . they were quite overwhelmed by all that they had seen . . . We are now all full of ideas for a new Environmental Resource Centre . . .

As for the second, Sue Humphreys, the head, has taught a prestigious early learners' course in the USA. Sue Rowe, her deputy, has been to Russia, and is a frequent visitor to Africa. Both Sues and Carole Cooke have been to Sweden to visit schools. Their international experience helps them put the National Curriculum into perspective. Their national and international reference set gives them strength and vision.

Engagement
Coombes teachers certainly found the National Curriculum constraining to some extent, but despite their reservations about the general

philosophy behind the changes, they seek to be positive in their response, and to use the National Curriculum, and to use it adventurously,

> as a baseline from which to grow, not to become slaves to it, but to actually use it and adapt it in the ways that suit our philosophy and don't perhaps narrow our outlook too much.

Their science curriculum policy statement, for example, says:

> Each area of the National Curriculum Science is covered over and over again in a two year cycle: much of the science work at the school goes beyond the requirements of the National Curriculum.

And:

> The National Curriculum defines the range of knowledge expected from the children in Key Stage 1, and the Science Policy at the Coombes encompasses this, and enhances it. The statutory requirements of the National Curriculum are seen as a base line of knowledge and understanding: the practice of the school is to take children beyond the base lines and the obvious, and to give them a deeper understanding of scientific issues.

The focus on certain areas formerly neglected was to be welcomed. Furthermore,

> [when] we do a big history or geography input specifically to cover certain points of the curriculum, we seem to be able to do it in a very imaginative way, a creative way which doesn't take away from the philosophy, and as long as we stick to that I think we'll be fairly happy.

An inspector who took part in a 'health check' on the school, took issue with their claim that they 'delivered the National Curriculum', saying:

> You do a lot more than deliver the National Curriculum, you actually use it as a sort of board to leap off. That's not to say that it's not without a lot of hard work, and it does sometimes feel like a huge weight on your shoulders.

There were exciting things they used to do which, with some ingenuity, they could still do. One recalled

> a very important module of work based on 'milk' – dairy products. We went to the farms, met the cows, the cows came here, we made cheese, butter, milkshakes, yoghurts . . .
>
> When I think of doing something like 'air', when we had the helicopter, the balloonists, the free-fall parachute people – that would be completely justifiable in terms of National Curriculum.

Submerged by the 'paperwork' for the moment, the vision spurs them on none the less. 'We think, well, we've just got to run with it this time'. This is what Lacey (1977) would call 'strategic compliance', wherein the individual accepts the prevailing system while entertaining private reservations. The 'compliance', however, is temporary, and there is an ongoing attempt at 'strategic redefinition', that is, to redefine the National Curriculum through their own values. Music, for example, has been downgraded in the National Curriculum. But Coombes manages to keep it going, not entirely in its full former glory, but 'once the SATs are out of the way, I hope we can get going again'. In general, Sue has hope and confidence for the future: 'I actually think it's going to be all right. One of my colleagues who gets worried at times, I keep patting her and saying "Don't worry! It's going to be OK"'. Another agreed: 'Stick it out'.

One colleague, newly returned to the school, thought:

> The staff here are really good, trying to get to grips with what is required of them, and they're adapting it and using everything they've got around them to present it in the best possible way that they can . . . Had I gone to some other schools I may not have wished to continue my career as a teacher. Having come here I feel that there is a way forward for me teaching . . . The spirit in a lot of other schools is very low, and I don't think I would have that commitment.

The development of the school grounds still goes from strength to strength. It is 'a fantastic resource' for the National Curriculum:

> When people were implementing science for the first time they didn't have the resources, but we've got a living laboratory . . . and we use it also for history, geography, technology, . . . we analyse more than we used to, as you have to justify what you're doing, whereas we used to operate a lot more on instinct.

The National Curriculum, therefore, has not inhibited their use of the school grounds: 'In fact, it's probably spurred us on to keep finding things out there to resource it'. One example is the 'turf maze'. Work on this followed the suggestion from one family, who had visited a maze in 1991, the 'Year of the Maze'. The following is an extract from the school's submission to 'The Royal Anniversary Trust Awards':

> Our children wanted to know why we did not have a maze! So, in the maths room, the children started work with simple grids and grid references, and they made models with bricks. In their technology work, the children used the mathematical models and began to translate these using rope, string and furniture. In the language area, the children heard the story of Theseus and the

Minotaur. They acted out the story; the children worked in pairs with a ball of knitting wool so that one child held the ball of wool while the partner unwound the wool and made a journey outside. He/she then had to re-wind the wool and retrace his/her steps to find their way back to the partner. Other traditional tales, such as Hansel and Gretel with the 'hunt and find' theme were enjoyed. Historical stories of perseverance and problem-solving were read, and the children could try out a variety of traditional maze designs in 2-D form.

Geographical skills were called into action when the children and staff had to identify an area of the school grounds large enough, and with the correct criteria, to contain a large turf maze. Scientific skills were drawn on as the children worked out how wide and tall the turf walls would need to be in order to be stable: they pondered what would hold the turves together, and the purpose of plant roots was identified and reinforced.

We enlisted a volunteer force of workers to help the children cut and transport turves, and to construct the maze. The maze has been an intriguing addition to the school grounds: it was the centrepiece for the acting out of the Epiphany Journey. The maze gave opportunity for every area of the curriculum to be called into action in an exciting and dynamic way.

Special mention might be made of science, which is the school's forte. Susan, and her colleague, Susan Rowe, have written two books on science teaching at Key Stage 1 of the National Curriculum, which aim to meet specified attainment targets *and* preserve their vision of science as a living experience (Humphries and Rowe, 1993a; 1993b). They deal with 14 themes, such as 'earth', 'water', 'air', 'fire', 'busy bodies', 'new life', 'death', 'how things move', 'light and colour', 'kitchen science'. They reflect Attainment Targets 2 (life and living processes), 3 (materials and their properties) and 4 (physical processes). The Coombes principles are stated in the introduction to the first book:

> Although the focus of each book is Primary Science, the method of presentation is that of an integrated, whole-curriculum approach, where sharing, discussion and theme-related activities set the children on a course of exploration and discovery in all subject areas. The activities are high interest ones which help the children to observe, experiment, research and relate their findings to real life situations . . . The chapter themes are rooted in the context of day-to-day events at home, at school, or in the immediate environment.

The authors aim to 'encourage the children to be active participants in experiences which are exciting, interesting and informative . . . We learn best what we enjoy doing. The books encourage the children to do, to discover and to evaluate . . . to be true scientists'.

This was the aim of 'Nuffield Science', an approach, popular in the Plowden era, with the emphasis on children engaging in 'real' experimentation and 'real' discovery, as opposed to the teacher simply imparting knowledge and illustrating by demonstration. The approach was articulated as long ago as 1898 by Henry Armstrong. He advocated 'heuristic' methods of teaching which involved children 'finding out' rather than being 'merely told'.

> Discovery and invention are divine prerogatives, in some degree granted to all, meet for daily usage . . . it is consequently of importance that we be taught the rules of the game of discovery and learn to play it skilfully. The value of mere knowledge is immensely overrated, and its possession over-praised and over-rewarded (Armstrong, 1898).

However, Atkinson and Delamont (1977), in a study of 'guided discovery instruction' at a medical school and an independent Scottish girls' school, argue that 'what appears as "discovery" is the recapitulation of the socially agreed nature of "science", "medicine" and the natural world' (p. 107). Typically, lessons would consist of 'mock-ups', situations designed to represent reality, though they are not themselves 'real science'. Atkinson and Delamont argue that 'such types of encounter are always precarious: they require a degree of careful creation and maintenance, and the borderline between bringing them off and spoiling them is narrow' (p. 97). The two science classes observed illustrate the dangers, one being 'stage-managed' by the teacher, the other not being managed enough and leading to 'muddle, confusion and anxiety' (p. 96).

The difference with the Coombes experiments is that they are real – using real materials on a real site for a real purpose. They do not recreate situations in a 'mock-up', and there are no artificial 'borderlines'. Atkinson and Delamont (1977, p. 106) affirm that

> The relationship between 'reality' and 'mock-ups' is dialectical. It is particular features of 'reality' that are selected and reconstructed to produce 'the working model'. In the same way, the model itself provides an interpretative framework whereby the reality may in time be understood. Through these 'reality-like' experiences, students amass a stock of typifications and recipes for action in typical circumstances in preparation for situations that are 'for real'.

One might argue that where the 'working model' is nature itself the correspondence to reality is closer, the pupil engages in more genuine discovery, the 'interpretative framework' has more of a unity, and rather purer (though applied!) science is produced.

All the practical experiments and activities suggested by Sue and Sue have been conducted and tested at school. They include digging holes and examining the soil for its structure and constituents, life and remains of life; the time capsule idea; growing crops; many experiments with water; many experiments and observations of plants and wild life; 'life counts' and 'safari hunts'; cooking; composting (recycling dead plant matter); collecting colours from the school grounds; listening for, and analysing, sounds; pushing and pulling; flying kites. Not all the activities use the school grounds, but they are the main resource. The young readers of these books are encouraged to ask their teacher to arrange for the local council to dump autumn leaves in the school grounds; and when these have decayed into rich soil, to try growing pumpkins, marrows or sunflowers.

Sue Humphries talked about their experiments with fire: preparing and lighting a bonfire (with an adult present), observing how different things burnt, noise, smells, colours, shapes, examining the ashes, using a biscuit tin as an oven for potatoes; experiments with candles, testing for light and heat; a visit from a fire engine (for which you need to plan weeks in advance); and various projects, including a candle vigil for Armenia. Again, the important thread running through the activities is that of life, in this case 'living fire'. For Sue, the National Curriculum 'doesn't open things up so that you can move off. Things are so well tailored that the spontaneous can be neglected. The magic cocktail of the children's reaction is missing.' Sue believes in a basic framework which you can then 'dress in all sorts of garbs. You need control of the basics before you can begin experimenting'. Sue tried to make the SATs as active as she could, doing things like planting and gathering. Similarly, with the National Curriculum, she and her colleagues have found ways of meeting requirements through their preferred methods. For example, they sent home requests for moving things and had a whole day of activity on 'push and pull', with bikes, skateboards, roller boots, scooters, sack-barrows, 'things with gears, bearings, axles'. Sue emphasized the social, as well as the physical and technological aspects, in the sharing of space and toys, and 'the considerate ways they rode round each other'.

This concern for social and cooperative learning is reflected in another book (Rowe and Humphries, 1994), which is a 'distillation' of their experience. This is a long way from the competitive, marketing ideology behind the recent changes (Ball, 1993), but such learning, which receives token acknowledgement in the National Curriculum, still figures prominently in the Coombes approach. The introduction states:

> One of the authors' aims is to raise the level of cooperative consciousness in children: they want children to catch on to the fact that all human beings can and must learn from each other. It is a struggle

to break down the competitive barriers which breed fear and suspicion amongst groups unaccustomed both to a cooperative ethic, and to sheltering all members. The common ground which gives children fun when working in teams and in small and large groups, and which fosters newcomers in the class, needs to be made explicit because it involves essential life skills. Curriculum provision for issues of race, gender and equal opportunity is partly covered through the playing of coooperative games and the involvement of everyone in a wide variety of social activities. It is in examining the outcomes of these exercises that the teacher is able to talk openly about fair shares, turns for everyone, vulnerability, risk taking and common needs (Rowe and Humphries, 1994, p. 3).

Coombes thus continues to blossom under the National Curriculum, and itself to provide a 'cutting edge' for learning through the environment for other schools.

Alliances
In the face of the considerable new powers of the Secretary of State and the range of directives, it is not easy for a single, small group of teachers to withstand the pressures, to take over and adapt, on their own. They may have strength in collaboration, but they also need allies and support. The Coombes staff realized this. They opted for a 'health check' – an unscheduled mini-inspection by two qualified inspectors. I asked the teachers if they felt their philosophy had been under attack and if they felt 'on the defensive'.

Oh no! That's the reason for having people come in to give us health checks, and to vouch for the effect of good hands-on experiences for children . . . Our two inspectors said: 'Your practice is far beyond your mission statement, get this sorted out . . . '

In other words, not only were they considered to be doing things right, they were not doing themselves justice in their accounts of themselves. This 'health check' had an enervating, morale-boosting effect on the staff:

When you actually read [the report], I mean it was wonderful that debriefing afterwards, because you do begin to wonder, especially when you go out and you're with teachers from other schools: 'Are we going down the right track? Is this right that we're doing this?' And all the things that were said . . . and that paper is very true to how they spoke to us that evening. It was really quite emotional because to have it affirmed that what we're doing is going down the right track by the guidelines that are set for a formal inspection meant a lot.

Even more reassuring was the news that the first full inspection under the new order would be led by the senior inspector who conducted the health check.

This feedback might be contrasted with that received from an inspection by Peter (Chapter 6), which was so critical, and which indicated such a culture shift from previous inspections, that it helped dispose him towards early retirement. Yet their philosophy of teaching was very similar. That had been Sue's fear:

> I thought: 'Well, if I've been encouraging my colleagues to do things which wouldn't be officially approved, it's got to be my neck on the block.' Having Dave and Anne here who have this Ofsted training and having them do the feedback afterwards made me feel for several days afterwards, 'My goodness! I'm like the cat that's had one of its lives handed back to it . . .'. We all felt very susceptible, I don't think there was any one of us who didn't feel exceedingly tender about the whole thing.

The chair and vice-chair of the governors were invited to hear the report – thus enlisting the support of another important group. The support of others was seen by the teachers as crucial in the survival of their vision:

> When people come in and say that what we're doing is good and important, they actually enhance what we're doing. It's so key, really important, and that's wonderful to hang on to on a day-to-day basis. But it's not reflected in what the government or LEA say.

There has always been a strong relationship between staff and parents at Coombes. Parents have free access to the school, and every day finds many helpers on site. They are strongly supportive of the school's philosophy. But

> the way we use parents has changed a lot. When they come in now you have to make sure that you see them before the start of the lesson and explain to them exactly what we'll be doing and why.

In other words, the parents' input is much more targeted.

A 'parent-helper' present at the discussion gave her opinion. She had left teaching just before the implementation of the National Curriculum, and was 'jolly glad to get out of it'. She had become reinvolved with education through her son's attendance at Coombes:

> I just think it's wonderful what goes on here and the way that they've adapted their ethos and their approach to education and tried to still carry on within the constraints of the National Curriculum. A memory that will go through with me for the rest of my life was of me coming to pick my son up, because I was picking him up at lunch

time, and then out in the car park the sunflowers and I thought this is just wonderful – that was revealing – his first day at school and he's been cutting down sunflowers, and he was working co-operatively with some of the other [older] children and they were counting seeds. I thought: 'This is what education is all about'. I don't know what went on before but I thought it's wonderful that they can still keep some of the traditions that have gone on and find a place for them within the National Curriculum and present them in such a creative way. I think it would be a very sad day if anybody ever came in and said that this wasn't the right way to go about providing education because I think this is what education's all about.

I have no means of knowing how typical of parents this is. But on all my visits to Coombes there have been large numbers of parents present, more than trebling the size of the staff, freely engaging with activities.

The staff are honest with parents, presenting their views and position to them

hopefully, with good grace . . . It would be immoral if we were saying: 'Look this is awful, and we're expected to do awful things with your children.' What we do is to tell them the truth, that we actually teach what we believe in, we adapt to what we believe in, that we adapt the National Curriculum . . . we do make them aware of the workload and what hoops the children will be expected to jump through, but we also assure them that their child will enjoy it, and we'll enjoy that process with them . . . It's a three-way thing that we'll all enjoy.

Their approach to the persuasion of other groups, therefore, rests on conviction and consistency. They do not employ strategic manipulation, presenting different truths to different groups:

They're far more confused. We're working with it and we're confused enough, but they're getting such mixed messages all the time. A lot of our parents have come from other schools where they haven't even met the National Curriculum. They've no idea what it is . . . So we feel we owe it to them and the children that we do keep them up-to-date with curriculum changes, and that we try to keep it as dynamic as we can. We all look a bit older and I've got some more grey hairs because of it, but we still try and do it . . .

And the support from the parent group is always very reassuring, isn't it? The feedback we get is one of understanding and sympathy.

Parents generally supported teachers in their dispute with the government that led to modifications in testing in 1993, and perhaps this was the decisive factor. The parent who, after the first year of SATs, 'turned up on the doorstep saying, "What are your SATs results?", and didn't want to know about the school and the school brochure, didn't want to come over the threshold' was very much in a minority. (In fact, the school has performed well at its SATs, regardless of the staff's views of the tests' inadequacy.) Numbers at the school – the acid test by the government's marketing philosophy – were bearing up well (nearly 200). It now had a nursery department, built with some of the proceeds from the Jerwood Award; and pupils were coming from outside the school's own area. If there were many more, Sue Humphries said, they would soon have to select.

The politics of appropriation

Through these various means – recognition, identification, engagement and alliances – the Coombes staff retain their distinctive identity and sense of purpose. But how real and secure is this appropriation? Is it possible, first, that they 'misrecognize' some of the signals? Clearly not in the way that this was conceived by Densmore (1987) and Apple (1986), where 'the increasing technicization and intensification of the teaching act . . . [is] misrecognised as a symbol of their increased professionalism' (Apple, 1986, p. 45). Such a misrecognition involves a strategic compliance totally at variance with the opposition and challenge adopted at Coombes. They see the intensification for what it is. They labour under it – they do not embrace it. The reforms somehow have to be made to work for them. They have a clear, strong vision of education, that is not amenable to compromise or distillation.

However, is it not possible that the appropriation is weak rather than strong, leaving them with the appearance of the Coombes vision rather than the substance, which has been taken over by the subject-dominated and standardized assessment driven National Curriculum? Maw (1993) points out that, despite this basic subject-based nature and structure, the National Curriculum Council (NCC) almost immediately attempted to reintroduce a discourse of 'the whole curriculum':

> Attainment targets and programmes of study are the bricks with which the curriculum must be built. Cross-curricular strategies bond these bricks into a cohesive structure (NCC, 1989, para. 19).

Maw draws on Bernstein's (1975) model of curricular types governed by different codes. The collection code curriculum is where

> contents stand in a closed relation to each other, that is, if the contents are clearly bounded and insulated from each other . . . Here

the learner has to collect a group of favoured contents in order to satisfy some criteria of evaluation' (p.87).

In an integrated curriculum, by contrast, 'the various contents do not go their own separate ways, but . . . stand in an open relation to each other' (p. 88). Integration does not involve simply cross-referencing between subjects, but 'refers minimally to the *subordination* of previously insulated subjects *or* courses to some *relational* idea, which blurs the boundaries between the subjects' (p. 93).

The NCC statement above, and the cross-curricular themes (which include environmental education) and skills (see NCC, 1990), suggest that the two ideas of 'collection' and 'integration' might be reconciled. However, Maw points out that Bernstein argued that any thoroughgoing reconciliation between the two was not possible, since they reflected basic societal differences in the distribution of power and principles of social control. They could only include weak elements of each other.

Was the Coombes appropriation, therefore, 'weak' in these terms? Certainly the core and foundation subjects are the power base of the National Curriculum as legislated, and this strength is consolidated by the assessment. Further, Bernstein stipulates a number of conditions if an integrated code is to be accomplished. There must be 'some relational idea, a supra-content concept, which focuses upon general principles at a high level of abstraction' (Bernstein, 1975, p. 101). There must be 'consensus about the integrating idea and it must be very explicit' (p. 107). The 'nature of the linkage between the integrating idea and the knowledge to be co-ordinated must also be coherently spelled out' (p. 107). A 'Committee system of staff may have to be set up to create a sensitive feed-back system . . . which will also provide a further agency of socialisation into the code'. And 'it is likely that integrated codes will give rise to multiple criteria of assessment compared with collection codes' (p. 107), involving 'a greater range of the student's behaviour', 'considerable diversity . . . between students . . . and [taking] more into account "inner" attributes of the student' (p. 109).

Maw points out that the high-level 'relational idea' is not present in the NCC texts. Though there are many references to holistic terms such as 'coherence' and 'continuity', their precise meaning is not stated. In the end, 'It must remain open to schools to decide how these themes are encompassed within the whole curriculum' (NCC, 1990, p. 6). The NCC texts are thus a kind of mediatory commentary on the National Curriculum, which does not provide 'relational ideas' itself, but opens up the possibilities for schools to do so. Maw (1993, p. 72) concludes that:

> The model of the whole curriculum which results is inherently unstable because it attempts an equilibrium between conflicting models of curriculum construction. Schools which read the texts as

unproblematic statements of intent will fail to recognise these constraints.

I would argue that Coombes does recognize these constraints and is exploiting that instability around its relational idea of the environment, which has a considerable and acclaimed history and such solid and secure everyday reinforcement in their school grounds. In the catharsis of the reforms, the 'relational idea' has, if anything, been made sharper and even more explicit in the minds of staff by comparison with the National Curriculum, their past experience and other schools. Their 'Curriculum Policy Statements' on each subject spell out the links between the idea and the knowledge to be co-ordinated. Their commitment, put to the test, has been strengthened. They have been further 'socialised into the code'. New recruits, students and returnees are soon inducted. Parents are incorporated into the 'collaborative culture' (Nias *et al.*, 1989), becoming a resource, rather than a constraint inhibiting integration because of their expectations of delivery of the National Curriculum (see Maw, 1993, p. 71). Coombes, also, is employing 'multiple criteria of assessment' over and above the limited and simplistic tests of national assessment. In all these respects, therefore, Coombes would appear to be meeting Bernstein's conditions for the establishment of an integrated code.

Underwriting this appropriation is a notion of power generated from below around a cause. Kreisberg (1992) has pointed out the limitations of defining power as 'power over', that is, a political act of domination, and draws attention to the possibilities of 'power with', that is a strength based on 'relationships of co-operation, mutual support, and equity' (Bloome and Willett 1991, p. 208). Acting in concert with this is a power deriving from the self. Heath (1993, p. 266) has written that, while appreciating the influence of external power, 'I believe also that internal motivations and desires to be something special for someone else empower individuals far more than we acknowledge when we talk of what happens within reform efforts of institutions such as schools'. These two aspects of power – the collective and the individual – interconnect to provide beleaguered schools with chances to promote their aims. Foucault has suggested how such power might be generated and utilized. For him, power is an ever-present, permeating force in social relations. The 'play' of power in everyday life produces knowledge that goes to the heart of how individuals are constituted. This view of power is positive and productive, rather than repressive and constraining:

> What makes power hold good, what makes it accepted, is quite simply the fact that it doesn't weigh on us as a force that says no, but that it traverses and produces things, it induces pleasure, forms knowledge, produces discourse. It needs to be considered as a pro-

ductive network which runs through the entire social body, much more than as a negative instance whose function is repression (Foucault, 1980, p. 119).

Two strategical notions from Foucault are relevant to the Coombes analysis. The first is the idea of 'surveillance'. He uses the metaphor of the 'panopticon' to make the point of a seat of power with all-seeing gaze. The analogy is easier to see in relation to a prison where the warders can see all activity from a central point, than to a school. In a case like Coombes, however, we might claim that the seat of power is in the school ethos, established, compelling, legitimated, from which individuals draw to sustain and develop their selves, and to which they contribute, thus consolidating and developing its power. The Coombes ethos permeates every moment of the day. There is continual reinforcement as one talks to colleagues, prepares lessons, evaluates work, or looks out of a window at children's activity. A common expression used at Coombes is 'That's what it's all about' – a reaffirmation of the ethos through the everyday, and what to others might seem trivial behaviour, unworthy of comment. It assails one at every turn. School situations are organised, furnished and decorated to convey the overriding perception of worthwhile knowledge (Dale, 1972). On the day of my second visit, the walls displayed photographs and pictures of children planting wild flowers. There was a record of how 'we went on a wild-flower safari'. There were pastel studies of bluebells and daffodils, pictures of sheep and lambs, seed packets pinned on the wall. Seeds were springing up in pots and trays everywhere. Self-made books displayed in the hall included volumes on the uses of pumpkins, on the sun, and the Coombes bog garden, and a word book on harvesting. Nature, the earth, and the environment were not the only subjects, but they were pervasive.

As an example of the almost imperceptible way in which the ethos bears in on one, I cite the following occurrences during the ten minutes of my lunch with Sue Humphries and Sue Rowe and some children outside under the trees:

1 A child came and told us about a dead bird that had been eaten by ants ('Nothing is wasted', said Sue, 'and birds will eat ants!').
2 Another brought some cuckoo spit, testing our joint biological knowledge.
3 Another showed me how some seeds were growing into plants.
4 Some children were playing under overhanging branches.
5 Sue Rowe pointed to the profusion of apples on a nearby Bramley which were just beginning to swell.
6 A beetle landed on my pudding.

The 'surveillance' here operates not through the eyes of a controlling group, as in a prison, but through one's own 'gaze'. Prominent among the messages assailing one's 'gaze' is the discourse through which the ethos is constructed – the second of Foucault's concepts.

> . . . power is enforced through discourse. Discourse, in turn, embodies knowledge, or what we take to be knowledge. In a sense, discourse constricts knowledge, making some things appear true and other things false. This discourse, like everything in a society, is constituted through institutions, institutions which are themselves constituted by power relations. Hence . . . the most likely place to search out power in an organisation is in the discourse which emanates from that organisation (Lovat, 1992, p. 188).

We have seen many examples of the Coombes discourse in earlier sections, how it is articulated and the purposes it serves (recognition, identification, forming alliances). An interesting effect is how it works to transform and subsume other discourses, for example, recasting the National Curriculum science programme into the school's own formula, or rejoicing at the imaginative way in which the children tackled the SATs (their own discourse), while the assessment did not require them to be imaginative (National Curriculum discourse). Also, some of their established activities are considered indispensable for the 'charismatic ideology' (Bourdieu and Passeron, 1977), for example, the hand-painted badges which are made by the teachers and given to every child in the school about four times a year. These are made of wood sent by a 'colleague's husband' from Dorset, sanded down, polyurethaned, decorated, printed, then polyurethaned again. The iconography consists of animals, such as sheep, frogs, fish, or trees or plants, or symbols (such as hearts for St Valentine's day) to mark traditions that 'we discovered in the less formal times, realized their value and we've set our teeth against not doing them', even though 'it scares us to death to have to do it, because of all the work involved'. This is because the badges are an important conveyor of culture. They are encapsulating symbols of all that Coombes stands for, part of the 'symbolic architecture' (Corrigan, 1989) that helps establish institutional identity, and succinctly delineates its goals (Symes, 1992). For Sue Humphries, they are important for

> cementing people in a group, giving children folk art, giving children something of real quality that a teacher or adult has done for them, celebrating individuals, showing some skills because you're lucky to have them . . . They're a joy . . . The next-door neighbour notices it, and their friend notices it. It's an important marker . . . and part of a social tradition at the school.

So well does this discourse work that parents will remind them if their children are a little late in receiving them, or if they do not receive ones similar to previous years. The badges work as a kind of ideological currency, treasured and sought after by the school's clientele, and banked in the school's community account. As long as they survive, the Coombes vision will survive.

Conclusion

The recent educational changes in England and Wales have been traumatic for many teachers and schools. They have raised basic questions of who they are, what they believe in, what aims they hold in life, and how they are going to achieve them. Teachers' investment of their substantial selves into teaching has been challenged, as has their commitment to certain values, to their view of knowledge, to pupils, to teaching. However, Coombes and Ensel teachers appear to be emerging stronger, from the point of view of values and beliefs, than when they entered the crisis. This may be reassuring for them and for others. It would be a mistake, however, to underestimate the power of the state and to deny the existence of structures within which schools have to work. Sue acknowledges that

> no school can sustain its beliefs and resolutely push out barriers if the climate out there is markedly hostile. Elements will survive, but they'll go underground, because at the end of the day you've got to pay the mortgage and get the children in. If you're ostracized in any kind of way, you just can't survive.

Another teacher agreed that, whereas the school had done quite well up to that moment at appropriating, 'there's always this sword of Damocles hanging over us'. Sue Humphries was confident that the school was well esteemed, but, as teachers, 'wanting to be tender to others and have that tenderness returned to you . . . we are exceedingly thin-skinned . . . and that makes it easy for people to injure you'. Also, it has to be recognized that in several respects teachers' work has become intensified. Recognition of these structures and processes is an important preliminary to the battle, and in itself a reassertion of professionalism. But teachers acting as a body have greater strength. The recovered collective power of teachers was demonstrated in the summer of 1993 when they refused to co-operate with the government's prescribed assessment programme. The Secretary of State gave way and instituted a review of procedures. This review made recommendations for further relaxations in curriculum and assessment requirements (Dearing, 1994), which the government immediately accepted.

In the spaces opened up by collective action individual schools can work to develop their own power base, refining and solidifying their collaborative cultures, developing their professional selves, articulating their values and learning theories, engaging wholeheartedly with those aspects of the National Curriculum which further their aims, forming alliances with other powerful groups. It is important that schools feel this sense of power. It is the dynamo on which schools like Ensel and Coombes run. Without it their teachers would be dull, emasculated, deprofessionalized technicians working to and reproducing others' specifications. With it, they are dynamic, creative, critical communities aiming to give their charges independence, life chances and justice. As ever, these things have to be fought for and struggled over. Ensel and Coombes show some of the possibilities.

4

The charisma of the critical other: enhancing the role of the teacher

A well-used strategy at Coombes was the use of people from outside the school on a large scale to enrich the work within. It has not been uncommon in primary schools, but seems likely to become even more important as a resource in the National Curriculum (see Jeffrey, 1994). It forms part of an adaptation of the teacher role which I term 'resourcing'. If combined with relief from low-level clerical aspects of the job, which Campbell (1993, p. 101) shows typically take up between five and six hours a week, the use of critical others on a systematic scale could assist developments in the teacher role which enhance creativity. This strategy was prominent during the 'critical events' research (Woods, 1993a), and I draw on that material here to explore what critical others can contribute to teaching.

At the centre of critical events, creating, co-ordinating and integrating, were critical agents – usually teachers – who had overall responsibility for the project. But there were also 'critical others'. These were 'critical' in that they made a significant input into the event, contributing special qualities and resource to the radical change that no other participant could contribute. They were 'others' in that they were not the central agents, nor indeed did they have any formal role within the institutions where the events took place. I shall draw here from five of the events: the making of a noted children's book, *Rushavenn Time*, at Brixworth Primary School, Northamptonshire, where Theresa Whistler, an author, was the critical other; the making of a film about their village by pupils of Laxfield Primary School, Suffolk, where the critical others were members of the community; the Chippindale Venture', involving the planning and design of a heritage centre on an actual site in Winchester by pupils from

Western Primary and All Saints Community Primary Schools, where the critical others were architects from various firms and planners from the local authorities; the 'Atwood Educational Project', involving the excavation of a Romano-British occupation site in the grounds of Atwood Primary School, Sanderstead, Surrey, with Gillian Batchelor, a senior archaeologist at the Museum of London, as the critical other; and the production of the musical *Godspell* at Roade School, Northamptonshire, where Nick Phillips, Head of Acting at the Central School of Speech and Drama, was a critical other. I shall use Atwood as the main source of illustration here, since the other events have been covered in more detail elsewhere (Woods, 1993a). However, they will be used for comparative purposes and to fill out consideration of the role of the critical other.

Basically, I argue that the critical other serves to enhance the role of the teacher (the 'critical agent') through the provision of a charismatic quality which is becoming increasingly difficult for teachers to provide themselves. This charisma derives from three main sources: qualities emerging from being 'other'; qualities emerging from 'self'; and qualities emerging from 'profession'.

The charisma of the critical other

The traditional culture of teaching is not conducive to the intervention of critical others. Gitlin *et al.* (1992, p. 17), for example, speak of 'the walls of isolation that so often surround teachers'. Where, however, teachers do 'teach together', spark each other off, and 'pull together', remarkable results can be achieved. As Nias (1989, p. 154) argues: 'The self is fulfilled and extended through and by means of the ideas and actions of adult as well as child others.' Going beyond fellow teachers, Golby (1989, p. 171) suggests that 'perhaps we need to look outside the profession of teaching to see how others assert a critical tradition'. However, as Nias (1989, p. 154) notes, this kind of collaboration 'does not always or easily happen'. Part of the problem is schools' struggle with the more problematic aspects of bureaucracy. Rizvi, (1989, p. 61), for example, claims that 'bureaucratic rationality remains all-pervasive in contemporary educational thinking and practice'. Rudduck (1985) has argued that the art of teaching is threatened by habit and routine, whereas lively teaching requires the continuous challenge of things that are taken for granted. Even with topic work, one of the more creative areas of primary school teaching, Tann (1988, p. 24) reports on research that shows that 'many teachers saw considerable potential for learning that was possible, but they often lacked experience of alternative ways of "doing" topic work in order to realize their own goals'. They tended to get 'locked in' to doing work in a particular way.

Bureaucracy in school has been intensified by the 1988 Education Reform Act. Emphasis is on the instrumentality of the teacher's role, how funds can be found, numbers on roll maintained, National Curriculum delivered, assessment conducted, records kept. Intensification has reduced the time available for critical reflection. There is increased specialization in the National Curriculum, an elaboration of rules and regulations, a greater emphasis on technical competence in the requirements of national assessment, a uniformity of provision that many fear will promote the development of routines and inhibit spontaneity and creativity. This has been exacerbated by the sheer number and variety of demands that are being made on teachers. In such circumstances bureaucracy is dysfunctional, inducing a growth of impersonality, a loss of personal identification and control, a sense of being taken over by the structures introduced to tackle their problems, increased alienation, greater boredom and a rise in 'bureaucratic consciousness' (Berger *et al.*, 1973). This threatens to hasten the general trend for bureaucracy to form 'a crust over society that might become too thick to permit the occasional eruptions of charismatic individuals' (Nisbet, 1967). Critical others offer one means of penetrating the crust and helping to sustain teachers' resolve and vision. In what ways, then, does the charisma of the critical other manifest itself in critical events?

Being other

Critical others are clearly different from teachers. There is, of course, an element of teaching in their work in the school, but they do not have a recognized formal role, nor can they take the place of teachers. At Atwood, for example, Gillian Batchelor's teaching skills were clearly recognized. One teacher, for example, said she was 'obviously used to handling children, had a good approach and did it well'. But however good critical others are at teaching, they are not 'proper teachers' (Blackie, 1980; Sikes *et al.*, 1985). The force of their contribution derives from the way they work with teachers as role-partners. They are able to leave matters such as general management and control, and overall responsibility for children's learning, to the teachers, allowing themselves as critical others to give free rein to their art and expertise, and to be bold and expansive. On other occasions, however, it is the extent of difference that is the important factor in yielding effect.

Strangeness

In qualitative research it is well known that 'making the familiar strange' can yield new insights into a situation (Delamont, 1992). Critical others do this in teaching to good effect. They cut across routines and rules, contesting institutional hierarchies, introducing novelty and strangeness, providing fresh perspectives, breaking down boundaries, re-establishing the personal. Like Schutz's (1964) 'stranger', these persons have to 'place in question nearly everything that seems to be unquestionable to the members of the approached group' (Schutz, 1964, p. 34). They have played no part in the development of the teacher culture, or school ethos, have none of the traditions integrated in their personal biography, are caught up in none of the routines and rituals. They perforce 'start to interpret the new social environment in terms of their thinking as usual'. While this might be disadvantageous in some circumstances, it can be a boon in teaching. Challenges to certain features of the basic system which have become taken for granted may lead to a review of the usefulness of those features. New insights derived from alternative frames of 'thinking as usual' can inform activity. Pam (deputy head, All Saints), for example, found her two architects refreshing.

> They were delightfully laid back and casual about it all . . . It was lovely. It was quite nice working with them . . . It's nice to go out and meet other professionals. It's a lonely job, teaching.

They had a considerable impact on some of the things that were taken for granted at school. For example, Pam said:

> There are things I forget as a teacher, like display and the children's presentation of their original ideas. They are very sort of scribbly. Yet the architects didn't seem to worry about the display and other things that I would be concerned about as a teacher. I would have trimmed it and double-mounted it . . . It is refreshing to see somebody else's viewpoint, and you think, 'Why am I so concerned about their handwriting?'. They are absolutely right. It's the ideas which are the key thing.

The architects explained how they were 'trying to get shot of any preconceived ideas', and encourage the children to draw freely, and how they valued the 'interesting sketches and doodles', which, to them, were 'the best, the ideas', but which 'upset the teacher because they were not neat drawings'. Similarly, at the other school children had been issued with squared paper by their teachers. But what teachers saw as an aid to design, the architects saw as an unnecessary constraint, the children 'ending up doing a lot of fairly rectangular drawings because they could only accommodate the brief within that framework'.

Role models
Critical others widen horizons by presenting new role models for students. They offer alternatives, and also dispel myth and mystery about what they do, while showing the required skills and qualities. In the process they open up new opportunities for students, and give them a

sense of the intrinsic rewards of the job. This is an exciting experience. Some of the Atwood children had never heard of archaeologists before. One said she 'couldn't even say it'. Most had simplistic, stereotypical views, depicting archaeologists as 'old men' who just went 'digging around' for 'old stones' or 'hidden treasures' or 'bits of old rubbish', and read 'loads of history books' and 'used big words that no one could understand'.

Students found out what archaeologists do, and what they are like. One class practised the basic techniques of 'probing and bozing'. 'Bozing', a student told me, is

> thumping the ground with a heavy beam of wood and detecting the different sound or vibration. The feel you get out of it can tell you whether the ground has been disturbed or not.

They found out how meticulous archaeologists have to be, for example,

> the way they dig. Usually you'd think that they'd just scoop the stuff out, but they have to really scrape, just delicately . . . in case they break anything that they come across.

David felt that the incredible thing was knowing where to dig, whereas 'we would think, "This looks a nice soft place to start"'. Rather than 'ease of digging', however, archaeologists went on evidence, such as the colour of the soil. A student explained:

> If you get some normal soil and then you look where the dig was, you find that the soil where the pottery and ditches and things were, it's much, much darker . . . because of the decayed matter in there.
> They're patient people. If they don't find anything in one place, they go down further. In one place they went down almost about three metres, and they were still scraping. Actually they found quite a few bits and pieces, but most impatient people would move on.

In fact many were amazed, in their letters to Gill, at what was discovered: 'all the pottery you found – it was a massive amount' and 'I was astonished that you had so much'. Another, speaking of the pottery, said:

> It was very wonderful and clever and the detail was lovely and I thought there was going to be nothing there. I was quite impressed.

Christopher wrote:

> I had never known that there was so much history under my feet. I had never seen anything like the site before and I think it is a great and important job you are doing.

David was impressed with the 'dedication' of the archaeologists, working all those hot hours. The skill of the work that goes into all your efforts digging up what looked like a non-interesting play-ground, transformed into a site full of interesting bits and bobs, bursting with imagination.

They discovered the precise way the archaeologists set out, and marked and numbered a site, using a grid and triangulation – which fitted well into their mathematics, illustrating the real, practical use of these tech-niques. Children acquired a sense of the values surrounding the activity, to do with human heritage (what Nicola described as 'the clever things people used to do') and the future as well as the past, generating a wider spirit of humanity. Interestingly, at first, they came up against the values of an acquisitive, market-oriented society. One child went home and told her brothers they had found something exciting, and their reaction was to ask how much it was worth. Gill explained that mostly their finds had little monetary worth, their value lay in their rarity. Mrs Rimmer (class teacher) thought such objects 'priceless'.

Several pupils said they would like to be archaeologists when they grew up. One told Gill: 'Looking round the excavation site in Atwood is one of the most exciting things I've done.' Tracey wrote: 'I admired the way you and your workers were digging away the soil'. Gill reported that

the children were amazed that I was a woman – 'a woman archae-ologist? This is very strange' – especially when I was seen driving the dumper truck. I used to have a lot of the girls run up to me, and talk, and some said 'I'm going to be an archaeologist when I grow up'.

Gill felt that, for many, she presented an arresting view on the site, because

I had these big boots on, and big muddy clothes and a hard hat. I must have looked like some sort of clown, because I wasn't like a teacher. I wasn't very smart and clean. It was all terribly exciting really, just because I was rather a different figure to be listening to.

Even more intriguing for them, perhaps, was the fact that Gill was the *senior* archaeologist on the site, with general responsibility, and with a number of men working under her guidance and direction.

In a sense, critical others are role models, too, for teachers, acting as a kind of 'looking-glass' self (Cooley, 1902). They represent a part of teachers that is undeveloped and unrealized – the professional artist, writer, histor-ian, musician, scientist and so forth. Teacher *and* other discipline would be impossible for one person to accomplish, but are achievable within the compound role. This, then, provides a new perspective which aids reflec-tion and is potentially liberating for both pupil and teacher.

Personal qualities

As Freund (1968, p. 232) points out, the foundation of charisma is emotional rather than rational. The whole force of its appeal rests on trust, faith and inspiration. A great deal of faith is evident in critical events – in the planning of them, in the abilities and aptitudes of people to respond and to co-operate, in securing the necessary resources, in the quality of the potential outcomes and in their general worthiness (see Woods, 1993a). Critical others contribute to that, but play a special part in the cultivation of trust and inspiration. These qualities are prominent in critical events.

Trust
The degree and nature of trust, affection and bonding which critical others helped to generate is illustrated in the development of *communitas* within the groups involved, marked by a strong feeling of camaraderie, a sense of common destiny, mutual support, the absence of stratification by age, ability, social class, gender or race, the transcendence of status and role as they apply in normal life, and great excitement and enthusiasm (Turner, 1969; McLaren, 1986). In 'Rushavenn', for example, it is clear that Theresa played a large part in generating the 'family feeling' within the group. She was well known in a way to the students since they had read her book, *The Riverside Boy*. When they came to meet her they were not disappointed. Stephen felt she was

> a very special person. I'd never met anyone like her before, not like a grandma, more of a great aunt, that sort of relationship. I felt very easy around her . . . The most important thing was that she made us feel as if we were making a very worthwhile contribution . . . Theresa was perfect for the job.

Sarah agreed:

> We were able to realize that she was a person, not just an author . . . She always made us feel at home.

Sarah's parents were sympathetic and helpful, but she didn't think she

> ever talked about it with them like I would do to Theresa, because it was something very personal to us. It was something special between us all.

Dawn thought that Theresa

> could have been a teacher, but teachers don't usually get that close to the pupils they're dealing with. She was a friend really.

At Atwood, the archaeologists had a similar effect if less intensively. The pupils adopted one old gentleman who was a volunteer. They were terribly fond of him, and would always ask over the fence, 'Oh, what have you found, Bob, what have you found, Bob?'. They took him several things that they found, and he cleaned them for them with his toothbrush and helped identify them. 'Even if he didn't think it was anything, he'd still clean it for us. He was really nice'.

The pupils thought

> Miss Batchelor was very kind and she taught us a lot about rocks, and what things were made of and how they looked. I think the archaeologists were very kind and thoughtful to help us because if they were people that just ignored us, I don't think we would have found out half so much information.

Another said:

> If somebody else had been doing that, someone who you didn't trust, we wouldn't have enjoyed it so much, and we wouldn't have actually felt something that was 2000 years old. Also I don't think we would have got the same amount out of it . . .

Others agreed:

> You could really trust the archaeologists. We would go to them and ask them what it was and they would tell us. They wouldn't just say, 'Sorry, I'm working, go away'.

Mrs Rimmer thought they had never met an archaeologist before, and

> probably thought they were a different breed of human, but they found them very helpful. It was their friendliness that impressed them – but also their discipline around the site.

Friendliness is clearly an outstanding feature, and an unexpected one. It softens the boundaries around institutionalized professionalism, and makes the mystery of its craft accessible. In Gill's favourite teaching organizational mode – a circle, where all are equal, and in the open air, on site, not in a classroom – this is promoted still more. The members of the circle are bound together, chiefly, in this case, by the artefacts that are passed round. Interestingly, circles featured prominently in 'Rushavenn' and 'Godspell', reproducing the sense of belonging to a social whole, like the family, that Lee (1915) observed about the 'ring game'.

Inspiration

The effect of charisma is to inspire and motivate. Critical others played a large part in providing this quality at all stages of the events. The Chippindale Venture in fact, was generated by a group of architects and planners in Winchester, and inspired by the memory of a noted local architect, Frank Chippindale. He had founded the Urban Studies Committee, and after his death an informal group gradually evolved the idea of the project. The head of the Teachers' Centre provided the link into teaching. Could schools have initiated this? They might, but it was pointed out that, for certain aspects of the work, you had to have fellow professionals dealing with each other – for example, asking for architectural time and funds.

In other events, while the idea for a project in a general area may have been the brainchild of a teacher, the particular shape that it took was initiated by the specialist. Thus, in 'Rushavenn', Peter had conceived the project for a book. It was a long-standing dream, and he had made considerable preparation for it. But Theresa provided the ideas for what the book was to be about – a long-standing dream of her own, to write about the home of her youth. Similarly, Gillian in the Atwood project controlled the conception of how it would unfold – necessarily so in this case as it was an archaeological event in the first instance. In these cases also, the specialists performed an anchoring role. They were the central force around which the events evolved. They helped to initiate, plan, prepare, enskill, diverge, converge and consolidate. Of these, the most significant were the enskilling and the divergence. The divergence stage of critical events is one where pupils are encouraged to be innovative and creative, explore opportunities, stretch their abilities, and experiment with different media and forms of expression. Architects, thus, in Chippindale, discussed with children principles of design and the generation of ideas, and encouraged them to be adventurous. Planners introduced a range of other factors they would have to consider, such as the effect of buildings on the environment. The relationship between architect and children seemed particularly productive. Joy (head of Teachers' Centre) reported: 'They were absolutely thrilled to bits with their own particular architect.' Debbie (head of Western Primary) said quite a lot of them told her 'the bit they liked best was getting to know their architect'. Similarly, in 'Rushavenn', Theresa sought to stimulate ideas for the book by various methods – taking in a large box containing some of her treasured mementoes, encouraging the children to take in and talk about their treasured possessions, having 'think-tank' sessions.

At Atwood, Gillian provided an information pack for teachers who 'might not know very much about archaeology, but knew their children would be interested'. These guidelines reported the results of previous excavations on the site, and what they might find this time, explained the role of the Museum of London, giving information on archaeology and presenting a list of possible resources and educational projects; and discussed site safety. She included information on related activities in London, and on various groups, such as the 'Young Archaeologists' Group'. She stressed how archaeology was interesting for primary school children because it could be particularly helpful with the concept of time, and with 'spurring their imagination as to how people lived in the past'. They 'loved the idea', for example, 'that they had actually played netball on an Iron Age farm, that there were other people living there hundreds of years ago, and that they built a hut which got totally demolished'. There were lots of questions like 'why did they build it under a school?', so there was a lot of reconstruction to be done.

One class converted one of the Portaloos on the site into a 'Tardis' (a time machine) and made up a play about visiting the past and portraying life as it was. They also planted beneath the new buildings a time capsule containing some of their writings and drawings on the project, and some of the pottery discovered,

> so perhaps in two or three hundred years' time, somebody will dig it up and see how children were in 1990 – what their interests were, what they found on the day, and so on.

This illustrates one way in which history can aid perspective for both past and future, giving an intellectual dimension which provides a basis for how we conceive social change. In this sense, it stands at the centre of what Egan (1992) terms the 'imagination-enhancing' curriculum. In yet another illustration of how history can contribute to such a curriculum, Gill suggested a range of possible related projects on the Iron Age, farms, hill forts, Celtic religion, excavation and field walking projects, and work drawing on historical fiction.

All were caught up in the excitement of these activities. Mrs Rimmer, for example, was inspired by the Atwood project to become a fully-fledged amateur archaeologist, complete with a set of tools and books, and spent much of her spare time putting them to use. She herself made some valuable finds on the site. Gill gave a lecture and a slide show to the children afterwards, and they were hugely delighted by slides of their teacher digging on the site, that is, 'being an archaeologist', and out of the role in which they usually saw her. Pupils, also, were motivated and inspired. With one boy, for example, said Mrs Rimmer,

> his construction was judged one of the best with two other boys. He's not the most able child but he is just fired by all this. The child who is less able and feels they can achieve, that's the greatest benefit. Then you can go on to the written work which they'll be satisfied to do when they have discovered and constructed – that's the way in . . . Gaining confidence, that's what it's all about, and enthusing them so that they want to go on and try to do something . . . small steps, big gains in confidence and they achieve more.

Gill mentioned

a very, very shy little girl who had found at home a prehistoric scraper – a flint artefact – and she actually had to have her mother come in with her to show it to me.

Gill thought it gave certain children confidence,

because it was an impartial thing, anybody could find something, you didn't have to have an ability'.

Mrs Rimmer demonstrated how the advantages could snowball, pointing to an illustration on the wall:

Look at the complications there, for a boy of ten. It's all mathematically drawn out. Then they said 'Let's try it on the computer', so they put it on the computer. Now that boy has found out that he can measure and join points with a rule and a pencil. He has produced those three up there and that's the best thing he's ever produced on paper or card . . . You know, you have to find ways in to these children.

One of the ways in is through the charisma of critical others. They can also provide ways *back* into something students have lost inspiration for. Nick Phillips, Head of Acting at Central School of Speech and Drama, worked with the cast of 'Godspell' on new skills, and reinvigorated them as they rebounded from the end of the school stage of this event. The play had run its course during the autumn term at the school, but had been selected for the National Students' Drama Festival at Cambridge the following Easter. After the great success of the school performances, the participants felt drained and listless. There was a feeling that it was over. Nick Phillips' intervention, however, helped them 'find the energy we thought we'd lost'. He 'finished things off', making the show 'a bit more flowing and professional'. He gave them confidence when they thought they would 'get booed off the stage', made them feel good about themselves, helped them squeeze even more enjoyment out of their performance. Coming in with his own brand of expertise and fresh vigour, he revived others so that their own abilities and spirits were restored and primed so that they could go on to even greater things.

Authenticity

The problems in sustaining the parallel between 'real' and school work, as illustrated in the work of Atkinson and Delamont (1977), discussed in Chapter 3, highlight the considerable contribution critical others make in this respect. Where there are genuine discovery and creative opportunities, they go some way towards producing authentic 'ways of knowing'. Consequently, verisimilitude is a prominent feature of the events – 'living history', a *real* book, a design for a building on a *real* site, a film that has meaning and purpose for the whole village, a play that aspires to *real*, as opposed to contrived, emotions. As one Atwood pupil said:

> When you get a book and you have to write it down, it gives you all the information, but it doesn't really help. I think it's better to go out and actually discover things for yourself.

Another said:

> I think it definitely makes history come alive because just reading from a textbook and writing it down, it just sort of passes through your mind and you don't really think properly about it. But if you've actually got something in front of you and it's 2000 years old, and a book and a piece of paper and pen, I think you can really get what it was like much better, because you've actually got something to show, and some people, somebody was living where you're sitting now, 2000 years ago. It really makes it exciting.

In Chippindale, children commented that you can understand 'what architects do', and 'what it's really like designing a building'. In Laxfield, the film about the village was judged by villagers a product of real community and historical worth. In 'Godspell', the students learnt to 'make sense in feelings of the subjective world of feeling, our capacity to feel intelligently, to find our way among feelings by feeling' (Ross, 1978, p. 43). In the early stages of production, Sara, one of the cast, felt she was 'losing touch with reality', but eventually she felt the experience brought her close to reality:

> We had created a kind of truth in the play. You believed in everything . . . It was so genuine (for this viewpoint, see Collingwood, 1966; and Stanislavski, 1972).

The critical others played a key role in helping to establish the high level of authenticity. The most obvious way in which they did this was by providing first-hand expertise and information and opportunities for hands-on experience. Gillian, for example, was keen for children to visit the Educational Department of the London Museum, for here they 'had a chance to handle lots of finds, have a lecture and a slide show, and visit the galleries'. This hands-on experience was then applied to their own site, centring the learning and grounding it in the real world. The children expressed their appreciation in letters to Gill. Lisa, for example, said:

> Thank you for letting us come to the archaeological dig. I found it interesting looking at Roman pottery, bones and arrowheads, but I liked feeling and looking at the arrowhead best. It was very smooth and shiny. I expected to go on the site, but not to feel things that had been dug up . . .

This illustrates the importance of sight, feel, presence, but especially handling. One boy with a sight problem enjoyed his visit to the site because he was able to handle the finds, like all the other children. When passing things around, you saw different responses. For example:

> We had a large polished pebble which was used in prehistoric times as a hammer-stone for pounding things. Some children would hold it correctly, some would just pass it on, others would hold it and try to hammer . . . There were lots of things going on – children trying to put pieces of pottery back together . . .

This first-hand experience informed role-play exercises, proving an effective package, heightening authenticity and arousing interest and attention. At one point, for example, when children were gathered in the school hall, there was 'this marvellous sort of hobnail noise' as two costumed burly Museum staff, who 'really looked like Roman soldiers' came 'clomping in', with much dramatic effect. Some hobnails had actually been found on the site, which added to the sense of reality. They then went round the school talking to children and answering questions, all the while maintaining their role. Pictures of the Roman soldiers featured prominently in the exhibition in the school hall at the end of the project.

Holism
Authenticity is further heightened by the feeling that things are all of a piece. They have a relevance, both to each other and within one's own scheme of relevancies. They are integrated within the self, and not bounded and compartmentalized. This integrity of knowledge was encouraged by and reflected in the holism of space, time and personnel.

With regard to space, critical others bring the outside world into school. At one extreme, sites merge into one another. At Atwood, the school and the archaeological site were on the same campus. As Gill pointed out:

> With the new legislation it's so difficult to go on any sort of school trip at all. We had an interesting school trip but actually in the playground.

It was easy for other local schools, too, to walk to the site. Also, 'the fields all around Atwood School are full of Roman pottery', so it was easy for pupils and teachers to practise their developing craft off-site, even, for some of them, in their own back gardens. Some pupils did take in examples which they had unearthed at home. On the site they would

> look through the surveyor's level and things like that, and watch all the archaeologists doing very different tasks, which were unusual things for them to be doing.

When a find was made, the news would spread very quickly, and there 'would be crowds of people at playtime craning over the fence to see it'. They were that close to seeing history made. There were many shards of pottery, some stone implements, bones and fossils. One particularly interesting find for the children was a 'late Bronze Age or Neolithic flint arrowhead, and they took that away and drew it, and did a project on it'. At times they were even closer, for example, when one of their own teachers, Mrs Rimmer, found a bronze brooch. On another occasion she excavated the jaw of an animal, which 'seemed to be sort of grinning at her', much to the children's amusement.

The importance of space, situations, props, the way an area is arranged, is all well known (Bennett and Bennett, 1970), as is the way differences of context can promote different definitions of the situation (Stebbins, 1975). Here was a real archaeological site under the children's own playground. 'The fact that they're not in the classroom' also seemed to matter to Gill: 'They're sitting out on the field and it's mid-summer, it's all quite a nice environment'. The pupils agreed:

> Sitting in the classroom is quite boring, so it's quite good to actually go out and find things yourself instead of reading it from a textbook.

Another said:

> Now that we've actually been out on the dig and found parts of old times for ourselves, we can actually picture in our minds what it would have been like and if we wanted to we could make a play of it, but if we're just looking at a book then it's not like reality really . . . You can't really imagine it like when you're there.

There were also lots of things happening out there:

> the site but with people planning or making tea; on the site, people recording and taking photographs . . . journalists and cable television . . . and us giving an educational talk at the same time.

One of the teachers said:

> The children enjoyed having it happen on their site – and they enjoyed being able to talk to a real live archaeologist . . . They got almost possessive about the site and weren't happy when the developers started to cover it up.

This was a complete contrast to the traditional enclosed classroom with its organization of teacher's desk at the front, and pupils' desks in rows. This may have its educational purposes, but it is for some matters a secondary unit, relaying knowledge derived from elsewhere, and modelling skills on those used elsewhere. It also conveys messages about relationships between pupils and teachers. Within the structure of the project, it might be seen as most functional in formal preparation, convergent and consolidation stages. The real site aids enskilling and divergence – the provision of inspiration, the development of ideas, the enthusiasm to explore new fields. Having both arenas side by side, therefore, was a powerful resource throughout the project as a whole.

Boundaries were softened, not only in relation to space, but also to people and time. For example, at Atwood, other members of the community were drawn into the event. Parents, for example, were greatly interested. There were many volunteers from among them at weekends, and they helped especially to excavate the post-holes. They took their time, too, when they came to collect their children. This is a reminder that formal school time is of little consequence in such a project. The archaeologists had only a limited period to complete the excavation (five weeks during the school's summer holiday, with a further three weeks at the beginning of the autumn term), so were always working against that deadline. Teachers and pupils made the most of their breaks and dinner-hours to catch up on the latest developments. Many spent time in the evenings to explore their own gardens or other areas. All were operating on what Lyman and Scott (1970) have called a 'humanistic time-track' marked by personal decision and self-expression, as opposed to 'fatalistic time-tracks', which are more coercible and restraining. These produce different 'rhythms of work' (Blauner, 1964). In one, people can be engrossed and emotionally engaged; in the other, they are more detached, going through processes for instrumental purposes (see also Hall, 1984; McLaren, 1986).

The other events exhibited the same kind of holism. In 'Rushavenn', for example, the event took place on Saturdays, outside normal school hours, and the main room used was the staffroom. There, as at Atwood, all 'were part of a circle, so that no one in that circle occupied a position which was more important than anyone else's'. The critical other, Theresa, was part of this circle and heightened the sense of difference from normal procedures. With Laxfield, clearly the project was centred in the village, with the villagers, in their clubs and places of leisure, as the main stars. 'Godspell' did not take off as an extra-special event until it had completed its 'school career' and been launched into its public stage in the run-up to the National Students' Drama Festival at Cambridge (where it won an award). Interestingly, a critical other played a key role in linking these two stages, as explained earlier. The architects and planners of Chippindale helped develop the sense of 'otherness' for the participating pupils. Apart from the main work at the site, some set up a visit to their offices for their group so they could see and experience how and in what surroundings architects worked, and with what equipment; and the project ended in a special day when the City Council Planning Committee considered the plans submitted in Council offices in as near a genuine format as possible.

Communication skills

Some of these activities can no doubt be provided by teachers. However, research (Southgate *et al.*, 1981; Avann, 1983) has shown that teachers lack 'information skills' in doing topic work. Critical others have these skills with respect to their own discipline. They know where and how to gather and generate knowledge and develop skills in their subject. Crucially, they have command of ways of communicating. Often, in critical events at least, teachers as well as pupils have to learn a new language. This manifested itself in various ways.

In 'Rushavenn', it was a matter of children developing their vocabulary and means of expression. All the pupils claimed great advances in vocabulary and expression. Julia, for example, said it gave her ideas as to what words to use to express feelings and to make descriptions more vivid. Jennifer had never thought of the characters in books she read as being real.

> But those in Rushavenn were real flesh and blood. You got to know them better, really created people out of words and you gave them life.

The project gave them a glimpse of the artist at work and of the artist's mind, which simultaneously unlocked doors to their own childhood vision. The book, according to Stephen,

> was a real, proper book . . . written for children. It isn't a book designed to show how cute 10-year-olds can be when they write poems about butterflies. It's a book that shows that children of 9, 10, 11 years old really do have something to offer in a poetic and literary way.

With Chippindale, they had to learn a new technical language and learn to communicate through design, acquiring what Phillips (1980) calls 'designerly' ways of knowing. One of the teachers commented:

> The children that have done Chippindale you could feel this vocabulary coming out. You could feel their way of looking at things coming out, not just through anybody trying to bring it out, but simply because it was part of them and these things spill over.

In Atwood, children were presented with a means of communicating with past ages, of 'hearing them speak'. For example, pupils found out about stratigraphy – how deposits get laid down over time and what clues they contain about the people who used them. Gill liked to use a dustbin with a Perspex front as a visual aid, with all sorts of domestic rubbish in layers. As you take them out – an empty can of dog food, a cigarette packet, a nappy – you discuss their significance, and their relationship to each other in terms of time. This illustrates that archaeology is a very interpretative subject.

If you dig something up, it can be whatever you want to make it really, although we try not to work like that . . .

Clare recognized the skill in this:

The hammer head you found, if I found it I would think it was just a stone and throw it away.

Another said the same about the flint arrowhead, which Gill described as

a beautiful object, almost transparent because it had been so worked, and also complete. It was very rare to find one of these.

It was also instructive to see how deductions were made from the post-holes about the buildings contained in the settlement. Gill had 136 post-holes, and even though she had a scaffold tower it was difficult to see the significance of their arrangement.

I really needed some sort of upright in them to show me the distribution. So we got about three classes and each child stood in a post-hole, which was quite an effective visual aid. It's also ideal, when talking about the project [in a lecture], to show the children on site participating. You can see how the post-holes take on a formation when you see them all laid out.

This was a particularly effective means of interpreting the significance of the post-holes on the site *and* demonstrating that significance to the children.

Validating
As well as shaping input, critical others were able to assess the authenticity of output, and to judge 'what counts' as a genuine product within their discipline. This takes a variety of forms.

Interpreting and identifying genuine archaeological products is a role for an expert. When Gill saw the relics Mrs Rimmer had found, she exclaimed 'That's it! That's it!', a joyful shout of recognition that here was the real thing, no substitutes, no secondary or tertiary sources, no photographs, drawings or reproductions. Similarly, she was able to say that the models the children did were 'very good and extremely accurate'. For example:

They would fill up a little glass fish bowl with soil and they'd have a little wall in there and a sandy pit. Then they'd put some tissue paper which had grass on the top, and they would demonstrate how crops will have stunted growth if there's something in the soil. That shows how archaeologists can see things from aerial photographs. By making the model they must have understood the process, and they were very accurate models.

The archaeologists encouraged the children to bring things to them, for example, if they found anything in their garden. One girl had a Roman coin belonging to her parents which 'we dated for them'. The girl then wrote a history of the coin, and this featured in the exhibition at the end of the project. Another girl found a key in a soil heap beside the site. It was actually a mediaeval key, but 'it was a wonderful find, and we took it away and dated it and had it conserved for her'.

They also encouraged the children to comment. If a comment was relevant,

> We would say 'Yes, now that's a very good idea . . .'. If what they brought wasn't anything, then we'd just say 'No, I'm afraid it isn't, but you want to look for something like this, but it would be a bit different because it would have such-and-such . . .'.

Similarly, children would volunteer knowledge that they had gained from somewhere else – parents or reading perhaps – and would be

> delighted if they knew something about the Romans which nobody else knew, or something about an archaeological site somewhere else similar to this – and I'd say 'Oh yes, they did!' – and that was really very rewarding for them.

In Laxfield, a prominent feature was the way the film was validated by members of the community. One villager, for example, felt they had captured 'the whole hurly-burly atmosphere of the playgroup'. She also thought the Horticultural Society 'came over very well, with its almost reverent atmosphere'. Several spoke of the integrating effect the film had on the community, 'drawing people together'. It roused a sense of pride in people, and showed 'there is a real lot going on in the village life, a lot more than people think'. It was also a motivational force, 'because some people very often are too scared to go along . . . Seeing things like that, you realise'. Mr High, retired agricultural worker, and a leading light of the Horticultural Society, thought 'the children done it well', and that the video gave a good picture of the Horticultural Show and was very informative about other things. The vicar thought 'they've done very well in picking out salient features'. Colin Emeny, builder, parent and school governor, thought it was

> brilliant, absolutely brilliant . . . I'm a local. I've been here all my life. I speak to other locals and they think it's remarkable . . . They covered literally everything and showed it as it is.

He thought 'the beauty of it would come out over the years'. This validation of the film by members of the community increased the sense of personal and educational gain among the participants.

In Chippindale, architects and planners recognized designs of merit, vision and possibility. Looking through some of the early designs, a planning officer pointed to one that he thought was

> quite extraordinary for a 10–11-year-old to have got to that stage with the concept of a building of that kind, and to be able to draw it in that way almost entirely on his own is a remarkable achievement.

One architect thought that children as young as 8 or 9 were already inhibited, and beginning to be 'moulded by society as a whole'. The task was to liberate their creativity, but within 'workable' limits. They were duly impressed with the 'pretty free ideas' and the 'character' of the designs. A planning officer thought that some of the schemes were buildable, and that some plans might have passed in a real meeting, though they might have 'raised a few eyebrows'. Some of them were 'sufficiently well thought out' to have stood a chance of being developed into a workable scheme.

Conclusion

To produce such results, teachers need autonomy. They also need knowledge. Indeed, Egan (1992, p. 156) argues that 'mastery of disciplined knowledge in a range of curriculum areas properly goes hand in hand with imaginative development'. He is not looking for superhumans with exceptional command of all subjects across the curriculum, but rather for 'the attitudes of mind that respect and pursue disciplined knowledge, especially in the area of teaching speciality'. Such 'attitudes of mind', however, are difficult to sustain in extreme rational-legal systems. Critical others provide one resource by which such attitudes of mind can be cultivated. They help to produce teaching that involves genuine, first-hand knowledge; purposeful work within the discipline area involved and actual processes, entailing 'skills' and 'modes of knowing' (Barrett, 1988, pp. 102–103), that induce thinking like an author, scientist, historian, architect, or whatever. Such teaching encourages learning that engages the students' full attention and powers. It motivates, stimulates, excites, unlocks and opens. It fosters a genuine spirit of enquiry and discovery. It leads to students' ownership of knowledge, internalized and integrated within their own systems of relevancies.

Critical events seem to work best where the 'substantial self' (Nias, 1989) of the teacher is in unison with the central demands of the role – 'the job is their life', in other words (Pollard, 1987). The same point, by analogy, would apply to critical others. Similarly, another favourable factor appears to be where the teacher's self fits into a set of professional norms, and where the teacher's work is a product of whole-school policies. Nias *et al.* (1989) show how one school developed a particular ethos. The headteacher worked for this from her appointment, including the selection of 'the right sort of people'. A strong normative environment developed in which the self and values of the teacher were integrated into the ethos of the school. At its fullest extent, Nias *et al.* argue, this is deeply fulfilling and liberating for the individual teacher. While critical others cannot be expected to develop such rapport with the school themselves – since it takes time – they can do it by association with the critical agent. The teacher provides the sureties in this respect; the other only has to ensure a consistency of aim and outlook with the teacher. For a number of reasons, therefore, selection is crucial. As Hughes (1962, p. 123) noted: 'It takes intelligence to find the "others" that will bring out the best in one's self'. Inevitably, Hughes argues, a number of significant others will be in the professions, which makes it 'the more important that the relations between profession-directedness and sensitivity to the others involved in the drama of work should be kept flexible, complex, and in balance' (pp. 125–126). Hughes goes on to speak of the complex person, 'finely tuned to many of the "others" in his/her life orbit', 'creative' and 'autonomous', a person 'of many sensitivities who would attain and maintain, by intelligent and courageous choice of the messages to which he would respond, by the choice of his "others", freedom of a high, but tough and resilient quality' (p. 126). Critical others present one way in which teachers can attempt to break free of any constraining strictures of their role, reinforce its professional base, and aspire to the heights of professional – and personal – satisfaction.

5

*Teaching, and researching the teaching of, a history topic: an experiment in collaboration**

Introduction

The critical events identified in Woods (1993a) occurred before the 1988 legislation took hold. All the teachers involved expressed grave doubt as to whether they would be able to mount similar 'critical' exercises within the National Curriculum. This was because of requirement over-load, which left them with little flexibility; the compartmentalization and differentiation of the curriculum, which offended their 'holistic' perspectives; and the bureaucracy, which took up all their spare time. This is now a familiar story. What is not clear is how long-standing and deep-seated are these initial reactions. Though creativity seems to have been threatened, as Day (1993, p. 87) points out, 'increased devolution of decision-making, albeit within a framework of centrally held values, presents a new potential power for teachers to assert not only their responsibilities but also their entitlements'. Thus, when the opportunity arose for one of us on the 'creative teaching' research team to join a teacher in teaching in a prescribed area within the National Curriculum, we decided to put 'creativity' to the test under these new circum-stances. A further interest was the form of collaboration between teacher and researcher. Could a researcher act as 'critical other', enhancing the role of the teacher and boosting the charismatic ambience of the activity? If so, what are the implications for the re-search element of the role?

* This chapter was co-authored with Peter Wenham

The work had the added attraction of the researchers trying to help the teacher to be (even) more successful. It was in an area – history – in which the teacher felt there to be a problem. Vass (1993, p. 23) tells of 'the shock waves that reverberated through the history teacher's world', following the arrival of the new history Orders, and primary teachers' awareness of their lack of subject and teaching knowledge. Gill (the teacher), however, argued that under the National Curriculum

> in a way you have to be more creative. You have got the framework, and you then have to make it interesting and attractive to the children and you have got to be able to present it in lots of different ways.

This applied to the ancient Greece topic which Gill first taught in the autumn term of 1991. She had had misgivings about this for two reasons. First, she had favoured, for the most part, a broad topic approach: 'I can't quite use the wide-ranging topics that I used to.' These, however, according to Noble (1990, p. 33) had 'failed to deliver the goods as far as history is concerned'. Second, she was uneasy about the suitability of this topic – 'very much dictated from above' – for her Year 2/3 children. This was the first time she had been required to teach a specific topic. It seemed a major challenge to her autonomy, as it did to many other history teachers (Phillips, 1991). As Phillips (1991, p. 24) notes:

> If we are genuinely concerned to ensure that the National Curriculum improves the historical experience of children, teachers have to be encouraged to believe that they still have a considerable degree of autonomy as far as the actual delivery of policy is concerned.

Gill very much needed to find a way, therefore, to teach this subject in a form that harmonized with her beliefs and values.

> Usually I have chosen a topic that has something in it that really attracts me. Ancient Greece I found very difficult to relate to, but I had to. So I had really to work at being imaginative about it and making it interesting.

We were concerned to do 'genuine research *for* teaching instead of simply research on teaching' (Noddings, 1986, p. 506). If our general research interest was 'creative teaching', we also had a practical one of collaborating in a particular event and helping towards its success. Thus the success of teacher and researcher would both be measured in large part by the success of the project (Scriven, 1986). This collaboration has raised interesting questions of research method. Peter Wenham joined the teacher as a participant observer, but also as a potential 'critical other' seeking to make a significant educational input. It would have been difficult for Peter to assess his own influence as 'critical other', so I joined them in the later stages of evaluation. I interviewed both teacher and researcher, and all the children, and saw the mass of documentary and artefact evidence. The reporting has followed these stages: first, Peter Wenham drafting a report from his perspective; second, this being commented upon by the research team and by Gill, and a report emerging agreed by both participants; third, me (P. Woods) adding parts of my evaluation; and fourth, this, in turn, being modified in the light of participants' comments. This shared product, we feel, covers all the major teaching and research aspects, and provides what we hoped would be an interesting and effective form of triangulation. In other respects, the research methods followed those used in Woods (1993a).

The topic and approach

The school was a first school of some 151 children aged 5–8, serving a multiethnic community. The teacher, Gill, was a fully qualified teacher holding an A incentive allowance mainly with responsibility for technology and display. She was a highly respected teacher who had taught in primary schools for twenty years, with a five-year break for child-rearing, concentrating on younger children for the last nine years. She took up the post she held in September 1991, and has led the school staff in implementing aspects of National Curriculum technology.

Up until December 1991, when he took early retirement and became a member of the research team, the researcher, Peter Wenham, held a post as senior adviser. He had a keen interest in history teaching – it was the subject of his first degree, and the one he taught himself for ten years. His teaching expertise, however, was mainly in secondary schools. Apart from the other aims mentioned above, Peter felt he had things to prove to himself – that he could still teach effectively, for example. Gill had a class of 30 vertically grouped children aged 6–8, four of whom spoke English as a second language. She had taken part in an earlier phase of the research, and Peter had found a 'considerable professional compatibility between them'. Apprehensive at first because of a feeling of her own 'inadequacy', she was reassured by the sharing of teaching and researching that was proposed, and by initial planning discussions. The topic was core unit 5 for Key Stage 2, 'Ancient Greece'. Lessons took place on nine consecutive Thursdays in the autumn term of 1992, culminating in a celebratory 'Greek Day'. The aims state that 'Pupils should be introduced to the civilisation of ancient Greece and its legacy to the modern world. The focus should be on the way of life, beliefs and achievements of the ancient Greeks.' There are specified contents, including 'the city state', 'Greek religion and thought' and 'the arts'. The National Curriculum Order, with its three attainment targets, focusing on knowledge and understanding of history, interpretations of history, and the use of historical sources, was felt by Gill to provide a useful basis for planning the topic. She agreed with Lee (1991) that the National Curriculum was good in some respects in having focused attention on schemes of work and presenting clear targets. It is also generally recognized that it rescued history in primary schools and gave it new status (Noble, 1991). But did it also allow for that excitement, that enthusiasm, that motivation for both teaching and learning that results when teachers and students are working at high levels of awareness?

Gill was sceptical at first since her previous projects had been holistic and not subject-based. However, the National Curriculum does not necessarily exclude holism (Bolton, 1993) and contributions to work in other subjects were planned. For example, Greek music would provide opportunities for listening to and appraising 'music from other cultures'. Work in art would be enhanced by observational drawings from artefacts and by considering ancient Greek styles in painting, sculpture and clothes. Making ancient Greek lamps and pots in clay, fashioning masks as worn by actors in Greek theatres, sewing in ancient Greek design and patterns, making straw models of Greek temples, cooking Greek foods, all contributed to technology. The topic of celebration in religious education would be informed by comparisons with the Olympic games and theatre festivals, and of caring and sharing by reference to Greek myths. Geography would be served by the study of photographs and maps, weather conditions and travel. Gill expected 'a great deal of language work to be based on the topic', with particular reference to speaking and listening, reading and writing. Gill mentioned in particular the value of the ancient Greeks 'as a vehicle for helping with language, spoken language, understanding and comprehension'. Thus, this teacher did not feel that her basic integrationist instincts were inhibited. Gill felt that the topic had lent itself to a 'good mixture' and 'a good blend – I like to blend from my topic quite a lot of my other work'. At the same time, her students stood to gain in historical knowledge, understanding and skills. It was the first time, apparently, that these children had done 'an entirely historical topic', and it was part of whole-school planning.

Nor was the topic to be closed and inflexible. Careful planning was important over the whole nine weeks, but there was a degree of openness to take advantage of unforeseen opportunities that might arise, and to take account of pupil reactions. Similarly, the principle of 'fitness for purpose' (Alexander *et al.*, 1992) was applied to classroom organization. Changes were rung between whole-class, group and individual work, and a variety of methods was used. A typical session began with a whole-class activity based on exposition and questioning by the teacher and a stimulus for the children, for example, a story, a model (e.g., of the

Parthenon), a statue (e.g., of the charioteer of Delphi), a video on ancient Greek theatres, or slides on an aspect of Greek life. The children would then break up into groups to do related practical activities, such as making sketches, creating theatre masks, constructing pots, role-play and writing. Sometimes each group worked co-operatively, for example in the 'dustbin' exercise (where they had a simulated bag of rubbish from a family for a week and they worked out all they could say about the family, the purpose of this being to give pupils experience of working on everyday artefacts to develop awareness of clues, and drawing tentative conclusions); sometimes in pairs, for example in role-play; and, more often, individually, for example, when each member of a group made a theatre mask. The core ideas underlying these activities were that they should begin within the child's experience, extend the child's thinking, involve the child in practical and experiential work, be varied, and provide opportunities for imagination and empathy. On the 'Greek Day' at the end of the event, they were to dress as Greeks and engage in a range of Greek activities, including hairdressing, cooking, sewing, designing plates, and, most excitingly, a 'mini-Olympics'. This final day brought the topic to a head, generating strong feelings of identification with the Greeks.

The philosophy behind the teaching might be described as 'pragmatic constructivism'. It was constructivist in its holism, child-centredness, teacher guidance, belief in involvement and discovery, children's ownership of their own learning, and emphasis on evidence (Edwards and Mercer, 1987). The child-centredness and teacher guidance are illustrated in the starting point, today, with holiday brochures, eating modern Greek food, globes, artefacts, pictures of Greece; in the strategy of 'one step back and two steps forward', revisiting the last point before continuing ('starting with the known and taking them into the unknown'); and in Gill's recognition that they would get different things from the project depending on their needs, seeing this topic as a 'vehicle' for that – a child like Jenny, for example,

> will take a topic on and I see myself as feeding that interest and helping her to develop it, going off at all sorts of tangents that take her interest. With another boy, you would use the topic to draw more spoken language from him, . . . and trying to see if we can get some understanding and him actually relating some of the things that we've learnt.

As Peter pointed out, much history is language-based, which poses an immediate problem for young children, and even more so for those who speak English as a second language. The 'hands-on' experience helps children to communicate. From this involvement, the children would be asked to be detectives, and then helped to build up their knowledge.

There is emphasis here, therefore, on discovery and evidence. This evidence has to be amenable to young children. Peter said:

> The teacher's got to be enthusiastic and make it *live*, make it exciting, and base it very much on evidence – visual evidence rather than documentary, because these children, on the whole, are not able to handle that.

Associated with this is the quest for authenticity, for using real, rather than 'mocked-up' (Atkinson and Delamont, 1977) evidence, for bringing pupils as close as possible to the real ancient Greeks (hence the involvement in cultural pursuits – language, dress, appearance, food, games, etc.), while at the same time conveying the understanding that history is a subject requiring skills of interpretation.

The educational principles on which the project was based were implicit in the teacher's personal practical philosophy (Clandinin, 1985). Gill saw herself as an instinctive and pragmatic teacher. She based most of what she did on experience, and believed in 'putting her own stamp on things, and preparation with a capital "P"'. She saw 'every child in my classroom as an individual, but my role is to make them gel as a class'. She encouraged children 'to offer their opinions freely', and wanted them 'to know they would not be shot down in flames'. She strove to be honest and fair with the children, and saw herself at times as a 'good parent' to them. As Peter noted:

> It was a very pragmatic approach. It wasn't always based on a lot of principles. It would be often at that level, just 'seat of the pants' business. 'Exploration' was the watchword of what we were doing.

In summary, the teaching method appeared to be:

1 integrated – based in history but cross-curricular where relevant;
2 child-centred;
3 grounded in evidence, particularly visual and tactile;
4 organized – carefully planned, structured and monitored;
5 'real' – involving a search for authenticity;
6 energized – by the enthusiasm and flair of the 'critical agent' and 'other';
7 triangulated – by the use of a variety of methods, aligned to a range of senses and abilities;
8 open – to be able to take advantage of unforeseen opportunities;
9 creative – encouraging both teachers and pupils to be innovative in certain respects;
10 pragmatic – responding to some situations as they arose.

Change and development

The children

Bage (1993, p. 280) has noted the inherent difficulty of telling whether a child has achieved a statement of attainment, as well as confusion among primary teachers about what such statements mean. Gill and Peter monitored the verbal response of the children and assessed their written work at intervals throughout the project. An example of the evaluation of children's developing capabilities with historical sources is an unseen source exercise based on a scene depicted on a Greek wine jar.

Two men and a seated woman were shown playing musical instruments, with ancient Greek lettering above their heads. Without any discussion the children were asked to respond in 25 minutes to two questions, 'What is happening in the picture?' and 'What does this picture tell us about ancient Greeks?'. Various responses to the question 'What is happening in the picture?' were offered. Most children were able to say that there were two men and a woman playing musical instruments. Most commented that they were wearing ancient Greek clothes and had bare feet. A few children were able to make more detailed responses – they named the musical instruments, describing them as 'harps' or 'lyres' and 'pipes' or 'recorders'. Some drew attention to the straight Greek noses and to the stool or chair on which the woman was sitting. The responses to what the picture tells us about ancient Greeks also varied. Some made little comment, others made two or three points while six children demonstrated some awareness of the 'provisional' judgements based on historical sources. Most children made comments such as 'It shows the ancient Greeks liked music'. Some said that perhaps they were a Greek group or band, while a few, perhaps remembering the study of the Olympic games, suggested that it might be a musical competition. Five commented that we have similar musical instruments today, while six drew attention to the ancient Greek lettering, and two suggested that it might depict their names. Rather more commented on the cool, flowing ancient Greek clothes, relating these to the hot climate. A few compared these clothes with those worn today. Some made reference to ancient Greek hairstyles and the stool depicted in the scene, and a few compared them to those of today. Three suggested that the man on the right was the winner or leader as he was wearing a laurel wreath. Two drew attention to the two stalks of wheat in the picture and wondered what they might mean.

From the evidence of this particular written assignment, 12 children in the class of 30 gave indications of being able to 'communicate information from an historical source', 'recognize that historical sources can stimulate and help answer questions about the past', and 'make deductions from historical sources'.[1] However, other children demonstrated a competent understanding orally.

Medley and White (1992) warn that, in assessment as in history, judgements cannot be made on a single piece of evidence. They recommend banks of exercises covering every level of each attainment target and a 'level of response mark-scheme' (p. 72). We are still some way from this. What these 'banks' and 'levels' presuppose, however, is motivation and enthusiasm for the subject, ensuring not just achievement, but the highest quality of achievement. They also leave out of account the degree of attraction towards and interest in a subject. In other words, they say nothing about emotional and aesthetic aspects, and privilege the cognitive. However, feelings, we argue, are of the essence in learning, and were particularly prominent in the ancient Greek project. In this kind of assessment, we believe that the pupils themselves (Qvortrup, 1990), their parents and their teacher (Nias, 1989) are the best witnesses to the quality and character of both. Pupils' and teacher's voices (Elbaz, 1990), therefore figure prominently in the evaluation.

Gill thought

the practical approach had paid dividends – the hands-on bit, the actual trying the costumes, the hairstyles, tasting the food, looking at slides.

As a teacher, she was

anxious to get something down on paper, quick, but . . . it's all gone in there. They've got it. They've taken it on board, and that has come through in other activities.

She felt that it had given the children a rich experience of ancient Greece.

We introduced them to a sense of history, possible for the first time in their lives. The children got a bit of a feel for the historical side, a bit of an idea of things ancient, some feel of a different culture, a different way of life, and I would hope it would encourage them to investigate for themselves. We've talked an awful lot about evidence – I really do feel we've hit that this time.

Lee (1991, p. 44) feels there are two aspects of 'real history': facts; and what constitutes good grounds for believing facts. There was an emphasis on both here. Peter was particularly pleased with the children's grasp of historical method, as in their work on the Greek vase, discussed earlier. Peter thought they had developed the skill of 'looking and drawing conclusions'. Furthermore, some of the children

won my heart because they'd say 'might', 'might show that', and I thought that was really wonderful – they'd got it!

There was 'aesthetic pleasure' and the development of motor skills in the practical work involved, such as the making of Greek masks; as well as language development and, among some, an appreciation that a lot of our words came from the Greek.

The learning benefits might have been variable across the wide range of ability in the class, but all, according to Peter, generated much enthusiasm, and a feel of excitement for the subject. This may have been the most important achievement:

> There is fire in their eye, they do have excitement, they look forward to the Thursdays.

Gill also felt that they had

> sown the seeds of enthusiasm for history, and many of those children, I hope, are going to begin to see history in a more lively way.

She said they had worked quite hard at trying to 'bring it to life', with some 'quite bold ideas really'. For example, they had two mothers coming in and giving the children 'Greek hairstyles', which could have been 'just a disaster'.

> But in fact the children got very caught up in that and thought it was wonderful. And it really changed their bearing when they were dressed as Greek ladies. Even down to the lady who came in and [spoke] Greek at them. That could have been way over their heads, but they were spellbound because it was all part of it. They've been like sponges, some of them, absorbing all this input and wanting more and more . . .

The 'Greek lady' had heard about the topic from one of the mothers, and had volunteered to become involved. She spoke Greek and had a love of Greece. She took in some books and aerial photographs, and even dressed in national costume. She demonstrated the value of the 'historical witness' (Vass, 1993).

> She was so interested in it, and her enthusiasm carried her along really. It was a gamble, but they thought it was wonderful.

This illustrates how enthusiasm spreads through a ripple effect, and generates more enthusiasm. There is a momentum and cumulation in the career of this kind of spirit in such events. Penny Joyce, the headteacher, commented on 'a sense of buzz' about the class on Thursdays.

Peter said of the final 'Greek Day':

> It was wonderful. Something was happening in the room which was special, and it was palpable. You could feel it. Gill had got them somewhere near being ancient Greek athletes and thinking in those terms.

Gill herself said:

The atmosphere was electric . . . The class loved it. They were all active. They were proud. They wanted to show how good they were to Peter. They had been involved in it from the beginning and had suggested things . . . There was a possibility of chaos with all the children milling around doing activities in the hall, but they were on their best behaviour. It was for them an Olympic games. The whole day was filled with exciting activities. There was a sense of reluctance to finish at the end. It was a fitting conclusion to the topic.

Here is the distinctive stamp of a critical event – the generation of uncommon awareness, excitement, expectation, fun. Gill

expected the children to be excited but instead they were spellbound. The atmosphere was different and special. They were so Greek. The children were definitely experiencing a kind of magic. There was a sense of expectation all day . . . Their faces in the photographs show how much they were concentrating and enjoying it . . .

When Peter (clad in Greek costume) was called on by Gill to award the prize to the best athlete, he also played the role of the 'historical witness', using

the evidence of his eyes, but he also consulted with Zeus, the god of the Olympic games . . . and they really got it. It was quite moving, really, that we got somewhere near where it really was true, what must have happened.

This empathizing illustrates 'the power of history. It adds to the children's humanity. They gain so much of what it is to be human . . ., breaking through to the thought patterns of different people'.

It might be claimed that the critical event builds up to this, gaining pace as skills are acquired, knowledge gained, enthusiasm kindled and relationships established, until on the final 'Greek Day' the empathy reaches new heights. Asked how he felt, one pupil replied: 'I feel Greek'. Gill said 'they were very much in character on that day. It was just the feeling it gave them.' Gill speaks about the cumulation:

It fell into place as the term went on, how it was going to work. It gathered momentum, too, because the children began to find library books about it, or to find pictures and bring things in. They also began to notice things, like the meander pattern round the mirror in the staffroom.

Though the Greek Day marked the final celebration, the event was still well remembered three months later. Gill observed:

The children often reminisce about the Greek topic and ask to see the photos. They see it as a high point . . . They don't hear or look at anything to do with Greece now without mentioning it.

Hannah's parents, for example, reported that she could not go into a supermarket without looking for Greek food. Karl found a Daedalus and Icarus story book in the library and proudly announced: 'I've got a Greek book!' The positive comments of parents in general at the parents' evenings were another indicator of success.

Some children sprang surprises, showing how such work can have uncommon appeal, changing attitudes and unlocking abilities. One of Gill's 'less able' children, for example,

> not a terribly good reader or writer, has been very articulate about it, surprising us with his comments about things that he's seen, and things that he notices when we're talking, things that he remembers . . . This has given him confidence with other things.

The children who speak English as a second language also found new means of expression, through the practical activities – for example, making pictures of the Parthenon from straws – which then aided them in their writing.

Another girl and her parents went to the British Museum in the second week of the topic, and 'brought back lots of bits and pieces' which they used. The fact that she had provided some of the evidence did wonders for her self-esteem within the group:

> She's quite a timid little girl, and if they feel that they've actually achieved something in that way, and you're pleased with them, then you can bring them into the topic somehow, and they're involved – it's theirs.

The same point was made about the child whose father constructed and presented them with a brilliant model of the Parthenon. Gill expresses the important point about 'ownership' here.

A child with considerable behavioural problems had his interest captured and 'went into great depths of concentration'. Gill 'was staggered sometimes by the amount he was looking up, what he was doing, and we were having a lot of chat about it'. He wrote some of this up, and

> we mounted it and presented it, and he was really pleased with that. And that was something he actually took it on himself to do. It wasn't even something I'd instigated in school.

Gill felt it may have had something to do with the mini-Olympics that they prepared for as 'he's quite a physical sort of lad, and I think that's what really captured his interest'. Peter talked to his mother, and was astonished to find he had told her in fine detail about everything they had done. Such a topic, with such treatment, clearly provides a number of 'ways in' for a range of children of differing abilities, ages and interests.

Having said this, all the children apparently exceeded expectations, in the way in which they had 'got down to it'.

> There have been times when I would have thought, 'Is today the right day?', or 'No, we won't watch any more of these slides now'. But they've all been watching and interested and trying to do what they were asked. They've really concentrated in a way that I wouldn't have expected, like a group that had the readings of Homer in the Greek – really taking them beyond what I might normally have expected of them.

The children themselves expressed their enthusiasm in many ways. One thought it was going to be 'dead hard, but it was very interesting, in fact the best topic we've done'. Another said: 'It was a good way to learn history'. In discussion with me, they all attested to their enjoyment and excitement. They wanted to go to Greece, some wanted to live there, and wanted more topics like this one. They explained what was special about the Greeks, how clever they were (at building, athletics, painting, writing, making pots), how they lived, the importance of myths, with full examples ('stories that were told but didn't really happen, but had a message in them'), the sexist arrangements of attending school ('girls were not allowed to go'), Greek gods, the Greek language, how to put broken pots together and how to interpret them, Greek food. They showed their folders of worksheets, Greek masks, pots and plates they had made, their 'time lines'.

They enjoyed having two teachers. It was 'fun', they 'learned more', 'you do a lot more things', and 'there was not so long a queue'. They appreciated the 'buzz' about the topic: 'It was nice to see people bringing things in. It showed we cared about the topic'; 'Our classroom looked lovely and Greek'. The stories were 'interesting' and 'exciting'; they were 'all mystery and magic'. The 'Greek Day' was 'special'. Everybody 'was happy – we didn't want it to end'. Several 'felt Greek' and it made Jennifer 'feel as though I was actually in Greece'. One said: 'We felt like a family.' Here, perhaps, was an expression of the feeling of *communitas* so distinctive of critical events.

Gill reported on some parents' reactions: Claire's parents said that the topic had 'really captured her interest straight away and she was very keen to visit the British Museum'; at the museum, she was delighted to recognize things she had already learned about. Jennifer was actively persuading her parents to visit Greece. She was eager to visit the ruins and see sites she had found out about. Sumbul's mother was pleased at her daughter's interest and enthusiasm about the 'Greek Day', even though they were going to Saudi Arabia the next day. Ben's parents commented on how he had been stimulated to want to research further on some aspects – for example, the army. Hannah's mother commented on her daughter's interest in Greek food in the supermarket. Stuart's parents mentioned his awareness of Greek-style architecture.

In summary, the documentary evidence and the testimony of teacher, researcher, the pupils themselves and their parents pointed to an uncommon degree of success in meeting the aims of the topic. In particular, the topic generated the enthusiasm, excitement and sparkle distinctive of critical events. Significant change also took place within the teacher.

Teacher development

Gill found the resource of the 'other' critical in several ways. It had been a different approach to her usual way of teaching, and

> having someone else there on a regular basis to teach alongside me is a first for me. It just doesn't happen like that in the teaching world. It would be nice if it happened all the time.

This echoes a point made by a teacher in May and Sigsworth (1987, p. 259): 'You can be in a small school for years and never see an adviser. There's no outside person ever coming to give you that bit of a lift really . . .' Gill continued:

> Having another teacher in the room gave me time which is precious. Not for many years have I had a colleague in the room. It was good to have the chance to work alongside another teacher. We worked well together and offered each other constructive feedback. Initially I was anxious about control of the class but once we had the rules set I was more relaxed. The brain-storming process of getting a topic together is an excellent way of bouncing ideas off each other and building up a topic. Also, being bold enough to try something that perhaps isn't quite your idea, but has come from somebody else, but you're getting the support from them in putting it across – that's been very successful, and has certainly expanded this topic. It perhaps made me a bit more adventurous – able to take a few gambles . . . It's given me a whole lot of extra insight. It's made me look fairly carefully at the way I teach and think about it fairly hard: Why do I do it this way? . . . It certainly made me take a far more critical self-appraising approach to my planning.

As well as material assistance, Peter helped rekindle inspiration and enthusiasm, after a contrasting experience in the previous year's project:

> The expansion of the ancient Greeks compared to what I did last year has been immense. Probably because I'd done it before, I'd found some of the pitfalls if you like, some of the things I wasn't happy about, some of the things that I felt I didn't do well enough . . . I had this strong feeling about not doing the same topic again. I've always tended to put my all into a topic and not re-visit it. Actually, revisiting it has been OK and I've been really pleased about it because I like to be enthusiastic and interested when I'm doing it as a topic, and I did wonder whether that would go.
>
> It's been a good way to do ancient Greece. It's given me a whole lot of extra insights. Peter's brought all sorts of evidence. That was the thing I found quite difficult before – finding something to ground it on, some sort of hands-on evidence to give it the visual impact. Having Peter to do that side of the research has been brilliant. It's given me something to work on for the next time that I have to present it.

So there is a sense of cumulation here. This had been much better than last year's, and next year's would be even better. Last time she didn't have so much hands-on experience. Now, 'it's been very good collecting together the materials and seeing how they can be used'. So it had given her 'renewed hope for doing ancient Greeks again – I can cope with that'.

In some ways the project had been an eye-opener to her, because she 'would not have singled out ancient Greece as something that young children would relate to very well . . . but it grabbed them amazingly'. Further, she has been able to *observe* the children's reactions. One of the things that 'gave her a lot of pleasure was to see them listening to someone else telling them a story'. And

> it's been good for me sometimes to actually be able to sit back, which you don't get a chance to do as a teacher, and actually see children relating to a topic . . . I've actually made very careful observation of what's going on, and I've tried a few things that perhaps I might not have tried before, successfully or otherwise – we've had one or two failures – but no, it's been very good for me.

There are several examples of the critical other challenging some of the teacher's basic assumptions, and causing her to think differently:

> There have been lots of times in the past when I would have thought, 'Right! Better stop and get this down on paper', which I haven't done so much this time. Every moment has been filled with all sorts of activities which, in the past, I might have thought, 'Well, that's enough for today'. But we've gone on and on and on, and the children have taken it on board. They've been able to cope with an

afternoon of more solid input . . . We've pushed them beyond. It's been most interesting to see how they've been able to cope. I wonder sometimes whether I've played safe maybe. I've been amazed, because they're quite young to do such a concentrated effort.

Gill is saying a number of things here. The children's concentrative powers have been a revelation to her. She has consequently revised some previous thoughts and bases for action. She has been able to observe them, and seen them in a new light. And their time has been filled more creatively and more solidly (Hargreaves, 1992). She has also changed her views on classroom organization. Hers used to be 'very much group-work based'. But this featured strongly as a subject in discussions between Peter and her, and she came to see more of a place for whole-class activity. She talked of one occasion when 'it wasn't what I'd normally do, but I wanted to show the best thing I could do'. So she set up a multi-activity day, including three separate art activities. These, however, showed all the problems associated with some forms of group work (Alexander, 1992; Galton and Williamson, 1992):

> It was an absolutely disastrous session. There were children milling around with glue spatulas and bits of stuff everywhere . . . and we ended up with a whole following week trying to finish each of these activities.

She had felt 'a bit anti' the idea of more whole-class teaching: 'My hackles came up immediately at the suggestion that I taught the whole class, because I felt that wasn't right'. But in reflecting on her practice, she came to realize that, in fact, on occasions that was what she did. Through the opportunity provided for reflection, and to engage in that reflection with a critical other, Gill came to realize that there was a discrepancy between her practice and her perception of her practice.

> That's very much how we've worked on this project, and I think it's been very successful . . . I would miss having Peter with me to do them but if I did the ancient Greeks again I would certainly use a lot of the ideas that we've done because I feel they're very sound.

The intervention of the critical other for Gill, therefore, has been catalytic, helping to bring her to new realization of her teaching and her beliefs, and, with that, recognition of new possibilities and opportunities (see Lather, 1986, p. 272; Gitlin, 1990; and Zajano and Edelsbert, 1993, for the 'catalytic' effect of this kind of research process).

Tann (1988, p. 24) reports on research that shows that

> many teachers saw considerable potential for learning that was possible through topic work [but] they often lacked experience of alternative ways of 'doing' topic work in order to realise their own goals.

It was very easy for teachers, and whole schools, to get locked in to doing topic work in a particular way which therefore limited the kinds of learning which could be expected.

It might be argued that the 'lack of experience' derives from pressures and constraints rather than personal qualities; and that the infusion of a catalytic agent can raise new awareness of possibilities and opportunities. Gill, for example, thought that

if I did the topic again, I would take on board this researcher thing. Having seen it work, having somebody looking for evidence and bringing in things to a topic as Peter has done, then I think I would put more time myself into that.

She is speaking here of 'extra research' (in the sense of looking for and assembling materials, for example) over and above the careful planning she does for all topics. In answer to the point that she might not have time for it, she replied: 'Well, you have to make time for things like that, don't you?' She spoke enthusiastically about the next topic they would be doing – a local study – how she would make use of 'several people who had done some interesting work on the school', and 'more practical evidence'. She has seen 'how it works and I know how to make it work':

Having seen it in operation and used Peter as a resource in that, I now would make even more of an effort to collect bits and pieces together and to find people like the Mrs Harveys [the Greek lady] of this world – because they're out there, aren't they?

We have to inject a note of caution here. Teachers have been enlightened before – by courses, by in-service education, for example – only to find the constraints on their work enforcing a return to 'business as usual', despite their best intentions. Only longer-term study could assess any deep-seated effects of Peter's intervention. What can be said is that this activity was successful in itself, as discussed earlier, and it established a bench-mark, an example of what could be done. Further, the topic was grounded in Gill's own practical experience. It was also tri-angulated, in the sense that the extra person added another dimension to vision and increased its range and depth, aiding distance and reflectivity. But it remained firmly part of the teacher's culture, and her voice spoke through the planning, decision-making, teaching and reporting.

Critical other development

If this were 'truly collaborative' (Day, 1991), it would be expected that the 'other' would also gain in some ways, over and above the contribution to the general research, that is, that there would be some personal benefit.

The participants would thus change each other (Lather, 1986). Collaborators contribute, draw upon, build, in an interactive, dialogic (Gitlin, 1990), spiralling process, developing a culture of partnership that is empowering to them both.

Peter, who had not taught on a regular basis in a school since 1972, certainly gained considerably:

It's given me a lease of life. It's proved to me I can still do it, which I had to do. It was necessary for me to prove I've still got the energy and the enthusiasm . . .

Peter did not have much experience of teaching 7- and 8-year-old children, so he was 'pleasantly reassured', though sometimes he had gone home 'very weary on Thursdays'. He was thus more confident about returning to teaching:

I thoroughly enjoyed coming to the school. Coming in on Thursday was a super routine for me, and I've enjoyed glimpsing school life.

It helped him with the overall research project in that he 'actually lived and experienced things that would not have been so real for me if I had merely been observing'. It had also added to his experience as a tutor to some students he was supervising on teaching practice. He could speak to them now 'not as a scribe, but as a person who had some recent experience of teaching'. He could draw on these Thursday experiences:

the very practical things which I'm not sure I would have been able to do if I hadn't the actual experience myself. There's been no aspect of it which has been bad for me. It's all been very good.

He was able to test a feeling he had about the 'art of primary teaching', that

Alexander [1992] was right in the sense that a good deal of class teaching is desirable and can be very productive, and that the activities going on in the classroom (divided up among different groups) should be limited.

Through discussion with Gill, and through experiment, they had reached agreement, as we saw earlier. Peter said:

This is where the collaborative mode has been quite useful, because Gill was certainly more of the group-work persuasion than I was. She's taught me a few things and I've taught her. I think we've learned from each other, and probably we've slightly shifted each other's perspective on it by working together.

Peter said that it had 'definitely been one of the highlights of my professional career'. It had given him satisfaction from linking his two recent professional roles, those of adviser and researcher; had appealed to the practical (teaching) and observational (researcher) sides of his nature; had confirmed his hunch about the benefits of collaboration; and had reinforced his view that the study of history had enormous educational potential for young children.

The collaboration, professional and personal

Much of the success of this topic appeared to derive from the collaboration between teacher and critical other. As Richards (1987, p. 10) has argued:

> If progress is to be made on the elucidation of general principles of teaching and learning . . . researchers have not only to focus more on learning and on the curriculum in the classroom but also to involve teachers much more as collaborators and 'critical friends' in the research enterprise.

We aimed to move beyond this model, continuing the quest for what Day (1991, p. 546) has called a 'truly collaborative approach': one that operates on principles of open professionality; where the aims of teacher and researcher are fused into one; where decision-making and products are jointly owned, where power is shared and both are 'empowered' by the activity (Elbaz, 1990). To do this, Day (1991, p. 546) argues researchers must 'first learn to walk in different ways, to converse in new languages, to listen to different voices, to care, and to establish educative communities made up of fellow professionals from schools, higher education, and government'.

In traditional collaborative research, the researcher often has a purely research agenda to which any aims within the school are subordinate. This model has a strong hold, since it is geared to the structure of expectations of researchers within their jobs, and enshrined in their culture. There are many other considerations, including nervousness about surrendering control (and being used for political purposes within the school or having the quality, as well as direction, of the research threatened), requirements to direct and manage research, and hierarchies within research teams. In addition, teacher culture, mainly owing to pressures on their time and the constraints they work under, in effect tends to support this model, though teachers might have strong reservations about much of the research that results. Though a collaborative contract might be jointly agreed, a researcher might still be met with courteous queries – 'Are you getting what you want?', 'Is this any use to you?' – as if it is the researcher's project alone. These 'polite forms of discourse' (White, 1989, p. 315) have been noted by Gitlin (1990, p. 445) as symptomatic of traditional research norms which separate researcher and practitioner. These norms are hard to break for both researcher and teacher. Establishing a 'truly collaborative culture' requires penetrating the different structures within which both work and forming a cultural bridge – a not inconsiderable task. While not completely free of these problems, we feel that a bridge was made through the following means.

Mutual aims

The aims of teaching and research were closely interlocked. Part of the researcher's main objective was to ensure the success of the topic – exactly the teacher's aim. There were no hidden agendas. However, the teaching and the research aims were still quite distinct, that of the teaching being to bring about pupils' learning in a specific situation, that of the research to analyse the processes involved and to compare them with others similar. In addition, there was a combined teaching/research aim, which was to contribute to teacher professional knowledge and development. We have seen what was achieved here in the previous section. Thus, aims were shared, and where there was a difference, it was complementary, not exploitative. Further, we recognized that neither side had a better way of knowing. As with Gitlin *et al.*(1989, p. 251), the approach was to 'use the differences between groups in a way that increases *both* groups' understanding'.

Power-sharing

Even if one neutralizes the researcher factor, there may be other issues affecting the balance of power in the collaboration. The 'other' can be, in some form or other, an authority figure, be it as an adviser, tutor, researcher, consultant, and this may permeate relations in subtle ways (May and Sigsworth, 1987). Among the other issues in our case is the fact that Peter used to be an adviser in the area, though he had never met Gill before in that capacity. Was there any residual power and status deriving from that post that affected the situation? As for any possible gender influence, did the collaboration show any division of responsibilities or patterns of decision-making that could be analysed on a gender basis and that led to inequalities?

All we can say is that we were aware of these possibilities, and did our best to guard against them. Gill's own testimony points to a feeling of joint control. Her participation was entirely voluntary. She saw considerable chances for her teaching and for her own development. She led and co-ordinated the teaching programme, of which she affirmed she was 'very much in charge'. In general, she commented, 'I don't like anything going on in the classroom of which I don't feel in control'. Further, she strongly supported teaching involvement from the researcher, 'rather than', as she said, 'a remote man sitting in the corner taking notes'. Peter's previous role as adviser helped here in reinforcing an earnest desire to support the teacher, in seeing the 'teacher as expert' and in regarding the needs of the client as paramount (Day, 1991).

The collaboration rested on this kind of friendly and persuasive basis, but it was essentially democratic – each had opportunities to persuade the other. For example, Gill's recognition of the whole-class aspects of her teaching was something she came to regard as a benefit. They regarded the collaboration as one of equals, each acting as 'critical friend' to the other. Peter said:

> I felt very welcome in the school and increasingly comfortable as Thursdays progressed . . . Above all, I was able to contribute to the teaching.

Gill was gratified that the researcher 'put emphasis on good practice for the children'. She commented:

> Peter has fitted in to what he knows is my sort of regime, my way of working, and my ways of dealing with the children, and he's backed me up. It could have been difficult otherwise.

This, therefore, is where Gill's power came into effect.

> I feel that I owe it to the children to give them as broad a spectrum of input as I can, and if that means making use of someone else's talent, why not? I have taught for long enough to realize the benefits of an extra pair of hands in the classroom.

Peter concurred with this, noting that he

> negotiated ideas, techniques, possibilities for teaching and learning with Gill. But she had the final say in this sphere.

Role-blending

Teacher and researcher roles meshed together to form one organic role that was greater than the sum of its parts. Nias has described relationships between teachers that are so close and interdependent that they are like 'one finger, one thumb' (1987) or 'Russian dolls' (Simmonds and Nias, 1989). This showed a similar kind of subtle dovetailing. We referred to Gill as a 'teacher-researcher', with main responsibility for the teaching but contributing to all stages of the research from planning to write-up; and to Peter, more uncommonly, as a 'researcher-teacher'. In some ways this might seem like the old-fashioned 'participant observer', but this did not fit Peter's role. Participant observation is part of the culture of anthropological and ethnographic research, and Peter's role was pitched more centrally into the culture of teaching. This was accentuated by the two-edged nature of Peter's research, for part of this was to do with research into the teaching of ancient Greece. His and Gill's roles were therefore mirror-images of each other.

The teacher-researcher co-ordinated the teaching and learning process. She had detailed knowledge of the children in the class and of the school and curriculum context. She provided schemes of work for the topic according to requirements, organized displays, co-ordinated planning, liaised with colleagues and parents, monitored assessment. She contributed to the research by joining in the planning, evaluation and analysis. The researcher-teacher co-ordinated the research, initiating the planning, collecting data, and beginning analysis and writing-up. He also contributed to the teaching by providing artefacts, visual material, worksheets and other resources, by contributing specialist knowledge on ancient Greece, and by direct involvement, especially story-telling and playing a leading part in the 'Greek Day'. On this basis, there was clear understanding of each other's roles from the outset, and the possibilities of role conflict and/or role strain (Musgrove and Taylor, 1974; Hargreaves, 1972) were minimized.

However, there was more to this collaboration than the filling and performing of roles. It was one that involved whole persons. In the culture of the primary school, staff interact as people, not just as role-occupants (Nias *et al.*, 1989). This takes us into personal qualities.

Personal qualities

Day (1991, p. 537) proposes a new form of collaboration in which 'affective, human-relating skills hold the same importance as the more traditional technical skills of the researcher'. In contrast to 'hit-and-run' research, this must be longer-lasting, founded on mutual respect and concern, and on feeling for the other as a human being. The researcher's connection with the teacher must be 'caring'. This is similar to a point made by Noddings (1986) about 'an ethic of caring', involving a concern for others, and for the effect one has on others. Only within such a relationship will there develop the kind of trust that will enable the participants to reflect fully and freely, to risk exposure and to engage in mutual criticism. Zajano and Edelsbert (1993, p. 151) write:

> we had to simultaneously learn to trust each other and to reflect on our work. Without the trust, we could not honestly question our own practice in the presence of the other; by questioning our practice in each other's presence, we learned to trust each other.

It is another ingredient that leads towards a productive catharsis. Gill noted:

We worked well together and we offered each other constructive feedback. I got a 'buzz' from it.

Collaborators, therefore, engage with the task full-bloodedly, just as the committed primary school teacher engages with her job. With such teachers, their 'substantial self' (Ball, 1972) is in unison with the central demands of the role – 'the job is their life', in other words (Pollard, 1987). Nias (1989, pp. 182–4) describes such teachers as having a feeling of 'wholeness' and 'belonging' about their teaching. There is something ethically suspect, therefore, about planned research involving them as principal actors that is less than 'whole', that compartmentalizes (separating teaching and research), that takes from the wholeness instead of contributing towards it. Instead of the formality, doubt and suspicion that mark some traditional research in schools, this kind of arrangement is based on mutual belief. There is a strong emotional stake. McLaren (1991, p. 163) concludes that 'a politics of field relations must be grounded in eros, in passion, in commitment to transform through a radical connectedness to the self and the other'.

Both participants saw the other as whole persons fully dedicated to the task. Peter describes Gill as

> displaying considerable energy, enthusiasm and animation. She plans and structures her lessons carefully, organizes her classroom effectively.

She told him: 'I have always had very high expectations of my classes and I push and push . . . '. Peter reported that

> there is frequently an air of excitement in the classroom, with Gill creating the impression that things are happening and what is being done is important.

Like most primary teachers (Nias, 1989), she relates strongly to the children. She knows their interests, makes her teaching relevant, cares for them and likes them all as individuals:

> I hope I am like a parent to the children . . . I encourage children to offer their opinions freely. I want them to know they will not be shot down in flames . . . I want to value what the children are and what they have done.

She has a sense of humour, communicates clearly with her children, preferring to consult and reason with them. But she will react strongly to inadequate work or to errant behaviour. She said: 'I can forgive a child anything if he or she tries.' She seems to have all the qualities of what students in general regard as a 'good teacher' (Woods, 1990b). Peter felt 'a special relationship between teacher and children is very apparent'. He thought his children exhibited a 'strong sense of belonging to her class'.

This high regard was mutual. Gill had great respect for Peter's specialist knowledge, seeing him as

> the sort of oracle really in terms of ancient Greece. That's why it's been brilliant to make use of that. I feel in a way I've been the one that's sort of been muddling along in the background, and he's been the one presenting all this wonderful evidence. I know he's put an awful lot of work into it, and that's been such a tremendous support. The children have come to see him as 'the Greek man', and that's been great. That's been a contributory factor in the success of the whole thing.

Peter's whole-hearted commitment to the project was never in doubt, right up to the final 'Greek Day', when he appeared dressed as an ancient Greek – the epitome of the 'charismatic other' (see Chapter 4). There were several aspects to this commitment. First, he has a great enthusiasm and liking for the ancient Greeks – 'so much of our culture comes from them' – developed from his history-teaching days. He also has considerable knowledge. He has visited many of the main archaeological sites and museums in Greece. He knew what resources were available and where to find them, visiting the Ashmolean and the British Museum, assembling slide sets, photographs, artefacts, and other materials – 'doing the legwork that Gill didn't have time for'. Second, he enjoys *teaching* history.

> I just love weaving a web from history. For example, I like to make little fantasies based on fact.

He gave the example of Clio, the muse of history, whom he presented in the form of a statue of a woman with a bird bath in front of her. They 'wove an elaborate web' around her of how and why one would make offerings to her, and acted out all the procedures, giving her history books and pure water (because she lived near a spring):

> We were somewhere near the way the ancient Greeks would have thought. The secret for me with history is the moment when you, as the teacher, get the children in touch with how it probably was at the time. That to me is real creative history teaching, when you make that breakthrough something happens, and it's really wonderful. It's getting in touch with the people who came before – a different civilization, different people – but we in the twentieth century in Chesham for ten minutes were somewhere near where ancient Greeks may have been, and that was precious.

Like the typical primary school teacher, Peter has

a very warm feeling with the children. They have been very positive, and there are some real characters. I shall miss them.

So well was Peter attuned that he felt he 'belonged' at the school:

I like the school, I like the staff and enjoy coming, so I don't feel like
a researcher. I feel just like really another member of staff. They
made me feel very welcome. I'm not one of the world's greatest
extroverts and the thought of me wearing Greek clothes is a bit
remote from the world in which I normally live. But I felt perfectly
comfortable because I felt I was amongst friends. I think that's been
a factor, this sense of belonging.

Peter was aware of the dangers in qualitative research of 'going native'
(Paul, 1953), that is to say, becoming submerged in the insider's view and
so seeing everything from that perspective and losing all objectivity.
Gitlin *et al.* (1989) raise a different question. They see the problem not as
involvement, but detachment.

The question is not whether the data are biased; the question is
whose interests are served by the bias. As we leave behind the goal
of objective knowledge, we are forced to consider the role social
relations have in mediating the construction of knowledge (p. 245).

Our answer was to aim for both involvement and detachment in a
different kind of research structure. Here we would say that Peter 'went
native' in full consciousness as a positive strategy. This gave him the full
benefits of involvement. Analytical distance was secured by his mem-
bership of a research team to which he regularly reported, and where
comparisons were made with other critical events and forms of collaboration. He felt equally at home here – but in a research capacity. This
kind of structure is one possible solution to the traditional problem
encountered by the lone ethnographer, and to that of whose knowledge
is constructed.

Policy implications

History has provoked more debate and controversy than most National
Curriculum subjects, fuelling one of the more prominent 'sites of struggle'. There are those who feared that the National Curriculum was retro-
gressive, privileging facts above skills, content over process, transmission
above interpretation, ethnocentrism above more broadly based study.
Some thought the National Curriculum would undermine teacher autonomy, creativity and individuality (Phillips, 1991). There has been concern, too, that the National Curriculum would mean the end of the

integrated topic. Webb (1993, p. 249), for example, noted in her research a 'definite move away from broad-based topics to subject-focused topics'.

Others feel that history has benefited from, indeed been revived by the National Curriculum. The Department of Education and Science (1989) reported that history 'was underemphasised or not taught in half the sample schools. The standards of work were very disappointing.' Noble (1991) opined that the National Curriculum had done much 'to rescue' primary history. Bage (1993, p. 270) points out that '[the] History Order does not need teaching as it is written, but requires interpretation before it is taught'. In other words, teacher autonomy is still there. Moreover, it might be seen in some respects to have increased. Thus, by introducing new areas within a reasoned framework, it could be argued that the National Curriculum has opened up a range of opportunities and possibilities that the teacher might not have realized were there.

This certainly seems to have applied to the ancient Greece project. For Gill, it has shown that the prescribed curriculum in the area of the ancient Greeks can be taught in an exciting way in line with her beliefs and values. After initial reservations, she has contributed to, and lived through, a teaching and learning experience that marks a considerable advance on the previous year's topic, and which sets new standards for the year following. She has retained her holistic approach, but 'inside out' rather than 'outside in', using the subject as base, in a way that recovers the historical imperative while preserving the integration of knowledge. She has broadened her methods in introducing her children to the historical discipline, to the excitement of exploration and discovery, to the value of 'the past', to the judgement and interpretation of evidence, and to taking part in the process of knowledge. Cooper (1992a) points out that before the National Curriculum not much history was taught in primary schools, and where it was, it was often 'based on television programmes and copying from poor text books'. The National Curriculum goes somewhat further than this, requiring pupils in the earliest years to 'have opportunities to learn about the past from a range of historical sources, including artefacts, pictures and photographs, music, written sources, buildings and sites'. It is, however, one thing to legislate, another to implement (Ball and Bowe, 1992). The History Order could still have been *experienced* as restrictive and controlling in this area were it not for the services of the 'critical other'. Like many other primary teachers since 1988, Gill has experienced the twin oppressions of general overwork and lack of specialist subject knowledge (Campbell *et al.*, 1991a). In some circumstances, Gill might have been tempted to follow a more traditional teaching line with the 'ancient Greece' project. The way it actually developed shows that there is nothing intrinsic in the Order that prevents teachers teaching as they would wish, at least with respect to this area. It is more a matter of resources, such as in-service provision to boost specialist knowledge, or the recruitment of specialist aid from outside. A combination of these is indicated. Alexander *et al.* (1992, p. 34) stated that 'teachers must possess the subject knowledge which the statutory orders require', but this seems hardly realistic without additional resources being provided.

The services of the 'other' here were seen to be critical, suggesting ways in which the teacher's role might be enhanced, and perhaps a new role for former inspectors and advisers, and for tutors in higher education. Teachers could clearly benefit from such a boost. But the collaboration has to be genuine. In this case it was one of whole selves, with mutual aims, equal power, dovetailing roles, strong personal accord, and a dialogic approach (Gitlin, 1990). The dialogue and interaction between Gill and Peter generated the ideas and exhilaration that underpinned the topic and spread to all. In aspiring to be 'truly collaborative', the researcher set out to submerge himself in teaching, and to work to the fullest extent with the class teacher for the success of the topic. The research team of which he was a member provided a 'research' reference set, and monitored the progress of the project. There are several advantages of such an arrangement. The research team provides a number of checks and balances – a kind of triangulation. It aids proportion and perspective. Not least, it reduces role conflict, providing reassurance and encouraging submergence in the teacher role and all that follows from that in terms of mutual aims, equal power, common strategies and joint investment.

The 'other' aids teaching, but also aids the teacher's reflectivity and research into her own practice. Cooper (1992b, p. 13) has argued that class teachers are in a good position to collect evidence of how the National Curriculum is working, and thus refine their own teaching, and Crawford and Rogers (1992, p. 25) argue that 'we need saturating in examples of good practice'. Teachers might thus help modify the National Curriculum in the way John McGregor advised: 'It is a living model which will undoubtedly evolve as the demands of education evolve . . . I strongly recognise the importance of teachers themselves being involved in this process' (quoted in Cooper, 1992b, p. 13). Bage (1993, p. 270) also maintains that 'the final classroom nature of history can still be heavily influenced by teachers'.

Any collaboration must beware of becoming technicist, that is, concerned simply with technical application (Weiner, 1989; Siraj-Blatchford, 1993), and reinforcing the status quo without question. We endeavoured to make the collaboration open and critical, and to help make teachers and pupils responsible for their own learning (Oldroyd and Tiller, 1987). The approach to history eschewed the 'social engineering' line in favour of an 'enlightenment' and 'empowering' model with emphasis on exploration, evidence, interpretation and self-worth. In the main, however, the teachers themselves were their own best defence against any danger of technicism. The headteacher encapsulated their approach when she said:

This may sound silly, but it helps having a throw-away attitude to the National Curriculum. I think it is getting the balance right between saying 'This is important, this is here to stay' and saying 'Fiddle! We are jolly good teachers and we will get on with the task of teaching'.

Note

1 These were government prescribed attainment targets in history at the time.

6

Managing marginality: aspects of the career of a primary school head

So far, the analysis has been, on the whole, optimistic in terms of teachers achieving their aims in education. However, many teachers have been frustrated and alienated by the changes. Cusack (1993, p. 7) is 'almost scared to do anything creative in case I fall foul of the law'. Some have felt compelled to leave the profession (see, for example, Anon, 1993; Jarvis, 1993). These have been among what many would regard as the best teachers. As Fullan (1992, p. 121) observes:

> Intensification-type reforms focusing on narrowly defined and im-posed curriculum and teacher competencies repel good people from entering and/or staying. Bureaucratic reforms may be able to guar-antee minimal performance, but not excellence in teaching.

One such teacher was Peter, who has decided to take early retirement from his position as a primary school head several years earlier than he would have wished. This chapter tells his story.

My acquaintance with Peter arose out of my critical events research (Woods, 1993a). Among the effects of such events is the confirming and preserving of a teacher's cherished beliefs, which often at other times are in danger of being undermined by forces beyond the teacher's control. These are peaks within the teacher's pedagogical career that sustain vis-ion and restore faith. Though they may occur rarely, they are as central to the teacher's sense of self and professionalism as they are to pupil learning.

One of these events occurred at Peter's primary school, where he had initiated the 'Rushavenn project'. This had resulted in a publication which won a prize for best children's book of the year (Whistler, 1988). In researching the processes that led up to this, I noted considerable advances in the children's personal and social development, and in the art of learning. Pupils involved, now sixth-formers at secondary schools, still recognized it as a high point in their educational careers, a kind of marker for what could be accomplished, and a guide to a truth, rarely experienced, but providing a perspective and insight for all else. This applied also to the teacher who devised and co-ordinated the event. For Peter, it was the culmination of a number of activities over the years in which he had sought to put his heartfelt views on education into practice. These views run counter to traditional forms, and at times he has found himself ploughing a lonely furrow, with only his convictions and his vision to support him. These convictions, however, have strong roots in his past, and are enshrined in his self. He explained this to me over a number of meetings at his school, and at his and my homes in discussions that enabled me to piece together a life history ranging from early childhood to the present. These discussions have continued at regular intervals up to the present day.

Peter's educational philosophy

Peter believes strongly in a largely child-directed approach to teaching and learning. Only through a measure of personal freedom can children give expression to the special and individual gifts which they all have but which are seldom recognized in traditional education. We should spend more time listening to children than talking to and at them, and should seek to elevate their creative skills to more of a central place. This means a holistic, interdisciplinary, integrated, largely thematic approach to the curriculum rather than a rigidly subject-based structure, and a recognition of the important role played by narrative and oracy in a child's development.

He does not advocate unstructured libertarianism. At his school, the children were regularly involved in some of the more formal processes of learning, since there were certain essential concepts and skills which they needed to acquire, sometimes through direct intervention. Peter said:

I would not go as far as to say that we provide our children with the foundations – for foundations predetermine the kind of edifice which will result. Rather, we try to ensure that they have sufficient knowledge and understanding to be able to choose an appropriate site on which to build.

Peter stressed the importance of freedom, space, latitude and flexibility. Context, also, is vital, and he is aware of the symbolic significance of classroom arrangement. Education, he believes, is for children, and not for a pre-ordained order of society into which they should be socialized. The teacher is a facilitator, catalytic agent, midwife, novice as well as guru, for the teacher also is always learning. Teaching should therefore be relevant to pupils' concerns, anchored in their personal experience, cognizant of the knowledge they already have, and responsive to 'the unique vision that characterizes the period of childhood'. It should capitalize on children's natural curiosity and inventiveness, not seek to shut them down. The formulation and basic legitimation of this educational theory comes not from teacher training or the study of theories set out by others, such as Piaget, Plowden, Dewey or Vygotsky (though the relevance of these can clearly be seen), but from his own experiences. That has been the motivating force. It has combined with study of such authors as these, and with his teaching experience, to form his own distinctive personal, practical knowledge (Clandinin, 1985). It has become validated through his own experience.

These views found their ultimate expression in the Rushavenn project. The aim was to create and write a book – a real book. The work for this was done in 1982, though the book was not published until 1988. The project was initiated and organized by Peter, and co-ordinated and written by Theresa Whistler, a well-known children's author, with the assistance of 15 children aged 8–11 who volunteered to take part. For some time, Peter had been inviting well-known authors to the school to discuss their work, and children had been encouraged to make and produce their own books. Rushavenn brought this work to a head. Great attention was paid to context. The emphasis here was on naturalism and freedom. The event took place on Saturdays, mainly in the staffroom, with, for Stephen (one of the pupils involved, now a sixth-former studying for A levels),

> a strange atmosphere really – as far away from the classroom as you could get. It was relaxed, comfortable, non-authoritarian, and a far better learning experience because of the one-to-one bouncing of ideas.

This is what it was designed to do, produce ideas, and many of them, which Theresa would co-ordinate and use to inform drafts which would then be put back to the group.

Peter emphasized the importance of instilling confidence in all members of the group. Some, he felt, were being held back because of apprehension about their abilities deriving from their experience of traditional schooling. The project opened doors for them by providing a range of opportunities – through writing, speaking, drawing, role-play, poetry and music. Some found expression in one medium, some another, but generally there was carry-over with other forms as they gained confidence. Relationships were also vital. Institutional roles and statuses were relaxed. There was a close, family feeling about the group. Theresa 'felt about them that they were children of my own. I got immensely fond of them'. To Dawn, Theresa was 'a sort of teacher, but a friend as well'. Sarah noticed a subtle difference in Peter:

> He wasn't being a teacher then. He was one of us. He had authority over us, but we didn't ever feel there was a teacher–pupil distinction.

To Stephen, Peter was not like a normal headteacher 'strolling around and looking officious . . . to see him come in in jeans and be human was great'. Both Peter and Theresa were acting here as guides and facilitators, trying to 'open doors'. The project belonged to them all. All identified with it, contributed freely, had a share in control of the process, and saw themselves in the final product.

The subject-matter clearly appealed to the imagination of all concerned. The nature of the setting of the book, the characters and their relationships was not based on ethereal sentiment, pandering to the 'innocence' of childhood as in the ideology identified by King (1978) and Alexander (1984), but on feelings generated in real life about real issues. The place 'Rushavenn' was in fact based on Theresa's family's north Devon home, where she had spent her childhood, and which was burnt down by accident during the war. Stephen, for one, had been inspired by that:

> At primary school you are fairly isolated, so to become somebody in your own right at the age of 9, 10, 11 is fairly special. To be able to move away from that isolated small world by writing, by listening to the stories that Theresa and Peter and the group had created . . . Even now I'd like to open the cupboard and find something in there.

Theresa said:

> It was lovely to have nobody who didn't want to be there, and that's the main thing that makes it unlike school.

The teaching philosophy was to lead out rather than force in. There were three prominent aspects to this. One was stimulation, as in the provision of props, mementoes, photographs, the children bringing in their own treasured possessions, and what Stephen called 'think-tank' activities, where they generated and developed ideas. A second aspect was encouragement. Theresa

> preferred not to correct their work . . . I think that people can only be creative when they feel encouragement . . . What I wanted was to help discover for each of them the kind of interior pressure that makes you want to create. I wanted each to feel like an artist.

The third aspect was example. Peter emphasized the importance of the adult setting an example, by listening to what the children had to say, appreciating their ideas and initiatives and honestly valuing their contributions.

The Rushavenn project yielded exceptional achievement for both pupils and teachers. For Peter and Theresa, in their separate ways, it fulfilled a lifetime's dream. In addition, it confirmed Peter's educational philosophy, so often, throughout his career and life, under siege. There is plenty of evidence showing how constraints almost pre-ordain a formal approach to teaching (Westbury 1973, Hargreaves 1988). Galton (1987) and Bennett (1987) have shown how difficult it is for teachers to use progressive methods, as conceived, for example, by the Plowden Committee (Central Advisory Council for Education in England 1967). Three questions arise, therefore. First, how did Peter acquire his educational philosophy? Second, how did he manage to sustain and develop it against all the odds? And third, why, after the triumph of 'Rushavenn', did he decide to quit teaching? For the answers, Peter searched deep into his past.

The self

Peter's teaching was an expression of the self. Pollard (1980, p. 38) remarks that 'teachers do hold particular opinions about the "right" way to teach and invest much of their self-identity in that chosen method'. For many of Nias's (1989, p. 182) teachers, 'to adopt the identity of "teacher" was simply to be "yourself" in the classroom', and for 'Sarah', the teacher in Aspinwall (1985), teaching, far from being peripheral, was 'so vital' to her; she could 'not divorce being a teacher from being me' (p. 43). What Pinar (1986) refers to as the 'architecture-of-self' is constructed over time as the result of numerous interactions in numerous contexts. There is no disjuncture between private and public here; the one feeds into the other. The personal dispositions and experiences accumulated over the years help shape the professional role of teacher as it is subjectively experienced. The self goes on developing, for it is a process, not an entity, formed in interaction with others and in interaction with oneself (Berger, 1963). Others act as role models, both positive and negative, and 'significant others' are especially important. These may be people in key positions, such as parents, friends or teachers. This does not necessarily assume a passive role for the individual: 'significant others' can also be sought out. They may reflect values, beliefs and behaviour highly esteemed by the individual. Interaction with these helps to construct and give shape to the chosen self, which finds new powers of expression as it grows. It acquires sharper definition by contrast with negative others; and new forms of articulation by internal debate, self-reflection, and interaction between the 'I' and the 'Me' (Mead, 1934).

The self is often represented as being multiple. Thus Ball (1972) and Nias (1989) talk of 'situationist' and 'substantial selves'. I also found this formulation useful in a previous study (Woods, 1981). In this conception there is a preferred self, but the individual adopts different guises in different situations. It is a way of coping with the world, and particularly with institutional, depersonalized life. A number of these situational selves may be contradictory and difficult to resolve – for example, between the traditional role of mother and that of career woman in paid work. Norquay (1990) argues that the self is not unified – at least there is no 'single narrative of a unified self, but rather several tellings with which we present and represent ourselves within different contexts and configurations of our locations in our gender, race and class' (p. 291). Thus, 'the process through which we work ourselves into positions in mainstream society as "normal" may entail the silencing and forgetting of experiences in our childhood that do not fit the position we strive to maintain' (p. 293). This may well be the case for some people, as they become subject to changing historical and social forces. But this is not the case with Peter, at least in his adult life. The outstanding feature of his account is how he strives to maintain the integrity of the self against many odds (though there were times during his own schooling when separate and different selves seemed the only answer to the problems that confronted him); how he uses contradiction and conflict to strengthen his preferred notion of self; how there is a fairly clear line of development (at least as he now sees it), with one or two hiatuses, from the very beginning.

The development of marginality

A critical divide

Peter's childhood focused on the contrast between the formal, alienating, intimidating, structured, world of school, and the natural world which he experienced himself at first hand, where he promoted what was, for him, real learning and developed his real self. He cultivated an alternative self for schools, and other such institutions, which largely followed the rules and met with moderate success in the school's terms, but which fell short of what he knew were his capabilities. School was like a prison for the most part, public, constraining, deadening and oppressing. The natural world was full of wonder and beauty, a rich environment that stretched his imagination and appealed to his creative instincts. He recounted the adventure and excitement of making new discoveries; and described some secret areas, which gave him a sense of freedom, privacy and ownership.

Contrast this with his portrayal of school. He is fond of imagery in conveying his feelings. For example, he recalls two objects from the conservatory of his grandfather's home which have metaphoric significance for him:

> One was a glass container shaped like a decanter. In the bottom was an aperture, the inside edge of which formed the outer lip of an internal groove in which was placed any sticky substance like jam or treacle. This was a fly and wasp trap. The insects would fly into the glass container from the underneath, attracted by the jam, and then die when they failed to find their way out. I used to stand by the top of the cupboard on which it was placed and watch the trapped insects flying around inside desperately trying to escape.
>
> The other object was an unusual mouse trap. I am not sure whether this was my grandfather's patent invention. It comprised a heavy block of wood suspended on a wooden arm above a narrow corridor made by two vertical pieces of wood fixed to the edges of a third which provided a floor area. In the centre of this floor area was a movable section which was attached to a simple release mechanism. A piece of cheese was placed on this 'trap' and when fractionally moved by an interested mouse would release a small wedge connected by string to the arm and this, in turn, brought the heavy block of wood down on the unsuspecting creature. The flattened mouse was then removed the following morning. I can remember the occasional sleepless night punctuated by the sound of this block of wood crashing down.
>
> I mention these two objects because there were times in my early schooling when I was made to feel as trapped as those insects and as flattened as those mice.

Critical incidents

While he kept the two worlds and selves apart, there was an absence of conflict. But inevitably, at times, it was a 'knife-edge' existence (Measor and Woods, 1984). Occasionally, as a pupil, he tried to amalgamate the two worlds, but this often produced a 'critical incident', that is, a 'highly charged moment or episode that has enormous consequences for personal change and development' (Sikes *et al.*, 1985, p. 230). He mentions one concerning cigarette cards. He had become something of an expert on these, his interest stimulated by his grandfather's collection. One day his primary teacher brought a cigarette card album into a nature lesson, and walked round showing it to each pupil. He noticed that some of the cards were out of order. He was a shy, retiring boy, who rarely spoke or volunteered an answer during lessons, but here was an instance where he could make a worthwhile contribution. He politely indicated that one or two of the cards were out of sequence.

> The next thing I knew was that my head was swimming and I had been dragged out to the front of the class. I had received a hefty clip across the back of the head. At that point I decided that if this was what school-based education was all about I wanted no more to do with it.

Seniority as a sixth-former at grammar school was no protection from such treatment in similar circumstances. The one thing that helped him through long, boring days at this school was the session spent on the beach after lunch:

> I could conceal myself amongst the marram grass and sand dunes and bird-watch – there were little terns and ringed plovers nesting on the North Beach then – and you could see different kinds of sea birds – duck and guillemots and cormorants and even the occasional 'exotics' like black-throated divers and sheerwaters, as well as a great variety of gulls and the more common coastal species. One day, however, it was decreed that if you did not go home to lunch you were not allowed to make these lunch-time sorties back into what was increasingly for me the 'real', the natural world. This was a considerable blow. In fact, I was to discover that it was the one sacrifice I just could not make. I, along with two or three others, disregarded the rule until, one day, we were reported by one of the second year sixth-form prefects. We were summoned before Reggie (the head teacher) and after being told how he had expected us sixth-formers to set a better example (I thought I was) we were given a good caning. This was the only time in my school career – primary or secondary – that I was caned by a head teacher and this had to happen to me when I was nearing the end of my school life. As I felt the cane eating into my buttocks I could feel the tears (of anguish rather than pure discomforture) welling up into my eyes. Again, I could not help reflecting that I was being caned by a representative of the un-natural world of the grammar school campus for wanting to preserve my contact with the natural world just at the end of the road. As with the primary school incident, the result was a reaction – even more severe in this case – to school and the imposed regime of schooling.

Degradation

There were also a series of officially sponsored degradation ceremonies (Garfinkel, 1956) attached to the routine procedures of school, which seemed to indicate Peter's total failure and lack of skill at some school-

defined activities (which were of dubious value and meaning to him), and
to celebrate this publicly; while he knew, and had abundant evidence to
show, that he did possess skills of the same kind when directed towards
what he regarded as meaningful tasks. His experiences in physical education are a good example of this.

Some parts of PE were enjoyable, but he

> detested the preliminaries – the pointless 'drill' and, even worse, the
> apparatus sessions. While nearly everyone else was vaulting
> straight over the horse I was the one who landed squarely in the
> middle and had to make an uncomfortable shuffle, under the none
> too sympathetic gaze of Lenny Major and the rest of the class, before
> dropping off the end. As a result of such sessions I was left in no
> doubt that my PE teachers regarded my physical prowess as being
> of the most elementary kind. Inwardly this made me feel very angry
> and frustrated – not because there were frequent demonstrations of
> my inability to clear, in a single leap, that curious-shaped box (I had
> never in my life met an object shaped just like that in village, town
> or countryside that I wanted or had need to vault over), but because
> I knew that that very weekend I had cycled 25 miles in a single day
> to get to a new birds'-nesting area and had, on arrival, climbed some
> 40 feet up a difficult fir tree to get at a clutch of crow's eggs. No one,
> however, seemed to rate these physical achievements as worthy of
> comment or record on my end-of-term report.

The irony of the dreaded 'box' and real fitness was brought out by Peter's
running prowess. Rather like the Borstal boy in Alan Sillitoe's *The Loneli-
ness of the Long-Distance Runner*, he took to lone long-distance runs on the
beach. After one 20-mile run he failed to clear the box even more ignom-
iniously, largely, he feels, through stiffness. The gaze of the PE teacher
seemed more disapproving than ever.

The degrader-in-chief was his mathematics teacher, an expert in the art
of acid wit and sarcasm. Those unfortunates, like Peter, who found mathematics difficult were lashed unmercifully in his stern, Yorkshire tones:
'Eh, lad, yer couldn't see wood in a forest!'

This man, with the headteacher, the PE master and his primary school
teacher, were prime examples of alienators, people who threatened to
mould him to their own preconceived image, to punish and pour scorn on
his alternative, to mortify him – in short, to deprive him of self (Goffman,
1968).

An alienated student teacher

It is, perhaps, curious that someone who was so opposed to the system
and its processes and who valued so much his own personal experience,

should continue through the system and become one of its practitioners. The truth is, however, that the initial conception of this career path was part of his alienated, situational self. He had to survive in the world that most others regarded as 'real'. He did enough in this world to scrape by – only just passing the 11-plus (after an interview), despite regular high form positions, passing five or six subjects in the General Certificate of Education, and staying on in the sixth form to study English, History and Geography. Shortly after entry to the sixth form he had a careers interview with the head. He really wanted to be 'an Egyptologist and devote my life to deciphering hieroglyphics and perhaps even discovering a new Rosetta stone'. But for this he would have needed to have Latin, which he had not been considered good enough at languages to study. This lack also debarred him from many universities. He was persuaded, therefore, to consider a more practical career:

Other than being the warden of a bird sanctuary in the Outer Hebrides (but, apparently, that was not the kind of answer which Reggie expected from a boy who had attended Grammar School – it was almost as bad as saying you wanted to become a ballet dancer), nothing else suggested itself to me as an interesting career. I then learned that the stock answer in this kind of situation – that is, if you had no clue what you wanted to do or to be – was to say that you wanted to become a teacher. That was the most respectable thing you could become if you were undecided and unlikely to make university. My parents also seemed pleased with my 'choice', which was an added bonus. This was how the decision was made (*for* me rather than by me and out of sheer desperation) that I should become a teacher. I honestly do not believe that I ever really wanted to become a teacher. Few, if any, of my educational experiences would have drawn me to teaching as a career. I began to discover, however, that having made such a response it was expected that I would live up to my avowed intention. Anyway, it was easier to go along with the general notion. It gave rise to far less hassle and you did not have the bother of dreaming up an acceptable alternative. Several of my peers went for further interviews, but it was not necessary in my case because I was 'going to teachers training college'. I have subsequently wondered how many others of my generation got into teaching in a similar manner.

Osborn and Broadfoot (1992b) indicate that this may, indeed, be a general trend among primary teachers in England. But so, too, is the tendency for them to become more vocational and dedicated as their careers proceeded. This also happened to Peter. Though it was the alienated Peter who went into teaching, he was to realize his true self there. The pattern of his career was set, however, not into lifelong alienation, with a more meaningful side-career in private life in which he indulged his interests to the full; but in the alternation between meaning and non-meaning, boredom and excitement, public sacrifice and personal attainment.

Managing marginality

How did this occur? Throughout his life, Peter has derived support from places and people.

Places

From childhood he learnt the value of private places and experienced the beauty of the natural world. These situations worked for him rather than against him, allowed him some autonomy and control, and enabled his self to feel in harmony with the world. As a young person, he could not wait to hear the bell signalling the end of the school day, so he could mount his racing bicycle and ride off into the countryside to one of his special places. As an adult this love of place has found expression in wider travel. He finds this a marvellous restorative. For example, his first teaching post was in harshly constrained circumstances. Disillusioned after five years, he gave up teaching for six months and hitch-hiked around Greece. He spends his summers travelling around Norway, Italy, Africa, the USA . . . Travel helps to sustain his vision, his perspective of what he sees as a greater truth.

> The crystallization of my educational philosophy really occurred during a visit, in the summer of 1981, to the north-western states of America – especially Craters of the Moon National Monument in the state of Idaho. The 85 square mile lava wilderness of Craters of the Moon was described by Washington Irving as follows: 'Nothing meets the eye but desolate and awful waste, where no grass grows, nor water runs and nothing is to be seen but lava.' This volcanic plain struck me as being analogous to large parts of the traditional British educational system: the overpowering aridity – sterility – of the landscape. Barely anything could be seen living or growing. The sudden appearance of a mountain bluebird, however, demonstrated that there was life amongst all this desolation. It merely had to be sought out and pursued. It was Idaho's national emblem – the blue-bird – that particularly interested me and this small but colourful bird was to achieve a particular symbolism for me in that barren landscape. The Rushavenn project was, in effect, an attempt to chart the flight of one such educational bluebird.

People

Peter had a number of alternative educators who acted as 'critical others'. They included his maternal grandfather (who had sailed tea-clippers to the South China Sea, and whose house was 'full of the most amazing objects'), and an uncle (who had been a major in the tank corps during the war). A prominent influence, far greater than that of the generality of teachers, was a gamekeeper whose 'beat' covered part of the territory into which Peter sought his alternative world. In a real sense the gamekeeper became an alternative teacher.

> I was far happier in his company and the experiences I had while accompanying him on his rounds were far more meaningful to me than anything I received from my secondary education.

Peter tells of his journeys to the remains of a Saxon-shore Roman fort, and his conversations with the labourers in the fields there. He comments:

> This was one of the things which really troubled me for long periods. Most of those people whom I had, up to this time (and subsequently), come into contact with who seemed to me to have a real grasp (understanding) of education were, like my gamekeeper friend, non-educationalists.

Some educationists were, however, to have a profound influence upon him. His alienated entry into teaching, for example, was transformed by his supervisors. Thus while opting for teaching was an unreal act in terms of self, he was to discover unexpected salvation. At Loughborough he met Jim Abraham, a senior lecturer in English, and Ernest Frost, a poet and novelist. He acknowledges his great debt to both these inspirational teachers of teachers. For the first time in his educational career he was asked what *he* thought, and his thoughts were valued. Here was someone (Jim Abraham) who

> had the wisdom and the humility . . . to recognize the contribution that other people and their ideas could make to his own thinking . . . Above everything else he was concerned with the autonomy of children . . . that we should value their opinions and experience. I was determined that as soon as I had an opportunity I would try to implement his philosophy.

Peter recalls being greatly helped by William Walsh's book, *The Use of Imagination: Educational thought and the literary mind* (1966). He expresses it thus:

> How little my teachers, and even my parents, knew what I had to offer and what was going on in my mind for large areas of my childhood and adolescence. I am sure that these experiences, which

did not worry me over-much at the time, developed – many years later – into a real concern that if I was to become an effective teacher I would need to probe and seek to understand that unique vision which characterizes the period of childhood. I also began to feel that I would need to be receptive – and to be receptive implies a degree of humility (a 'condition' which I have always felt lies at the heart of true understanding, i.e. 'education'). Any sadness that I had at this time derived from an ill-defined, barely articulated feeling that no one was really interested in my vision of the world which, being so important to me, I felt must have something worthwhile to offer, and that my teachers were so concerned with *imparting* (i.e. *giving out*) knowledge that they had no time (or desire?) to benefit from what they could *take in* through what they experienced in *my* presence. In their ignorance of the uniqueness of the child's perception of the world, they probably had no conception that there was anything of value in this diminutive vessel or others of its kind. It was not until I read William Walsh's marvellous book that I began to comprehend how thinking adults could believe in a system of education which was entirely didactic and not a two-way process. Through reading that book I came to realize how Victorian notions that children should be seen and not heard, that the role of a responsible adult was to ensure that their offspring were moulded in their image at the earliest possible moment, and that the expressions of childhood were expressions of immaturity and not to be encouraged (let alone probed), lingered even in the post-Second World War period. William Walsh was a landmark in the later development of my particular brand of educational philosophy in which literature and childhood played an important part.

Most important, perhaps, was the quest for self through research into the English novelist, Leo Walmsley. So much of his own past, feelings and incidents, were discovered and rediscovered in Walmsley's writings. He felt that his own past illuminated his understanding of Walmsley, and vice versa. He told how his experience of Uncle Bill after the Second World War seemed remarkably similar to experiences of Walmsley's after the First World War; Walmsley published articles in *The Wide World Magazine* and *The Captain*, so dear to Peter's memories of his grandfather's shed; Walmsley had also lived for a time in a converted ex-army hut, and his experiences there were better understood by Peter as a result of his own recollections of living, when very young, in a converted railway carriage. Above all, Walmsley's (1935) account of his childhood in *Foreigners* captured the essence of Peter's recollections of his own. The book recounts the experiences of a young boy in a seaside town where his family had recently taken up residence and hence were, to the locals, 'foreigners'. The feeling of isolation and separateness, and the opposition of alien forces, were things well known to Peter. Like him, Walmsley 'hated school, because it stopped me doing so many things I liked'. Peter identified strongly with 'Worms', the hero of *Foreigners*.

Foreigners is not so much a novel as a cross-section of the life of a young boy ('Worms'), seen through the eyes of that boy, but with the accumulated wisdom, powers of expression, descriptive and organizational skills of an adult, redrawing and reliving his own childhood with precision and affection, but without sentimentality. Walmsley has a crisp and direct style, but he is more than a 'literary photographer' (as some of his critics described him). The description gets below surface features and feelings, and by seeing things 'in the round', holistically, a pattern is constructed. We understand the parts better by seeing them as pieces of a whole. Peter commented that one of the reasons why he can relate so readily to Walmsley's writing is that

> he has demonstrated that the gap between fact and fiction, between reality and the literary creation, is less real than imagined. His was a very holistic approach to life and experience.

Foreigners does not offer explanations in the sense of theories of why 'Slogger', the schoolteacher, for example, behaved as he did. However, the precision and sensitivity of the account arouse empathetic feelings that aid readers' understanding both of *Foreigners* and of their own childhood experiences.

Here is one of Peter's favourite passages in *Foreigners*, (Walmsley, 1935, pp. 24–25).

> At the best of times I hated school. The room itself, which was under the chapel gallery, was small and dark, and its windows were heavily barred, for the narrow playground that separated it from the edge of the cliff was actually above the level of the floor, so that really we were half underground, and it was gloomy as a prison. Through the bars you could see patches of sky, so that you always knew whether the sun was shining or not, but the sun itself, even in summer, never entered the room, and while you could hear the sea breaking on the cliff foot, or on the scaur ends if the tide was down, it was not visible. I could always think of a hundred places where I'd rather be than in this gloomy room. I hated having to sit still. I hated writing, and doing sums, and learning poetry off by heart, and learning about nouns and pronouns, and history. I liked looking at maps, and imagining I was seeing the places marked on them, but I hated having to learn off by heart the names of capes and rivers and mountains. I liked reading, but you only got one reader a year for the standard you were in, and you could read it through by

yourself in one lesson (skipping the poetry) so that even the interesting bits became dull when you had to go through them word by word, spelling the difficult words out aloud, or writing them on your slate. And while you sat in school you heard all the time the sound of the sea, and the cries of the gulls which often would alight on the playground railings, and stay there, making a queer laughing sound, just as though they were laughing at you, and mocking you because you had to stay in. No matter what time of the year, there was always something exciting to do at Bramblewick.

Peter comments:

Whilst Walmsley's works contain numerous passages which have made a lasting impression on me, this is one of the most meaningful. I think that it beautifully conveys the manner in which so-called educational experiences can exclude the real world (and hence relevance). All the boys in that Edwardian classroom knew that the sun was shining outside, but inside gloom and darkness prevailed – through the exclusion of the light of practical experience and relevance. They could hear (but not fully appreciate until they escaped from that environment) the cry of the gulls and the sound of the sea – the living and the elemental worlds. Walmsley also manages to capture the manner in which that drabness is transferred to such learning as takes place. Throughout this short passage we see the dichotomy of thoughtless repression on the one hand and untapped enthusiasm on the other – note how the passage begins in a negative way – 'At the best of times I hated school' – and how it ends with a note of affirmation – 'there was always something exciting to do at Bramblewick'. Against those things he did not like doing – arithmetic, grammar, history, learning poetry and the names of geographical features by rote – he sets down those things which he did enjoy – reading and studying maps. Here is another example of someone searching out those elements in an adverse experience which could provide the foundations for an alternative personal development. Here we see a determination to survive against all the odds. Here we have a child who, whilst at primary school and secondary school, loathed poetry and grammar and history, and probably writing too, who – through *real-life* experiences – was to develop into a fine novelist with a deeply rooted interest in archaeology and things historical. This poses an important question: how did Walmsley acquire his literary talents and his lasting fascination with the ancient world? It was certainly not through the conventional education which he received in the Bay Wesleyan or the Scarborough Municipal Schools. (Like D.H. Lawrence, Walmsley was to undergo a brief, and deeply unsatisfying, spell as a teacher. Yet what Lawrence and Walmsley were subjected to at the turn of the century is not all that far removed from the ideas of those 'educationalists' and politicians who are advocating a return to 'real learning' today.) This was the question which I decided I had to resolve for myself those many years ago. If Walmsley had not acquired his education in a typical classroom context, was there not some other alternative, and much more relevant, approach that we ought to be considering? This was really the starting point of the educational journey which I have made in my post-formal schooling years and which has gradually given rise to that educational philosophy which I hold today (and which is still evolving). My point of departure was not one without hope of successful resolution. Although I did not articulate it at the time, I probably received some kind of inner encouragement from the unexpressed belief that if Lawrence and Walmsley could survive – *so could I*!

Peter acknowledges that Walmsley has been a strong formative influence on his life and on his notion of self. Over the last 20 years or so, he has collected copies of all his published books, long out of print, and many other papers, articles and stories published in newspapers, periodicals and magazines. He has also accumulated much unpublished work and correspondence, and travelled around Britain and overseas to interview those still alive who knew him. He has begun the process of writing a series of monographs on Walmsley and his work. The desire to do this in nine monographs rather than a single volume was sparked off by his conception of

the composite self [as] like the facets of a diamond – each being highlighted as the jewel is turned through a full circle.

In this way Peter retains a notion of self as both multiple and holistic. In more senses than one the Walmsley biography has become a life's work. The more he discovers about Walmsley, the more he discovers about himself. The deeper he goes, the more he validates the past insecure impressions of himself, and the more he grows as new indices, details and patterns come to light against which to compare his own life.

The pains and pleasures of marginality

Through a mixture of internal attributes to do with resolve, commitment, faith and application, and external motivators and supports such as significant people and places, Peter managed not only to preserve a sense of holism but also to carry that into his teaching persona. Some adaptations were necessary, but by and large he stood against the traditional picture of alienated teachers, disempowered by constraints, and falling back on time-honoured routines; and against the view that child-centred teaching is unachievable given current resources and management procedures and/or unproductive in terms of children's learning. Further, the relationship between internal and external factors is one that suggests the former are pre-eminent. Like 'Glenda' in Butt and Raymond (1990), the key for him and for his pupils was 'self-directedness'. This involves 'putting significant others in a facilitative relationship to self as opposed to a source of self' (p. 16). As with 'Glenda' too, the self-directedness occurred most strongly during periods of alienation, with clear and decisive 'turning-points' and occasions which unlock caverns of meaning when required.

Peter's experiences suggest a new way of looking at the teacher's career as a quest for, and as an expression of, self (see also Woods, 1990a). Given the integrity of his approach he, like many of the teachers interviewed by Nias (1989), would not accept, that 'personal dignity, with its basis in genuineness and authenticity, is not to be found in the performance of institutional roles which only hide or distort the true self' (Musgrove, 1977, p. 225). Peter's professional career, role and interests are indistinguishable from his personal career, role and interests. They have a history as long as his memory, for his professional self, as we have seen, is rooted in his childhood. The self is not a static set of attributes, but undergoing constant fashioning and development. In this view of career, the self, not a formal career structure, nor the professional role, is central. Careers, role and other features are part of a network that the individual constructs through the preferred self.

Through taking this course of strong self-direction in a climate not always conducive to that inclination, Peter was inevitably in something of a marginal position. But marginality had become enshrined in his self. It was established in his childhood in those altercations between the formal, official, public world and his own private, alternative world. But while he could spend some time communing with nature, he had to make some progress through the formal curriculum. He could give neither his full attention. The rebellion he indulged in was typical of one in such a position – cerebral rather than behavioural, for this

> was much more conducive to a reflective, inward-looking child – but it increased the sense of isolation, both socially and intellectually.

He was alone, as a youth too, in his view of education. He semi-achieved at examinations. There was a 'chasm between teachers' expectations and what I knew about myself'.

The situation was possibly compounded by a social class factor. The grammar school had not long been admitting non-fee paying pupils as a result of the 1944 Education Act. There may have been some resentment among the staff against the new type of entrant, the working-class 11-plus success. The whole culture of the school was geared to the public school ethos. The knowledge purveyed was in accordance with a hierarchy of subjects and a form of procedure that privileged a particular group. Its social referents had at least as much significance as its educational (Young, 1971). Peter was not the only one to be disadvantaged in these circumstances. However, because of his introspection, solitude and reserve, he felt it, perhaps, more keenly than most. He records:

> Like many other boys I was desperately trying, and in lonely isolation to make sense of a system which seemed to defy logic or explanation. Most of my peers, perhaps because they had not been saddled with such sensitive natures and thought less about their immediate circumstances, were able to shrug off such disconcerting thoughts and accept their new surroundings in an admirably philosophical sort of way. I was envious of this ability. I was left confused and disorientated, not knowing whom to believe. This early conflict has continued to haunt me over the years.

However, while there is inevitably a feeling of discomfiture in such a position, there is also considerable potential strength. Berger (1971) comments that to move into the margins is to experience ecstasy, but it is also to experience terror. Turner (1969) argues that, '"threshold experiences" liberate us and renew our humanity; and in closely structured societies, it is the marginal man who comes to symbolize not incompleteness, but a wider, more embracing, humanity' (Musgrove, 1976, p. 105). Aoki (1983, p. 325), commenting on his probing for the essence of what it means to be human, remarks that:

> This kind of opportunity for probing does not come easily to a person flowing within the mainstream. It comes more readily to one who lives at the margin . . . It is, I believe, a condition that makes possible deeper understanding of human acts that can transform both self and world, not in an instrumental way, but in a human way (see also Turner, 1979; Plummer, 1983).

McLaren (1986, p. 237) suggests viewing the student as 'pilgrim'. By association, this might also be a useful concept for the teacher. The pilgrim's stance is one of 'active waiting, hopeful expectation, power in innocence and weakness, and acceptance of strangeness of others as a possible source of transcendence' (Holmes, 1973, pp. 63–64). To be a pilgrim is to be outside institutional structures and 'to free the imagination for the discovery of what is new' (p. 64). It also connotes the image of a traveller on a journey, perhaps to a holy place – Durkheim's 'sacred' as opposed to the 'profane' – reflecting the notions of *communitas* and structure. There is strain, restlessness, and inventiveness involved in the exploration of new worlds.

The relevance of this to Peter's case is clear – the marginality, the emotional, spiritual and cognitive experience of it, the holism, the sense of ordeal, the penetrative insight, the recognition of two worlds, the alienating and the alternative, the solitariness, the perception of others and theirs of him. There is a sense of conflict and struggle, but also triumph, or 'ecstasy'. There are several indications of this – his joy on the occasions of his 'escapes' to pursue his 'self-directed' journey, the establishing of communion with other like-minded souls, and, above all perhaps, as a teacher, when he has facilitated the experience of *communitas* among his pupils. As Peter, for example, faced his 5–11-year-old children from year to year, he saw himself in their place, remembered the mousetrap and the glass jar, but also the exhilaration of escaping into the real world from the prison-like constraints of school, the sense of achievement in accomplishing self-directed, arduous tasks, and the feeling of excitement and wonder at the simple beauty of a bird's egg ('like a piece of sky fallen to earth').

The pain of intensification

The changes in the education system following the 1988 Education Reform Act have been catastrophic for Peter as a teacher, but ultimately triumphant in terms of self. All the pleasures of marginality have been squeezed out by the pain of the reforms which run directly counter to his philosophy and leave him no room for manoeuvre. *Rushavenn Time* had been published in 1988 – the same year, rather ironically, as the Education Reform Act. After four years of trying to come to terms with the changes, Peter decided to take early retirement at the age of 57. He would have liked to continue for another five years or so to try to spread the gains of 'Rushavenn' to a wider population of children over a wider range of activity, and to have encouraged his staff in developing those ideas and techniques. But a combination of circumstances forced him to reconsider and to reroute his career. Why, then, did he choose to retire, and withdraw from the margins once and for all?

In essence, the coping strategies that Peter had fashioned and used throughout his life were not capable of counteracting the massive alienation that now confronted him in the system. In the end, the preservation of self demanded a more radical strategy – rerouteing. Peter's experience illustrates the subjective side of intensification. There was the huge increase in bureaucracy. He bemoaned

> the proliferation of administration . . . the more bureaucratic approach . . . the number of questionnaires . . . the quantification to the nth degree . . .

So much more direction was being given to teachers, so that they were beginning to feel de-professionalized. Isolation made the possibility of teachers joining together to resist increasingly difficult. There was little movement between schools since there was no staffing flexibility to allow inter-school visits, and promotional opportunities had been reduced. Schools themselves had become isolated as a result of the changes to the LEAs.

Even more problematic was the headteacher's role. Soon after what he perceived as the achievement of an ideal conjuncture of person and role, all was suddenly thrown into confusion. His natural tendency was to support his staff in their teaching, and to try to inspire them to even greater heights, but there were strong pressures on him now to take on more responsibility for finance and administration, as well as stronger leadership across all subjects of the curriculum. Consequently, he found himself 'doing a whole range of jobs somewhat inadequately'. Even worse, the officials exercising pressure – inspectors – seemed to have no conception of what the new headteacher role would involve, other than the accumulation of a whole new range of 'different and diverse' responsibilities. In consequence, the role was becoming depersonalized. Peter said that it

had gone beyond the point where it was being used to challenge the person to progress further within the context of their own personal development, and was making demands on them that would ultimately have a clone-like effect, a stereotyping effect, that I felt I needed to resist quite strongly.

Peter is objecting to the view of education as a commodity, and to 'scientific corporate management' structures that are being introduced in the increasing drive for efficiency, with their implications for depersonalization, top-down management structures, and division of labour between heads and their staffs, which turn the head into a 'chief executive' rather than 'leading professional' (Ball, 1990). These effects have been noted quite widely in primary schools since the mid-1980s (Hellawell, 1990). Others derived from the sheer pressures on his time and personal resources, which 'dissipated his energies' and robbed him of reflective space. Peter referred to George Orwell's *Nineteen Eighty-four*,

where the proles are fed very mundane, low-level forms of literature to keep their minds deadened to cut down the level of adverse response from them . . . In one's more cynical moments, one wonders whether what is being promoted at the moment is deliberately aimed at deadening the creative, imaginative response.

The central motivating force in policy towards teaching was changing. There was a movement away from education being an experience for personal development to seeing it as a business . . . which is so alien to my philosophy.

Managerialism has gained the moral ascendancy (Inglis, 1989). The policing through four-yearly inspections he saw as politically rather than educationally biased. He had

less confidence in the motives behind those who have been entrusted with the provision of education in our country these days than I ever have in the past.

Even in its own terms he considered it a failure, since

so much of current educational thinking is at best ill-conceived, and at worst totally illogical, that it is no longer capable of resolution by logical measures.

This is far removed from the rationalized and 'extended professional' role of the head preferred by Peter (see Hoyle, 1973; Coulson, 1976). The intrinsic rewards for him in teaching (Lortie, 1975; Nias, 1989) were rapidly diminishing.

Thus, Peter felt once more marginalized. As a child he had sought salvation in his beloved marshes, seeking redress from the impersonal, authoritarian, constricting, oppressive world of school. He was doing the same now – on a permanent basis. Why permanent? Such matters, it might be argued, are for working out on the ground through pain and struggle. But Peter was at a stage of career and life where such activity could take its toll. If he stayed for another four years, until he was 61 or 62, say, in view of

the steep upward gradient in workload . . . there is good concrete evidence that my life expectancy could be reduced considerably.

It was also a stage where his personal development was even more critical to him, for

there comes a point when you know that there are so many things you want to achieve while you still have your faculties and your strength to be able to do it.

If he stayed in teaching, he saw little prospect of the

avenues for the continuing of the kind of development in which he was interested being reopened.

The fulfilling 'trade-offs' that had helped to balance out the less rewarding aspects of teaching had almost totally disappeared. The only realistic prospect was to 'get out of that situation'.

This was one of the basic differences between Peter and the teachers of the other schools discussed earlier, who were not dissimilar to him in philosophy and beliefs, but who made more accommodatory adaptations within teaching. The teachers at Ensel, for example, were at an earlier stage of their careers, on a 'rising curve' in career terms (Sikes *et al.*, 1985). It would have been difficult for them to legitimize their 'right to enter a phase that is not clearly institutionalized' (Strauss, 1962, p. 81), whereas retirement for teachers of Peter's age has become a *de facto* legitimized passage. The classroom teachers, too, though overloaded, had less pressure on them than heads, and retained their interaction with the children. Some of them had been trained in the National Curriculum, their conception of the teacher role being grounded and validated within the new system. Another key factor, perhaps, is that Coombes and Ensel, as well as Gill's school, were lower schools (Key Stage 1), whereas Peter's was a primary (Key Stage 2). Though intensification bears on them also, it is arguably less intense (see Campbell, 1993). Their smaller size and smaller age range also reduce the impact of the changes in teacher role felt so acutely by Peter, enabling their heads to preserve democratic management styles. The staff at both Ensel and Coombes had distinctive causes at their schools which they championed. They also had strong, stable, collaborative cultures. Peter used to have one, but its members had all gained promotion, and he was inducting a new group – under vastly different circumstances. Here, 'identification' worked for the other schools but against Peter's (though for him personally). For example, Coombes's teachers contrasting themselves with other, more normative schools, served to consolidate their own culture. Peter's views contrasted with those of others, for example, other heads, many of whom he found to have 'secondary' rather than 'primary' views of education, that is to say, views almost wholly dependent on others which they had not synthesized into a personal philosophy of their own. But whereas Coombes became marginalized as a school, Peter became marginalized as an individual.

Then there was a series of critical incidents which Peter experienced. One was a general inspection, which he found very traumatic. He had had several inspections in the past, which he had always found 'constructively critical' and 'very, very fair'. This inspection, however, had given no credit for things the school did well, and was almost entirely critical. New forms of accountability that involved publication of the inspectors' report, policy documents and action plans left no room for manoeuvre and undermined morale. Peter had suddenly found his situation transformed

from . . . where you've received plaudits for what you've been doing, with a measure of criticism, to one of almost total criticism.

Neither of the other two schools had had a general inspection as yet, though Coombes was preparing for one through 'alliances'.

At the same time, there were critical incidents in his domestic life which bore on his position. His wife, also a teacher, had also reached a stage in life where there was 'potential for retirement'. Discussions between them helped to lay the basis for this often most traumatic of status passages. But its timing was forced by a number of 'unfortunate circumstances', after which, nevertheless, 'everything seemed to fall into place'. His wife's school had to lose a teacher, so she offered herself for voluntary redundancy. Then she was awarded a disability pension. Shortly after this, Peter's mother died, leaving him a house and a small legacy. These incidents removed any problems of material circumstances from consideration. There was nothing left in teaching for Peter, not even the salary. His history of lifelong marginality both predisposed him towards and prepared him for a radical solution. As we shall see in Chapter 7, for him this was a positive move, almost a triumphant act in the end, an advance rather than a retreat, which marked the end of marginality. For the education system, it meant the loss of a creative teacher at the height of his powers.

7

Self-determination among primary school teachers

The teachers featuring in this book have many things in common. They all have strong vocational and professional commitment to teaching (Sikes *et al.*, 1985). For them, teaching is the activity and the arena in which they become whole, achieve their ultimate ambitions, become the persons they wish to be. They are dedicated professionals who have given their lives and their selves to their job.

All teachers have certain primary interests. Pollard (1985), in examining how considerations of self bear on teachers' actions, identified certain interests associated with maintaining a sense of self in the classroom: maximizing enjoyment; controlling the workload; maintaining one's health and avoiding stress; retaining autonomy; maintaining one's self-image. All of these are important for our teachers, but the last is particularly so as the others are integral to it. From their perceptions of self arise their philosophies of teaching and their values. Prominent here is their concern for the children, who are placed before knowledge, teachers, adults generally, and the state. They care about their children greatly. Children's needs and aspirations come first, as defined by them (the teachers) and other representatives of the children in the local community, not by some remote government department. A related concern is their attention to equality issues, to recognizing aptitudes for, and constraints on, achievement, to wanting to bring out the best in all children, and to not prejudging them. The 'equality' point applies also to their relationships with each other, which operate on a basis of creative collegiality, in a democratic-participatory management structure. This collegiality is not consensual or 'contrived', but operates in a culture of constructive critique. This is a means to their own development – they learn alongside the children. They have open minds on many issues, therefore. They are reflective professionals who think deeply about their work, and discuss it among themselves at length. They are very articulate, both in speech and actions; and they are creative, as defined in Chapter 1. The 'I' part of the self, as defined by Mead (1934), the part that is the source of initiative, novelty and change, is well to the fore. They have a measure of the 'Me', the agent of self-regulation and self-control, for without it the 'I' could not operate. But it is from the 'I' that novel acts 'emerge'. It is the main ingredient behind social change and adaptation. Mead argues that people develop different propensities for using the 'I' or the 'Me'. The conventional form of the 'Me' may be reduced in some cases. Mead (1934, pp. 209–210) gives the example of the artist, for whom 'the emphasis upon that which is unconventional, that which is not in the structure of the "Me" is carried as far, perhaps, as it can be carried'. Creative teachers are like artists in this respect. They acknowledge the benefits, indeed indispensability, of a measure of routine, but for them, as for Mead (1934, p. 213), the health of both self and society depends on the abilities and freedom of people to 'think their own thoughts', 'express themselves' and 'be original'.

Neither self nor creativity, however, is constant. Both are social products and are influenced by social circumstances. Berger (1963, p. 106) affirms that 'the self is no longer a solid, given entity that moves from one situation to another. It is rather a process, continuously created and re-created in each social situation that one enters'. It is therefore in continual need of defence, maintenance and promotion. Some occasions and periods may be more favourable to promotion. Others may bring teachers' preferred perceptions of self under attack. Inasmuch as their work has become intensified, creative teachers would appear to be going through one of the latter periods. In some respects, and for some teachers, the whole state education system has become like one of Goffman's 'total institutions', where

> [the] recruit comes into the establishment with a conception of himself made possible by certain stable social arrangements in his home world. Upon entrance, he is immediately stripped of the support provided by these arrangements . . . [and] begins a series of abasements, degradations, humiliations, and profanations of self. His self is systematically, if often unintentionally, mortified. He begins some radical shifts in his moral career, a career composed of the progressive changes that occur in the beliefs that he has concerning himself and significant others, (Goffman, 1968, p. 24).

This, thankfully, may be a little too stark for what is happening to teachers, but the threat to selves during intensification is real and potentially radical. To the extent that teachers' work is becoming intensified, so their selves are in danger of a degree of debasement – less autonomy, less choice, less freedom, less reflection, less individuality, less voice and, ultimately perhaps, less commitment, and/or a change to a more instrumental form. Working to prescribed programmes might also undermine their child-centredness.

White (1993), in a discussion of the principles behind his ideal national curriculum, lists 'self-determination' as a core value in a liberal democratic society. Our creative teachers would subscribe to this, emphasizing its relevance to teachers as well as pupils. Throughout all the adaptations discussed in previous chapters, they illustrate a number of ways in which self-determination operates. Prominent aspects of this are defence, reinforcement, realization, and renewal of the self. I shall examine examples of each.

Self-defence

Nias's (1989) teachers, though undergoing continual professional development, were always at pains to protect their substantial selves from uncomplementary change. She notes that the most effective form of self-protection was the reference group (p. 204).

> Regular contact with other people who shared their beliefs about the social and moral purposes of education and about how children learnt, not only reinforced their view of themselves but also enabled them to filter and even distort messages reaching them from other sources (pp. 204–205).

We have seen how, in resistance at Ensel School, perceived assaults on the self threw people even closer together. But the self in these circumstances frequently has a resilience of its own, which contributes to the strength of the whole-school perspective. The interplay between individual and group is revealed to some extent when we consider some of the foundations of the whole-school perspective at Ensel (see Chapter 2), for it did not arise simply in response to the changes. I identified the following factors (see also Pollard, 1985; Acker, 1990).

Individual biography

In several instances, this seems to be the origin of the perspective, however ill formulated at inception. Teachers' theories are grounded in their own lives. The nature and significance of the perspective might not be realized at the time. It may be little more than vaguely but acutely felt experience, not articulated, but sedimented in the self in embryo. We have seen in

Chapter 6 the formative influence of one teacher's childhood years. The following examples from Ensel School show other ways in which teacher beliefs have strong roots deep in their past. Mardle and Walker (1980) have suggested that teachers draw on their own experiences as pupils, using similar strategies as were used on them in a kind of continuing latent culture of teaching. These Ensel teachers claim that their practices are in large measure a *reaction* to their own earlier personal experiences.

Susan's story

Susan as a child went to a 'very, very formal school', where you

> had to memorize and spew out information in examinations . . . You sit at a desk, listen, teacher imparts knowledge, you take it on board, do a spelling test, a maths test . . . and you don't really have much of a stake in your own learning.

Susan has also been a student teacher in such schools, producing, to her mind,

> children lacking in independence, completely needing to be told every single move they make. So I have to admit I don't like what I saw, and I don't like what happened to me through school.

Susan felt she 'only just succeeded' aided by

> a very traditional kind of middle-class family, who really valued education . . . It wasn't easy, and I was always on the borderlines.

She would love to have done

> coursework, finding out about things, taking part in my own learning a lot more . . . That would have been better for me. I'm not an exam sort of person, so I think I felt disadvantaged by what I had to go through.

Susan describes her first teaching post as a

> very difficult situation but with very, very, positive, constructive, supportive staff. Had it not been quite like that, I would have thought, 'Oh no, this progressive way of working doesn't work'. But I was supported, and it was a very good, positive, model to start working, because it put into action a lot of things I'd been told at college.

Following that, she moved to an all-white, middle-class school where teachers practised more traditional methods:

> I couldn't really cope with that . . . There was no centrality and no basic philosophy . . . I was fighting and saying 'I don't believe in

rote learning, they don't understand what they're doing. I'm going to teach differently', and they were saying, 'No, it's always been done like this' and 'we demand that you give my child spelling lists', and the head was supporting them. I thought, 'I can't work somewhere that doesn't really believe what I believe', and then I came here. So apart from that one year I've been very lucky.

Penny's story

Penny came into teaching 'very late', and only as a result of starting helping in her own children's school. She was delighted to find that the teaching matched the philosophy she was using with her children. She had always wanted to teach, but that gave her the impetus. She found it very exciting that learning was seen as an intrinsic thing and valued in its right, rather than measured by the products of formal tests. Penny considered herself

a total failure at school, because I cannot spell. I've read all my life, and everybody told my parents that if I read I would be able to spell. Therefore, if I couldn't spell it meant I was lazy, or careless, there was something wrong with me. It took me to get to college before I realized that all my work at school was good, but poor spelling and punctuation. I never saw that good.

She recalls experiencing a sense of *déjà vu* at college when her tutor read out one of her assignments. She was back sitting in a classroom and her English teacher was reading out her essay. She suddenly thought: 'If I'm so bad at English, why is my teacher reading out my essay?' She did not realize that it was because it was good. This message 'didn't come across until 30 years later'.

So this is what you do to children by picking on the weakness they've got. You can totally destroy their own ability in themselves.

Penny refers here to the consequences of 'labelling' (Becker, 1963; Hargreaves *et al.*, 1975). She has a constant reminder in her own experience of

how children feel when all you do is criticise them, and you're not looking at really what they can do.

She was able to apply her views to her own children. Her son (at age 12–13), for example, thought his English was poor, as she had done, because of spelling and punctuation, but she

was able to look at the sentence construction and say to him that the way he was putting his sentences together was very mature.

She recalls 'a passage of intellectual growth' with her own children.

Using my knowledge of language and understanding to search in your brain with them talking, questioning, and that was so search-ing, it made my brain ache. That's what we should be aiming for in the classroom, where the child is using the adult to search out and extend into areas that he couldn't do without the adult.

Penny here gives expression to the Vygotskian notion of teacher assisting the child through the 'zone of proximal development' (Vygotsky, 1978; Bruner, 1986). The experiences, reinforced by theory, have led to such strength of feeling that,

if the government really changed how we had to teach in schools, I wouldn't teach. I really wouldn't. I wouldn't teach rote learning without understanding. I just wouldn't be able to.

Vanessa's story

Vanessa reported similar experiences:

At 15 or 16 I was told: 'You've developed very well up to here basically, but now you've stopped.' The kind of person I was then (I'm not now!) said, 'OK, all right, you've told me I've stopped, you're a teacher, you know better', so I stopped, which is why I didn't get to my degree until my late thirties. You've got to be so aware of the messages that you give to children.

Vanessa came from a working-class Irish Catholic family, very support-ing, but not well off, and feeling

there were areas you didn't go into because of your background. But because I was a Catholic I could get to a grammar school, otherwise we couldn't have afforded it. So there was always that doubt at the back of my mind that I shouldn't be there anyway . . . I didn't have a lot of confidence and I didn't believe in myself and the headmistress stopped me even trying.

Vanessa here articulates the loss of confidence and belief in oneself that particularly afflicts many girls and women (Spender, 1982). But Vanessa also points to the social class factors. The school

related very much to economic factors . . . there was a difference in attitude, and lots of things, like we didn't have a proper uniform.

Cultural capital (Bourdieu, 1971), in other words, was of the essence. She 'hit the gender issue at age 22' when she applied for day release from her local government job to study for a Diploma in Management Studies. The training officer said no, although two men who were with her were given leave. When she asked why, she was asked:

Are you courting?' I said 'Yes'. 'Getting married?' 'Well, not at the moment, in the next couple of years.' 'Well, that's it, we won't train you', and his words were almost word-for-word. 'Why should the Council put money into you when you're going off to have children?' In fact, I stayed there another eight years . . .

All these experiences fed into Vanessa's conception of childhood. Her approach to parenthood was very different from the authoritarian style of her mother and mother-in-law. She saw her children as individuals and 'valuable people in themselves'. She remembers her 10-day-old baby smiling at her, and being told 'This is wind'. But 'it's absolutely not, this is a reaction, this is human recognition!'

How did Vanessa get into teaching? She was told at 7 years old by a 'very, very good teacher' that she would go to university and would teach, and 'she gave me a feeling that I could do things'. Then 'everyone else who came after seemed to knock it down'. Even as a child, though, she was an organizer among other children.

Not getting my A levels and my parents not being educated enough themselves to know different, I realized I wasn't to be a teacher . . . So I went on and had my own family. Then I became involved in mother and toddler groups, playgroups, setting them up, manning them, helping in schools, always involved with children. Then a teacher at school said: 'Why aren't you teaching?' I told her my story about how I always wanted to do it, but . . . , and she said 'Oh, you can! They take mature students'. So I rang college and that was that.

She now feels

totally at home. Sometimes I get a little cross because I think I should have done this 20 years ago . . .

Vanessa here illustrates the importance of 'critical incidents' (Sikes *et al.*, 1985; Tripp, 1993) in her life, and how teaching, and her view of how it should be done, is very much part of her substantial self (Nias, 1989).

Teacher training

Ensel teachers' initial training and educational studies introduced them to a range of theory and practice that confirmed their intuition and cast new light on some of their own experiences. As with Peter in Chapter 6, their experiences contrast strongly with those of others recorded in the literature (for example, Otty, 1972). Training illuminated and legitimated their partially formed but keenly felt views, by introducing them to theory, literature and research; illustrating their application to prac-

tice; and giving realistic assessments of how they might become modified over time.

Penny thought college was 'brilliant'. It reinforced what she thought
she already knew, introduced her to some wonderful thinkers: 'I really
am very keen on Vygotsky! It's tremendous, it really is . . . '. When she
first went to college, she was

> questioning college's philosophy because if they weren't going to be
> right for me, if the philosophy wasn't matching . . . but I found it
> matched very, very well . . .

Vanessa also found her experience confirmed:

> Just realizing when I went to college and had access to the theory that
> that's what I had been doing naturally with my own children, and
> had seen them learn. So it's a very personal thing. It's not that I've
> been 'dogma'd', and read them and thought, 'That's good'. I've actu-
> ally thought 'Yes, yes! That's right, and this is somebody who's stud-
> ied this and who's an authority on it'. It's bringing together what I'd
> come to believe and understand, and that gave the theory to it . . .

Vanessa here is arguing against the accusation that she may be unduly
influenced by child-centred 'dogmas' (Alexander *et al.*, 1992). Theories that
she met at college explained much in her personal experience.

There are other testimonies available concerning the value of training in
the formulation of a personal philosophy of education. For Peter (Chapter
6), for example, it was a crucial, disalienating experience, which helped
give his teaching real meaning (see also Wilcock, 1994). Dave was keen to
emphasize the transformational as well as confirmatory nature of teacher
education, its catalytic as well as legitimatory qualities. He cited his own
experience of an in-service course with a

> very highly talented and intelligent English adviser, who created an
> immense amount of question marks in my head which led to some
> very, very fundamental changes in the way I taught.

Dave cited:

> the way I organized my teaching, the complexities of group work, the
> way I actually taught, the way I interacted with children in the
> classroom.

The adviser developed ideas of how children actually learn:

> It was at a time when Plowden was just coming out, and it was a
> complete eye-opener for me. It was a message I'd only partially
> grasped before. It was a catalyst which changed my whole way of
> thinking, because in a sense he was ahead of his time.

Professional experience

Their own practice as teachers *validates* the perspective. The particular circumstances of Ensel School, with its large proportion of children who speak English as a second language, stress the *relevance* of the perspective. There is a strong emphasis on issues of equality, social justice and multi-culturalism. Access to the National Curriculum is a current major concern, with a strong focus of attention on language. Constructivist theories of learning seem to have a special relevance for such issues. 'Starting where the child is at', for example, seems even more of a priority where language issues and different cultural traditions are involved (see, for example, Heath, 1982). Having 'assimilated cultural awareness', as Dave expressed it, teachers then proceed through trial and error. They refine approaches that work, modify those that do not, and reflect on circumstances that affect them. They build up a stock of experience, an accumulating resource with which to help meet new situations.

Collaboration

Working and discussing with like-minded colleagues *consolidates*, defends and fortifies the perspective. Cavan (1962, p. 535) notes that 'the necessary elements for forming, maintaining, or modifying self-conceptions are socially approved self-images and social roles for their expression, and a group that supports these self-images and roles'. It is difficult for creative teachers to survive on their own. Together, they are a potent force. Penny, who was at the time acting as mentor for Vanessa, said:

> It's lovely with Vanessa, because she shares the philosophy 100 per cent, and it's very easy for us to see the value in what each is doing. If I look in her classroom I can see all the good things that are going on.

By contrast, as Susan noted, 'If you've got rifts in the staffroom about various philosophies, then I think you've got problems'. She believes strongly in the idea of 'a team all working together to achieve the same ends'.

It would seem important, therefore, for staff to select, and be selected, with care, to maximize the opportunities for collaboration. Vanessa, for example, did her second-year practice at Ensel.

> Dave had just started as head then, and I just loved it. I loved his attitude to the children and the community and to children's learning. I was going to get in touch with him, and he got in touch with me when he knew a vacancy was coming up. So it was the school I wanted.

Dave, as head, had appointed all the other members of staff. He noted that 'the collegiality has come out of a common view, and of course I've appointed people in that image'. All teaching ideals are vulnerable in the maelstrom of the classroom. Those associated with child-centred ideologies are currently particularly under attack. There is strength in numbers and in the links between them. The whole-school perspective, especially where also supported by governors and parents, as at Ensel, is both a knowledge and a power base. It expands the range of thought and experience, offers therapy in times of difficulty, and resolve and determination when challenged. It may be stronger in such circumstances. The perspective is not just a matter of cognition, but is part of the self (see below), infused with aesthetics and emotions. These find a productive outlet in collective expression.

Constraints

Constraints *delimit* the perspective, bringing it to earth and gearing it to practicalities. Things like class size, lack of material resources, and the heavy demands of the National Curriculum can impede the prosecution of strategies indicated by theories emphasizing individualism, space and creativity. Where constraints apply in force, teaching can assume a hand-to-mouth appearance, teachers making decisions on the spot in a way that is difficult to relate to a consistent set of principles (see Berlak and Berlak, 1981). However, all teaching is constrained to some extent, and a modicum can lead to more creativity. The ideals guiding the perspective are principles to inform one's approach rather than ends to be met. The creative teacher is always trying to find ways to apply her principles, and to manage the constraints, which might involve outflanking them or using them to advantage (when, of course, they cease to constrain).

These examples illustrate how teaching is very much part of these teachers' substantial selves, and how they come to a view that, they would rather withdraw from teaching than succumb to directives from central government in which they did not believe. Their resolve is strengthened by their experience of the discovery in adulthood of new insights and a new truth about themselves, giving them an enlightened perspective on their own childhood, and an inspired vision of teaching.

Self-reinforcement

Collaboration has been represented here as operating in self-defence. But it also operates in a more expansive sense. The 'resistance' teachers will develop their notions of self in interaction with each other. Nias (1989, p. 154) argues: 'The self is fulfilled and extended through and by means of the ideas and actions of adult as well as child others', though this 'does not always or easily happen'.

The use of critical others (Chapter 4) illustrates another way in which the self can be reinforced. Critical others can help teachers recover their creativity, bring a long-standing ideal project to fruition, develop new interests, gain new insights into their selves through challenging basic assumptions, help cultivate charisma. Currently, there is demand for more specialist teaching in primary schools (Alexander, 1992), and for greater flexibility in the teacher role (Campbell, 1993; Brighouse, 1994). Flexibility, however, is not a prominent attribute of extreme rational-legal systems. Critical others add to teachers' specialist knowledge, while still leaving the teacher in control as 'orchestrator' (Woods, 1990a). They help them to be 'extended professionals' in Hoyle's (1980) sense of being interested in theory, involved in non-teaching professional activities, and reading professional literature. They help swing the always precarious balance between the preferred, principled mode of teaching, in this case constructivism, and pragmatic, dilemmatic action forced by circumstances.

The teaching of the history project shows what a powerful resource critical others can be within the full context of the National Curriculum. We saw in Chapter 5 how the intervention of the critical other was catalytic for Gill, helping to bring her to a new realization of her teaching and her beliefs, and, with that, recognition of new possibilities and opportunities. The project also increased her self-esteem, and its favourable reception among colleagues and others boosted her morale, at a time when it was flagging. She felt the gains to her professionalism were permanent. She would apply the gains to next year's and other projects. The indications were that what had been learned was not something gained from external or disembodied theory or case studies, or some other school, class or teacher, but from her own 'lived experience' (Smyth, 1991, p. 85). It had become part of her professional apparatus as a teacher, to be called on as and when required and possible.

Critical others also played a key role at Coombes, enhancing the charisma of the teacher. Sue overlooked no opportunity to use the knowledge, expertise, experience and equipment of others in advancing her aims. The local shepherd, Hugh, had been coming for nine years to wash and shear the sheep. 'He used to bring a pair of hand shears and do it very slowly, talking to the children while he did it'. Alan, the traveller, also visited the school. A book records one of his visits, and how he cares for his horse, 'Jolly Roger'. The children helped, using currycombs to groom his coat, cleaning parts of the tackle, observing how Alan cleaned each shoe, and why. The book included excellent black and white photographs, and concluded it was 'A job well done'. This provided an entry into considering the social and cultural life of travellers, children of whom formed a minority group within the school. Rural craftsmen are invited in to demonstrate their skills – wood turning, besom broom-making, carpentry, bread-making, weaving – as part of the school's attempts to trace local traditions. George, the caretaker, exercised his skills in building playground furniture and contributing to features in the grounds (see Mortimore and Mortimore, 1994, for innovations since 1988 in the role and deployment of associate staff). Hot air balloonists, helicopter pilots, illustrators (such as Anthony Browne) padres, circus performers, and many others have demonstrated their skills and shared their experiences at Coombes. A school document stresses the need to work together:

> We offer children opportunities to meet, observe, and converse with a wide range of adult models. Every person who crosses the threshold of the school is valued as a teacher. Our professional role is to provide a laboratory staffed by people with a range of experiences and expertise. Local craftspeople, professionals, parents and visitors work alongside teachers.

Self-realization

Whereas self-defence is aligned against perceived threat, and self-reinforcement strengthens existing tendencies, self-realization is about coming to fruition. Though I have divided these three aspects of self-determination here for analytic purposes, there are elements of all of them in many of the examples given. So we have already some illustrations of self-realization, for example at the 'resistance' school, where teachers were defending the realized self. But perhaps the best example is in 'appropriation' at Coombes. At the centre of the Coombes achievement is the charismatic agent, the head, who had the vision, faith, values and beliefs to launch the project, the resolve and patience to sustain and develop it, and the personal skills and judgement in surrounding herself with and inspiring like-minded people to contribute to the enterprise. Fullan and Hargreaves (1992) recall Tom's (1984) view of teaching as a moral business, firstly in helping to shape the generations of the future, and secondly in the discretionary judgements teachers make in classrooms. 'Because teaching is a moral craft, it has purpose for those who do it. There are things that teachers value, that they want to achieve through their teaching' (Fullan and Hargreaves, 1992, p. 29). Too often, teachers' purposes are overlooked by reformers and they do not have a voice. At Coombes, there is a strong sense of purpose. At heart, there is a clear conviction about the central importance of environmental issues, a love of and deep respect for nature, a concern for the future of the planet. I asked Sue Humphries how she managed so often to get her own way with exterior bureaucratic forces, and she replied: 'Well, I think having a reputation as an eccentric helps.' Part of this 'eccentricity', perhaps, is Sue's ability to challenge the 'givens' of school, which Sarason (1982) feels is one of the most important factors in inducing change. Some of these 'givens' are the inside classroom as the main context of teaching and learning, the sharp division between inside and outside school, the playground as a plain hard surface, the National Curriculum, and assessment. At Coombes, Sue retains her independent vision. Certain aspects of the National Curriculum are welcome, others are an irritant, but, by and large, it is subsumed within their grand design. Sue makes capital in other ways. To run and develop such a project requires funds and services from others:

> We need money for repairs. For example, a pond cracked in last year's drought and will cost about £600 to put right . . . We also need money for ephemeral things, like feeding sheep, paying vets' bills, giving expenses to people like hot air balloonists . . . You can't actually see what they've left you with. They are the intangibles, but they are the things that give a quality and a certain edge to this kind of education, if it's what you believe in.

It also means entrepreneurial skills, powers of persuasion and considerable determination. To get opera singers, under-belly horse riders, internationally acclaimed writers, helicopter pilots, parachutists, etc., to the school, Sue feels rests on

> the way you present the case, the tone of the approach, and the doggedness of the approach . . . and, of course, the way a group decides how it spends its money.

A colleague reported that 'when a small circus visited the area, Sue was absolutely determined we were going to get this camel into the playground . . . and she did it'. Why was it so important?

> It was to do with the Epiphany and the journey of the wise men, and it was really something that just put that special memory into all the talk that had gone on . . . Children are talked at by teachers for hundreds of hours, and so much of it must sail directly over them.

In many ways, Coombes is an expression of Sue's self. I have argued elsewhere that a teacher can both find a means of expression and give expression to a curriculum area (Woods, 1990a). Despite the constraints and opposing pressures, teachers can engage with the curriculum at a deep personal level. Sue shows that this can apply to the school itself. As with many of the teachers interviewed by Nias (1989), it provides opportunities to 'be yourself' and to 'be whole' and to 'be natural'. As a major, long-term project, with many branches and operating at a number of levels, Coombes represents a considerable part of a life's work. Holistic in its aims, it has been holistic in its claims on the time, energies, creativity, patience, perseverance and enthusiasm of its sponsors. This includes the staff as a whole, and the body of parents. Sue's colleagues

> aren't just in this for money. They're in it for a certain amount of personal power, and that personal power has to be released. They have to be part of the decision-making. They've got to see their personality reflected in the overall school pattern.

As for parents, Sue makes the same point about 'ownership' as she does for pupils and staff. They make an enormous contribution to the school, but

> there are always letters that come back here that are saying 'Thank you for letting us be part of the school. We had a lovely time.' It's them actually that should be thanked for doing it!

Sue feels that they are making 'some sort of recompense for what school didn't give them when they were children', and that they derive considerable self-gratification from being so highly valued.

Self-renewal

Self-realization is never complete, but needs what Sue calls 'self-renewal'. Just as the self has a long history with deep biographical roots, so it has a constant dynamic which drives it on.

> The fact that we are deeply immersed in the work and energized by it is going to be the most significant thing, because if you're not, you become terribly tense and stressed. You avoid that with the constant novelty. [She mentioned things that were happening next term for the first time around the theme of 'the performing arts': an early harp recital, a brass quintet, street buskers . . . .] Most teachers want to go back to teaching because they actually want to finish off their own education. This is a calling for us, but actually it's from needs which were never met when we were at school. You have this great hunger to continue to learn. If the teachers don't get satisfied, the children don't get the buzz out of it.

New themes, or new ways of approaching the same themes, was a deliberate policy. They believed in

> first-class experiences for adults and children, so that they can resonate with those experiences and be energized next day.

A concert, for example, provided

valuable reflective time . . . a chance to reorganize their thinking, to be refreshed, and up-and-running the next day.

It might take you away from a task, but 'you get back to it with renewed vigour'. Sue 'believed passionately in the ability of certain experiences to regenerate everyone', 'reflective nuggets' she called them, which were

even more important now than formerly because of the mechanistic approaches induced by current developments.

Self-renewal was a major factor behind Peter's retirement. With his experiences of marginality, he needed disalienating experiences from time to time to retain realistic sight of his preferred side of the margins, and to reaffirm his perception of the substantial self. Even more than this, however, he felt that that self had not yet been fully realized, and still had great potential. Peter was fully committed to the integrity of the self. However, the strategies that he had developed over the years to protect that integrity were no longer sufficient. Retirement was a catalyst not only to save the self, but also to provide it with a springboard to new endeavours.

I hope my retirement is not perceived as someone abandoning ship. Rather, it's transferring from one ship to another ship that's going rather more in the direction that I want to go.

He pointed out that the initiative for his ideas about education originated from a time of working in isolation, when he took time out from teaching at a low point during his early career to 'wander around Greece for six months'. He has now

reached the point where I need to isolate myself to re-engender or renew those lines of development, and to pick up the threads which I have had to let drop, and really take off from there.

Retirement, therefore, is a strategy to save and to promote the self. In those terms it is less radical than it may appear, since it is an act entirely consistent with his holistic philosophy. It is expansive and forward-looking, rather than traumatic and retreatist. In terms of self, Peter had, rather ironically, an alienated entry into teaching, but is making an empowered exit. For some, retirement might mean 'putting their feet up, having a rest, taking life easy'. But for Peter, retirement offered reinvigoration and rebirth through 'restoration', 'continuity', and an 'end of marginality'.

Restoration

Teaching is being restructured in a way that stifles your ability to care for and stimulate your students and to make use of your own skills and experience, but also prevents you from attending to

> yourself . . . To be able to do your job you must give to yourself, and
> you are prevented from doing that. So you mustn't . . . see leaving
> school as being driven out . . . but an act of valuing those qualities
> which have made you such a brilliant teacher who can still give so
> much to other things (Anon. 1993).

This is how one teacher was advised by his daughter. Peter's position was
not dissimilar. After only a month of retirement, he was feeling 'better
and better both physically and mentally'. As the days went by, with the
unburdening of responsibility, not only did he feel less tired (when it
came to the evening he could now continue jobs involving deep thought
processes and remain awake), but also his mind was a lot clearer. This
was a 'wonderful aspect of retirement'. He had been overweight while
teaching, but already was back at his optimum weight, and thus much
better equipped for the things he now wanted to do. He and his wife had
taken up swimming again, going to early morning sessions and taking
lessons, and feeling 'much fresher and fitter'.

Even more significant, perhaps, was his emotional state, so under siege
during his final years of headship (see Revell, 1993, for the affective
nature of primary headship). Asked if he would miss anything in teaching, he replied:

> I must be honest. So far, I have experienced so much relief at the
> unburdening of the pressures, and the . . . *ecstasy* of being able to be in
> a position to broaden the area of my research . . . those two things are
> so wonderful and so important that they completely outshine any of
> the things I might miss in teaching, especially the last four to five years.

If there was one thing he would miss, it was the special contact he had
had with groups of children from time to time, such as had developed in
the Rushavenn project. However,

> because of the reduction of staff, the administrative pressures, and
> the doubling of responsibility (which is not an exaggeration – you
> were required to do two jobs simultaneously) . . . this so eroded
> your physical and mental powers. It's not just age. If I felt as I do
> now and the National Curriculum were not there, I could do Rus-
> havenn again. I feel now as I did then – fresh, alert, physically able.
> That's a wonderful asset to me, and by comparison, anything else I
> might miss pales into insignificance.

Further testimony to this came from some supply teaching Peter had
already undertaken at the request of some headteacher colleagues. He
commented:

> I can honestly say that going into these schools has been a real
> pleasure and I have not enjoyed teaching so much for many a year.

He acknowledged that he did not have the responsibility of a full-time class teacher, but felt his enjoyment was not unconnected with his 'increasing feelings of dissatisfaction as a headteacher'. Above all, it was the close contact with children that he cherished, which had almost dried up when he was in post. Here, then, somewhat unexpectedly, was some restoration of what was, for him, the essence of teaching, and which also contributed to continuity.

Continuity

Ironically in some ways, retirement offered Peter a more meaningful continuity – with his childhood, with the world beyond school, and of endeavour in valued activities.

Continuity with childhood

All his life Peter had tried not to lose contact with his childhood. The travels that he and his wife were planning were

> all part and parcel of taking a broader look at education as I see it, and to discover more about myself, and get a greater understanding of childhood and the part it plays in one's organizing development.

High on his list of priorities was the completion of the autobiography of his childhood, with the emphasis on the educative aspects. The intervening years had given him the experience and knowledge to understand it better. With time now to research and write he could make a decent job of it, and produce something worthwhile, perhaps, for the literary and/or educational world. His main motivation, however, was 'an inner need . . . a very personal thing'. The quest was the achievement of a more complete picture of the self. Peter described his life as like

> sitting down to undertake a limitless jigsaw. All the time you are filling in the pieces . . . You don't know what the final picture is, you don't have a lid. As you fill in the pieces, you realize it's not a traditional jigsaw scene, but of yourself, and every extra bit you fill in adds something to that image. You can have all the mirrors in the world, but the image you get never gives you a complete picture of the self, but the 'jigsaw of life' that you can work on over a long period gives you a more complete picture.

Peter's childhood also figured prominently in the other two aspects of continuity, discussed below.

The world beyond

Peter employed his favourite device of imagery to explain the extension of vision that was now offered him, drawing again on childhood memories. In his teens, there used to be a precious half-hour following his homework, before it grew dark, when he would go into the adjacent recreation ground to search in the roofs of the stands for birds' nests. The ground was surrounded by a concrete wall. There were exciting things within, like the discovery of a new nest, but from the top of the stand you could see over the concrete wall to the world beyond and the promise of even more exciting things. So with his teaching career. There were exciting things from time to time – like Rushavenn – but on the whole it was constrained, with little opportunity to explore the exciting world beyond.

As a child, he had gone off at weekends on his bicycle into this world – the countryside – and this image had stayed with him. His retirement was like

> a prolonged weekend of his childhood, not a period of relaxation, but a reaching out into the wider world, not retreating from what one was doing in the week, but extending outwards from that and looking at the same kinds of problem but in a much wider context.

Continuity of endeavour

One of the things retirement gives you that education does not is

> continuity of endeavour in those areas that particularly interest you. These may not be an important part of your work in education in the more limited way as defined by the LEA or government.

In addition to his autobiography, Peter has always had a great interest in the classical world and in archaeology. It was an important part of his early life, and he came to favour the Greek holistic view of the person. From time to time he had done some exciting work, for example on the development of late Belgic and early Romano-British kilns, which was published in *Britannia*. He has resumed collecting ancient coins, and has uncovered his previous collection. He was resuming research broken off years ago. One line of enquiry was to involve visiting classical sites in Syria, Jordan and Israel, where he hoped to work on some archaeological sites, and fill in more 'pieces of the jigsaw'. His new fitness made him much better equipped for travel, and for 'scrambling around archaeological sites'. He would aim to publish his results. In a way, this is but an extension of his childhood activities at the Roman fort.

Peter later sent me an account of his visit to the Middle East, which included sites of ancient monuments at Petra and Palmyra. He comments:

> As I stood looking up at the slightly weather-worn, but nonetheless impressive façade of the Treasury at Petra, which, on that site, is only matched in concept and execution by the Deir or Monastery, my mind slipped back to my recent early-morning experiences at Palmyra and over a decade ago at the Craters of the Moon National

Monument in Idaho [see Chapter 6]. At Craters of the Moon I had chanced upon a bluebird amongst an arid and hostile landscape. Although I was only able to watch it for a few minutes, that fleeting encounter was sufficient to help me to understand that some kind of transient flowering was possible even in the most unpromising and uncompromising environment. This experience was soon to take its place in that parcel of special, and mostly unexpected, occurrences which can help fashion the bastions of a lasting philosophy of life. But Petra and Palmyra were different. At both of these sites, not only had something impressive been created in the face of enormous odds, but there was an over-riding sense of permanence against which the twin destroyers, Time and Climate, had not prevailed and which my earlier bluebird had not conveyed. Here was added a new dimension to my thinking and philosophy joining the earlier experience with the delicate thread of continuity.

An end of marginality

In some ways, Peter's sense of marginality continues. As a child he had frequented the countryside, where he found more value and meaning than in what he experienced as the impersonal, authoritarian, constricting, oppressive and unnatural world of school. He is doing the same now. He feels disaffected with current educational policies. His best years in teaching were during the 1960s and 1970s – the heyday of the Plowden era – presenting periods of 'flowering and opportunity that I wouldn't have missed for the world'. The constraints were bearable then, necessary even, but since 1988 they had come to predominate. He also feels that he is pursuing a 'minority course of action', so there is a sense in which he feels marginalized from society. But from the point of view of self, he has become demarginalized. Retirement offers him rejuvenation, a return to the romanticism and the basic values of his youth (on this, see P.J. Woods, 1993; also Jackson, 1992), and, with the experience of a lifetime's teaching, the best hope yet of realizing them. Looking back on his childhood, marginality offered him both pain and pleasure. At school he had experienced the pain of alienation and degradation; but in his experience of the wider world, he had also felt pleasure and ecstasy, strength, power and control, fulfilment and holism. For most of his career he had held the two sides in balance, but since 1988 this had become increasingly difficult. Education was no longer the world of William Walsh and Jim Abraham, but was regressing into that of Reggie and Lenny Major. Now, however, he had more personal resources at his disposal, material as well as knowledge and experience, and was able to select a path that offered to maximize the positive side of marginality. For the first time in his life, he was offered the prospect of becoming whole, of making significant advances with the jigsaw, of discovering some of the innermost secrets of the substantial self.

The changes have been cathartic for some teachers' sense of self. They have raised basic questions of who they are, what they believe in, what aims they hold in life, and how they are going to achieve them. They have induced 'critical career phases' (Sikes *et al.*, 1985) and what Denzin (1989) calls a 'major epiphany' in their lives: 'In these existentially problematic moments, human character is revealed, and human lives are shaped, sometimes irrevocably' (Denzin, 1989, p. 128). It has opened up reflection on the 'I' component of the self (the individual, creative part that induces change), when the 'Me' (as others are perceived to see us) is the part more usually contemplated (Nias, 1989). Teachers' investment of substantial self in teaching has been challenged, as has their commitment to certain values, to their view of knowledge, to pupils, to teaching. Some teachers, no doubt, have experienced a 'spoliation' of self, a deprivation of opportunity and meaningful work (see, for example, Casey, 1992). The teachers featuring in this book, however, are emerging stronger, from the point of view of knowledge of self, than when they entered the 'epiphany'. This may be reassuring for them and for others. Whether it is sufficient to counter-balance other forces at work in the educational system, or to effect change in that system, is another matter.

Epilogue

In Chapter 2, I noted that there 'are dangers in resistance. It is not an easy route to follow . . . and makes heavy demands on physical, mental and emotional reserves'. As this book was on the point of going to press, I heard that Dave, the head of Ensel (Chapter 2), was applying for early retirement on the grounds of ill health. He described to me the factors behind his 'burn-out' – for that was how he described it – causing him extreme frustration and deep anxiety. They were very similar to those recounted by Peter in Chapter 6: quantity driving out quality; the frustration of 'getting a lot done with the minimum amount of reflection when reflection is the greatest need'; writing reports and policy statements which you know need more thought than you are giving them; decisions having to be made in a hurry. Two years previously, Dave, thinking long-term, had initiated the research that took me into his school. But gradually and relentlessly since then

> [the] increasing pressures are creating a shout for help which is not necessarily directed towards research, but towards 'how are you going to help me with today's situation?', because it's survival and 'how are we going to overcome that particular problem?' . . .

As for the headteacher role, it

> has changed so much that I was beginning to feel a dinosaur . . . The type of thing I was having to do in terms of administration was taking me away from some of the ideals that I got into the job for. I felt that the kind of person they were looking for was somebody completely different. I was not the kind of headteacher that they needed or wanted.`

It was not only the change to more financial administration, which he saw as 'clearly important', but also the diminishing contact with the children, and the pressures for a new style of management, for heads 'who will actually manage the hierarchical decision-making process that will operate within a very, very strict management structure'. Thus, as with Peter, he found the transition from one role model of headteacher to the other traumatic. As Strauss (1962, p. 76) points out, 'personal stress can arise if motivations are inappropriate for further passages'.

Above all, in the end, the resistance structures discussed in Chapter 2, strong in discourse, were, like the appropriation at Coombes (Chapter 3), inevitably precarious. Strauss (1962, p. 77) asserts that 'when organizations are expanding, forming, disintegrating, or in any way changing radically, the personal lives of their members are rendered more tortuous and uncertain and at the same time more dangerous and more exciting'. We saw some of the excitement in earlier chapters. Dave's enforced retirement brings home the dangers. Inescapably, the danger and uncertainty are increased when the system is promoting a change you wish to resist. As Dave pointed out:

> Where you're trying to transform national orders to actually fit the needs of your pupils . . . in the context of a single school that's a very fragile process, and one that can perhaps be knocked down very easily.

Where the self is invested heavily in the situation, the fragility in the latter is readily transferred to the former. In such situations, the self also can be 'knocked down very easily'. In truth, I should not have been so surprised. In England and Wales, 5549 teachers under the age of 60 retired on grounds of ill health in 1993–4, compared with 2551 in 1987–8, the year before the National Curriculum was introduced (MacLeod and Meikle, 1994). Peter had the option of a legitimized alternative route within the teacher career structure. Dave did not. His only option was to change himself, or to construct a 'façade' (Hargreaves, 1972, p. 20). However, as I have argued elsewhere (Woods, 1990a, p. 185), for some teachers,

> redefinition or adaptation for some reason or another, is difficult, painful, or impossible. Among these are those teachers who are

highly committed, vocationally oriented and 'caring', for there is no
escape route open to them. They will not weaken their commitment.
There is nothing left to give way but themselves. The best teachers,
arguably, are the most vulnerable.

Among these I would include 'creative' teachers. It is not surprising, in
the end, to find them both resourceful and susceptible, strong-minded but
sensitive, ebullient but, at times, despondent. I had expected this book to
have a defiant and triumphant ring, celebrating some teachers' success in
sustaining their selves through a challenging period, and offering encouragement to others. I hope it does do that. But Dave's case reminds us of
the fine line that creative teachers tread, how near to the edge some of
them are, and how their finest aspirations can be destroyed despite all the
resolve, patience, commitment and strength one can muster. Self-
determination takes its toll and has its limits. The self's defences can be
penetrated. It can be weakened as well as reinforced, ruined as well as
renewed.

I am reluctant, however, to let intensification have the final word.
Clearly it cannot be discounted. But the book's message is still an optimistic one, in terms of the principles for which these teachers stand, the
degree for manoeuvre that is there between policy-making and implementation, teachers' undoubted successes, and the strength of their resolve. If it is a high-risk strategy, and there have been, and will be more,
losses, depending on the various different factors at play in different
situations, even then, we have to ask how permanent these losses are, or
whether such teachers seek to make their voices heard in other situations,
perhaps through research, writing, teaching in some other form, or as
'critical others'. Peter feels reinvigorated by retirement. Perhaps, too,
Dave will find new opportunities. The future depends to a large extent,
however, on a new generation of teachers, trained in the National Curriculum, but remembering the principles that others have fought for, and no
less creative and self-determined.

References

Acker, S. (1990) 'Teachers' culture in an English primary school: continuity and change', *British Journal of Sociology of Education*, 11, 3, pp. 257–273.

Adams, E. (1990) *Learning through Landscapes: A report on the use, design, management and development of school grounds*, Winchester, Learning through Landscapes Trust.

Alexander, R.J. (1984) *Primary Teaching*, London, Holt, Rinehart and Winston.

Alexander, R.J. (1992) *Policy and Practice in Primary Education*, London, Routledge.

Alexander, R.J., Rose, J. and Woodhead, C. (1992) *Curriculum Organisation and Classroom Practice in Primary Schools: A discussion paper*, London, HMSO.

Anon. (1993) 'Dear Dad, no one can fight forever', *Times Educational Supplement*, 17 September, p. 2

Aoki, T.T. (1983) 'Experiencing ethnicity as a Japanese Canadian teacher: Reflections on a personal curriculum', *Curriculum Inquiry*, 13, 3. pp. 321–335.

Apple, M.W. (1986) *Teachers and Texts: A political economy of class and gender relations in education*, New York, Routledge & Kegan Paul.

Apple, M.W. (1988) 'Work, class and teaching' in J. Ozga, (ed.), *Schoolwork: Approaches to the labour process of teaching*, Milton Keynes, Open University Press.

Apple, M.W. and Jungck, S. (1992) 'You don't have to be a teacher to teach this unit: teaching, technology and control in the curriculum', in Hargreaves, A. and Fullan, M. (eds.) *Understanding Teacher Development*, London, Cassell.

Armstrong, H.E. (1898) 'The heuristic method of teaching or the art of making children discover things for themselves; a chapter in the history of English schools', reprinted in Brock, W.H. (ed.), *H.E. Armstrong and the Teaching of Science*, Cambridge, Cambridge University Press, 1973.

Ashley, M. (1993) 'Tarmacadam classrooms', *Times Educational Supplement*, 19 March, p. 5.

Aspinwall, K. (1985) 'A biographical approach to the professional development of teachers', MEd thesis, University of Sheffield.

Atkinson, P. and Delamont, S. (1977) 'Mock-ups and cock-ups: The stage-management of guided discovery instruction' in P. Woods, and M. Hammersley, (eds), *School Experience*, London, Croom Helm.

Avann, P. (1983) 'Information skills teaching in primary schools: An investigation', MEd thesis, University of Loughborough.

Bage, G. (1993) 'History at KS1 and KS2: Questions of teaching, planning, assessment and progression', *The Curriculum Journal*, 4, 2, pp. 269–282.

Ball, D. (1972) 'Self and identity in the context of deviance: The case of criminal abortion' in R.A. Scott, and J.D. Douglas, (eds), *Theoretical Perspectives on Deviance*, New York, Basic Books.

Ball, S.J. (1981) *Beachside Comprehensive*, Cambridge, Cambridge University Press.

Ball, S.J. (1982) 'Competition and conflict in the teaching of English: A socio-historical analysis', *Journal of Curriculum Studies*, 14, 1, pp. 1–28.

Ball, S.J. (1990) *Politics and Policy Making in Education*, London, Routledge.

Ball, S.J. (1993) 'Education markets, choice and social class: The market as a class strategy in the UK and the USA', *British Journal of Sociology of Education*, 14, 1, pp. 3–19.

Ball, S.J. and Bowe, R. (1992) 'Subject departments and the "implementation" of National Curriculum policy: An overview of the issues', *Journal of Curriculum Studies*, 24, 2, pp. 97–115.

Barrett, J. (1988) 'Topic as a way of working' in C.S. Tann, *Developing Topic Work in the Primary School*, Lewes, Falmer Press.

Becker, H.S. (1963) *Outsiders: Studies in the sociology of deviance*, Chicago, Free Press.

Becker, H.S. (1964) 'Personal change in adult life', *Sociometry*, 27, 1, pp. 40–53.

Bennett, D.J. and Bennett, J.D. (1970) 'Making the scene' in G. Stone, and H. Farberman, (eds.), *Social Psychology through Symbolic Interaction*, Gini-Blaisdale, Waltham, Mass.

Bennett, N. (1976) *Teaching Styles and Pupil Progress*, London, Open Books.

Bennett, N. (1987) 'The search for the effective primary school teacher' in S. Delamont, (ed.), *The Primary School Teacher*, Lewes, Falmer Press.

Berger, P.L. (1963) *Invitation to Sociology*, New York, Doubleday.

Berger, P.L. (1971) *A Rumour of Angels*, Harmondsworth, Penguin.

Berger, P.L., Berger, B. and Kellner, H. (1973) *The Homeless Mind*, Harmondsworth, Penguin.

Berlak, A. and Berlak, H. (1981) *The Dilemmas of Schooling*, London, Methuen.

Bernstein, B. (1975), *Class, Codes and Control, Vol. 3: towards a theory of educational transmissions*, London, Routledge & Kegan Paul.

Blackie, P. (1980) 'Not quite proper' in S. Reedy, and M. Woodhead, (eds), *Family, Work and Education*, London, Hodder & Stoughton.

Blatchford, P. (1989) *Playtime in the Primary School: Problems and improvements*, Windsor, NFER–Nelson.

Blatchford, P., Creeser, R. and Mooney, A. (1990) 'Playground games and playtime: The children's view', *Educational Research*, 32, 3.

Blauner, R. (1964) *Alienation and Freedom*, Chicago, University of Chicago Press.

Bloome, D. and Willett, J. (1991) 'Towards a micropolitics of classroom interaction' in J. Blase, (ed.) *The Politics of Life in Schools*, London, Sage.

Bolton, E. (1993) 'Perspectives on the National Curriculum' in P. O'Hear, and J. White, (eds), *Assessing the National Curriculum*, London, Paul Chapman.

Bourdieu, P. (1971) 'Systems of education and systems of thought' in M.F.D. Young, (ed.), *Knowledge and Control*, London, Collier-Macmillan.

Bourdieu, P. and Passeron, J.C. (1977) *Reproduction in Education, Society and Culture*, London, Sage.

Brighouse, T. (1994) 'Magicians of the inner city', TES/Greenwich Lecture, *Times Educational Supplement*, 22 April, Section 2, pp. 1–2.

Bruner, J.S. (1983) *Child's Talk*, London, Oxford University Press.

Bruner, J.S. (1986) *Actual Minds, Possible Worlds*, Cambridge, Mass., Harvard University Press.

Burton, L. and Weiner, G. (1993) 'From rhetoric to reality: Strategies for developing a social justice approach to educational decision-making' in I. Siraj-Blatchford, (ed.), *'Race', Gender and the Education of Teachers*, Buckingham, Open University Press, pp. 137–153.

Butt, R.L. and Raymond, D. (1990) 'Studying the nature and development of teachers' knowledge using collaborative autobiography', *International Journal of Educational Research*, 13, 4, pp. 403–449.

Campbell, R. (1992) *Reading Real Books*, Buckingham, Open University Press.

Campbell, R.J. (1993) 'The National Curriculum in primary schools: A dream at conception, a nightmare at delivery' in C. Chitty and B. Simon, *Education Answers Back: Critical responses to government policy*. London, Lawrence and Wishart.

Campbell, R.J., Evans, L., St. J. Neill, S.R. and Packwood, A. (1991a) *Workloads, Achievements and Stress: Two follow-up studies of teacher time in Key Stage 1*, Policy Analysis Unit, Department of Education, University of Warwick.

Campbell, R.J., Evans, L., St. J. Neill, S.R. and Packwood, A. (1991b) 'The use and management of infant teachers' time – some policy issues', paper presented at *Policy Analysis Unit Seminar*, Warwick, November.

Campbell, R.J. and St. J. Neill, S. (1990) *Thirteen Hundred and Thirty Days*, final report of a pilot study of teacher time in Key Stage 1, commissioned by the Assistant Masters and Mistresses Association.

Casey, K. (1992) 'Why do progressive women activists leave teaching? Theory, methodology and politics in life-history research' in I.F. Goodson, (ed.), *Studying Teachers' Lives*, Routledge, London.

Cavan, R.S. (1962) 'Self and role in adjustment during old age' in A.M. Rose, (ed.), *Human Behaviour and Social Processes: An interactionist approach*, London, Routledge & Kegan Paul.

Central Advisory Council for Education in England (1967) *Children and their Primary Schools* (Plowden Report), London, HMSO.

Clandinin, D.J. (1985) 'Personal practical knowledge: A study of teachers' classroom images', *Curriculum Inquiry*, 15, 4, pp. 361–385.

Collingwood, R.G. (1966) 'Expressing one's emotions' in E.W. Eisner and D.W. Ecker, (eds), *Readings in Art Education*, Lexington, Mass., Xerox College Publishing.

Cooley, C.H. (1902) *Human Nature and the Social Order*, New York, Charles Scribner's Sons.

182 *Creative teachers in primary schools*

Cooper, H. (1992a) *Studies in Primary Education: The teaching of history*, London, David Fulton Publishers.

Cooper, H. (1992b) 'Young children's thinking in history', *Teaching History*, October, pp. 8–31.

Corrigan, P. (1989) 'In/forming schooling' in D. Livingstone, (eds), *Critical Pedagogy and Cultural Power*, London, Macmillan.

Coulson, A.A. (1976) 'The role of the primary head' in R.S. Peters, (ed.), *The Role of the Head*, London, Routledge & Kegan Paul.

Cox, B. (1993) 'The right is wrong on English teaching', Times/Channel 4 lecture, reprinted in *The Times*, 1 March, p. 10.

Crawford, K. and Rogers, G. (1992) 'Delivering the primary history curriculum', *Teaching History*, October, pp. 22–25.

Croll, P. and Abbott, D. (1993) 'Whole school change and the National Curriculum: Headteachers' perspectives', paper presented as part of the Symposium on *The Changing English Primary School*, British Educational Research Association Conference, Liverpool, September.

Cusack, I. (1993) 'Looking back in anger, aged 28', *Times Educational Supplement*, 8 January.

Dadds, M. (1992) 'Monty Python and the three wise men', *Cambridge Journal of Education*, 22, 2, pp. 129–141.

Dale, I.R. (1972) *The Culture of the School*, Unit 4 of E282, *School and Society*, Milton Keynes, Open University Press.

Day, C. (1991) 'Roles and relationships in qualitative research on teachers' thinking: A reconsideration', *Teaching and Teacher Education*, 7, 5/6, pp. 537–547.

Day, C. (1993) 'Reflection: A necessary but not sufficient condition for professional development', *British Educational Research Journal*, 19, 1, pp. 83–93.

Dearing, R. (1994) *Review of the National Curriculum: Final Report*, London, School Curriculum and Assessment Authority (SCAA) Publications.

Delamont, S. (1992) *Fieldwork in Educational Settings: Methods, pitfalls and perspectives*, London, Falmer Press.

Densmore, K. (1987) 'Professionalism, proletarianisation and teachers' work' in T. Popkewitz, (ed.), *Critical Studies in Teacher Education*, Lewes, Falmer Press.

Denzin, N. (1989) *Interpretive Interactionism*, London, Sage.

Donaldson, M. (1978) *Children's Minds*, London, Fontana.

Drummond, M.J. (1991) 'The child and the primary curriculum – from policy to practice', *The Curriculum Journal*, 2, 2, pp. 115–24.

Edwards, A.D. and Furlong, V.J. (1978) *The Language of Teaching*, London, Heinemann.

Edwards, D. and Mercer, N. (1987) *Common Knowledge: The development of understanding in the classroom*, London, Methuen.

Egan, K. (1992) *Imagination in Teaching and Learning: Ages 8–15*, London, Routledge.

Eggleston, S.J. (1992) *The Challenge for Teachers*, London, Cassell.

Elbaz, F. (1990) 'Knowledge and discourse: The evolution of research on teacher thinking' in C. Day, M. Pope, and P. Denicolo, (eds), *Insight Into Teachers' Thinking and Practice*, Basingstoke, Falmer Press.

Elliott, J. (1991) *Action Research for Educational Change,* Buckingham, Open University Press.

Foucault, M. (1980) *Power/Knowledge: Selected interviews and other writings,* edited by C. Gordon, New York, Pantheon.

Freire, P. (1970) *Pedagogy of the Oppressed,* New York, Herder and Herder.

Freund, J. (1968) *The Sociology of Max Weber,* London, Alan Lane, The Penguin Press.

Fryer, M. and Collings, J.A. (1993) 'Teachers' views about creativity', *British Journal of Educational Psychology,* 61, pp. 207–219.

Fullan, M.G. (1992) *Successful School Improvement,* Buckingham, Open University Press.

Fullan, M. and Hargreaves, A. (1992) *What's Worth Fighting for in Your School?,* Buckingham, Open University Press.

Galton, M. (1987) 'An ORACLE chronicle: A decade of classroom research' in S. Delamont, (ed.), *The Primary School Teacher,* Lewes, Falmer Press.

Galton, M. (1989) *Teaching in the Primary School,* London, David Fulton Publishers.

Galton, M. and Willcocks, J. (1983) *Moving from the Primary Classroom,* London, Routledge & Kegan Paul.

Galton, M. and Williamson, J. (1992) *Group Work in the Primary Classroom,* London, Routledge.

Galton, M., Simon, B. and Croll, P. (1980) *Inside the Primary Classroom,* London, Routledge & Kegan Paul.

Garfinkel, H. (1956) 'Conditions of successful degradation ceremonies', *American Journal of Sociology,* 61, pp. 420–424.

Geertz, C. (1973) 'Thick description: Toward an interpretive theory of culture' in C. Geertz, (ed.), *The Interpretation of Cultures: Selected essays by Clifford Geertz,* New York, Basic Books.

Gitlin, A. D. (1990) 'Education research, voice and school change', *Harvard Educational Review,* 60, 4, pp. 443–66.

Gitlin, A. (1992) *Teachers' Voices for School Change: An introduction to educative research,* London, Routledge.

Gitlin, A., Siegel, M. and Boru, K. (1989) 'The politics of method: From leftist ethnography to educative research', *International Journal of Qualitative Studies in Education,* 2,3, pp. 237–253.

Glaser, B.G. and Strauss, A.L. (1967) *The Discovery of Grounded Theory,* London, Weidenfeld and Nicolson.

Goffman, E. (1968) *Asylums,* Harmondsworth, Penguin.

Golby, M. (1989) 'Teachers and their research' in W. Carr, (ed.), *Quality in Teaching,* Lewes, Falmer Press, pp. 163–172.

Goodson, I. (1983) *School Subjects and Curriculum Change,* London, Croom Helm.

Grugeon, E. (1988) 'Children's oral culture: A transitional experience', in M. MacLure, T. Phillips, and A. Wilkinson, (eds), *Oracy Matters,* Milton Keynes, Open University Press, pp. 159–173.

Grugeon, E. (1993) 'Gender implications of children's playground culture' in P. Woods, and M. Hammersley, (eds), *Gender and Ethnicity in Schools: Ethnographic accounts,* London, Routledge.

Hall, E.T. (1984) *The Dance of Life*, New York, Anchor Press/Doubleday.

Halpin, D. (1990) 'The sociology of education and the National Curriculum', *British Journal of Sociology of Education*, 11, 1, pp. 21–36.

Hardy, J. and Veiler-Porter, C. (1990) 'Race, schooling and the 1988 Education Reform Act' in M. Flude, and M. Hammer, M. (eds), *The Education Reform Act 1988: Its origins and implications*, Lewes, Falmer Press.

Hargreaves, A. (1978) 'Towards a theory of classroom strategies' in L. Barton, and R. Meighan, (eds), *Sociological Interpretations of Schooling and Classrooms*, Driffield, Nafferton Books.

Hargreaves, A. (1984) 'The significance of classroom coping strategies' in A. Hargreaves, and P. Woods, (eds), *Classroom and Staffrooms*, Milton Keynes, Open University Press.

Hargreaves, A. (1988) 'Teaching quality: A sociological analysis', *Journal of Curriculum Studies*, 20, 3, pp. 211–231.

Hargreaves, A. (1989) 'Cultures of teaching' in I. Goodson, and S. Ball, (eds), *Teachers' Lives*, New York, Routledge.

Hargreaves, A. (1990) 'Teachers' work and the politics of time and space', *International Journal of Qualitative Studies in Education*, 3, 4, pp. 303–20.

Hargreaves, A. (1991) 'Contrived collegiality: The micropolitics of teacher collaboration', in J. Blase, (ed.), *The Politics of Life in Schools*, London, Sage.

Hargreaves, A. (1992) 'Time and teachers; work: An analysis of the intensification thesis', *Teachers' College Record*, 94, 1, pp. 87–108.

Hargreaves, A. (1994) *Changing Teachers, Changing Times*, London, Cassell.

Hargreaves, A. and Tucker, E. (1991) 'Teaching and guilt: Exploring the feelings of teaching', *Teaching and Teacher Education*, 7, 5/6, pp. 491–505.

Hargreaves, D.H. (1972) *Interpersonal Relations and Education*, London, Routledge & Kegan Paul.

Hargreaves, D.H. (1991) 'Coherence and manageability: Reflections on the National Curriculum and cross-curricular provision', *The Curriculum Journal*, 2, 1, pp. 33–41.

Hargreaves, D.H., Hester, S.K. and Mellor, F.J. (1975) *Deviance in Classrooms*, London, Routledge & Kegan Paul.

Harries, J. (1994) 'Accountability coming out of our ears', *Times Educational Supplement*, 29 April, Section 2, p. 4.

Haviland, J. (ed.) (1988) *Take Care, Mr Baker!*, London, Fourth Estate.

Heath, S.B. (1982) 'Questioning at home and at school: A comparative study' in G. Spindler, (ed.), *Doing the Ethnography of Schooling*, New York, Holt, Rinehart and Winston.

Heath, S.B. (1993) 'The madness of reading and writing ethnography', *Anthropology and Education Quarterly*, 24, 3, pp. 256–68.

Hellawell, D. (1990) 'Some effects of the national dispute on the relationships between head teachers and school staffs in primary schools', *British Journal of Sociology of Education*, 11, 4, pp. 397–410.

Holmes, U.T. (1973) 'Revivals are un-American: a recalling of America to its pilgrimage', *Anglican Theological Review*, supplementary series, no. 1, pp. 58–75.

Holt, J. (1964) *How Children Fail*, Harmondsworth, Penguin.

Hoyle, E. (1973) 'Strategies of curriculum change' in R. Watkins, (ed.), *In-service Training: Structure and content*, London, Ward Lock.

Hoyle, E. (1980) 'Professionalization and deprofessionalization in education' in E. Hoyle, and J. Megarry, (eds), *World Yearbook of Education 1980: Professional development of teachers*, London, Kogan Page, pp. 42–54.

Hughes, E.C. (1962) 'What other?', in A.M. Rose, (ed.), *Human Behaviour and Social Processes: An interactionist approach*, London, Routledge & Kegan Paul.

Humphries, S. and Rowe, S. (1993a) *The Big Science Book: All about living*, London, Forbes Publications.

Humphries, S. and Rowe, S. (1993b) *The Big Science Book: Materials and forces*, London, Forbes Publications.

Hunter, J., Turner, I., Russell, C., Trew, K. and Curry, C. (1993) 'Mathematics and the real world', *British Educational Research Journal*, 19, 1, pp. 17–26.

Hutchinson, M.M. (1961) *Practical Nature Study in Town Schools*, London, National Froebel Foundation, p. 1.

Inglis, F. (1989) 'Managerialism and morality' in W. Carr, (ed.), *Quality in Teaching: Arguments for a reflective profession*, Lewes, Falmer Press.

Jackson, P.W. (1992) *Untaught Lessons*, New York, Teachers' College Press.

Jarvis, A. (1993) 'Why I'm glad to be going', *Times Educational Supplement*, 20 August.

Jeffrey, R. (1994) The art of primary school teaching, paper presented at CEDAR International Conference, *Changing Educational Structures: Policy and Practice*, University of Warwick, 15–17 April.

King, R.A. (1978) *All Things Bright and Beautiful*, Chichester, Wiley.

Kreisberg, S. (1992), *Transforming Power: Domination, empowerment and education*, Albany, State University of New York Press.

Lacey, C. (1977) *The Socialization of Teachers*, London, Methuen.

Lakoff, G. and Johnston, M. (1980) *Metaphors We Live By*, Chicago, University of Chicago Press.

Larson, S.M. (1980) 'Proletarianisation and educated labour', *Theory and Society*, 9, 1, pp. 131–175.

Lather, P. (1986) 'Research as praxis', *Harvard Educational Review*, 56, 3, pp. 257–277.

Lee, J. (1915) *Play in Education*, London, Macmillan.

Lee, P. (1991) 'Historical knowledge and the National Curriculum' in R. Aldrich, (ed.), *History in the National Curriculum*, London, Kogan Page.

Little, J.W. (1984) 'Seductive images and organizational realities in professional development', *Teachers' College Record*, 86, 1, pp. 84–102.

Lortie, D.C. (1975) *Schoolteacher*, Chicago, University of Chicago Press.

Lovat, T.J. (1992) 'Models of power: Power relations in and over schools' in T.J. Lovat, (ed.), *Sociology for Teachers*, Wentworth Falls, NSW, Social Science Press, pp. 183–189.

Lyman, S.M. and Scott, M.B. (1970) *A Sociology of the Absurd*, Appleton Century Crofts, New York.

McLaren, P. (1986) *Schooling as a Ritual Performance*, London, Routledge & Kegan Paul.

McLaren, P. (1991) 'Field relations and the discourse of the other: Collaboration in our own ruin' in W.B. Shaffir, and R.A. Stebbins, (eds), *Experiencing Fieldwork: An inside view of qualitative research*, London, Sage.

MacLeod, D. and Meikle, J. (1994) 'Education changes "making heads quit"', *The Guardian*, 1 September, p. 6.

Mardle, G. and Walker, M. (1980) 'Strategies and structure: Some critical notes on teacher socialization' in P. Woods, (ed.), *Teacher Strategies*, London, Croom Helm.

Martineau, W.H. (1972) 'A model of the social functions of humour' in J.H. Goldstein, and P.E. McGhee, (eds), *The Psychology of Humour*, New York, Academic Press.

Maw, J. (1993) 'The National Curriculum Council and the whole Curriculum: Reconstruction of a discourse?', *Curriculum Studies*, 1, 1, pp. 55–74.

May, N. and Sigsworth, A. (1987) 'Teacher-outsider partnerships in the observation of classrooms' in R. Murphy, and H. Torrance, (eds), *Evaluating Education: Issues and methods*, London, Harper and Row.

Maybin, J., Mercer, N., and Stierer, B. (1992) 'Scaffolding learning in the classroom', in K. Norman, (ed.), *Thinking Voices: The work of the National Oracy Project*, London, Hodder & Stoughton.

Mead, G.H. (1934) *Mind, Self and Society*, Chicago, University of Chicago Press.

Measor, L. (1984) 'Pupil perceptions of subject status', in S.J. Ball, (ed.), *Defining the Curriculum: Histories and ethnographics of school subjects*, Lewes, Falmer.

Measor, L. and Woods, P. (1984) *Changing Schools: Pupil perspectives on transfer to a comprehensive*, Milton Keynes, Open University Press.

Medley, R. and White, C. (1992) 'Assessing the National Curriculum: Lessons from assessing history', *The Curriculum Journal*, 3, 1, pp. 63–74.

Mortimore, P. and Mortimore, J. (1994) *Managing Associate Staff: Innovation in primary and secondary schools*, London, Paul Chapman.

Murphy, R. and Torrance, H. (eds) (1987) *Evaluating Education: Issues and methods*, London, Paul Chapman.

Muschamp, Y., Pollard, A. and Sharpe, R. (1992) 'Curriculum management in primary schools' *The Curriculum Journal*, 3, 1, pp. 21–39.

Musgrove, F. (1976) 'Marginality, education and the reconstruction of reality', *Journal of Curriculum Studies*, 8, 2, pp. 101–109.

Musgrove, F. (1977) *Margins of the Mind*, London, Methuen.

Musgrove, F. and Taylor, P.H. (1974) *Society and the Teacher's Role*, London, Routledge & Kegan Paul.

Nias, J. (1987) One finger, one thumb: A case study of the deputy head's part in the leadership of a nursery/infant school' in G. Southworth, (ed.), *Readings in Primary School Management*, Lewes, Falmer Press.

Nias, J. (1989) *Primary Teachers Talking: A study of teaching as work*, London, Routledge.

Nias, J. (1991) 'Changing times, changing identities: Grieving for a lost self' in R.G. Burgess, (ed.), *Educational Research and Evaluation*, London, Falmer Press.

Nias, J., Southworth, G. and Yeomans, R. (1989) *Staff Relationships in the Primary School: A study of organizational cultures*, London, Cassell.

Nias, J., Southworth, G. and Campbell, P. (1992) *Whole School Curriculum Development in the Primary School*, Lewes, Falmer Press.

Nisbet, R.A. (1967) *The Sociological Tradition*, London, Heinemann.

Noble, P. (1990) 'Time to rectify past mistakes: The case for investment in primary history', *Teaching History*, 59, April, pp. 33–34.

Noble, P. (1991) Editorial Introduction, *Primary History Today*, Historical Association Occasional Paper No. 2.

Noddings, N. (1986) 'Fidelity in teaching, teacher education, and research for teaching', *Harvard Educational Review*, 56, pp. 496–510.

Norquay, N. (1990) 'Life history research: Memory, schooling and social difference', *Cambridge Journal of Education*, 20, 3, pp. 291–300.

Oldroyd, D. and Tiller, T. (1987) 'Change from within: An account of school-based collaborative action research in an English secondary school', *Journal of Education for Teaching*, 12, 3, pp. 13–27.

Osborn, M. (1993) Changes in teachers' professional perspectives, paper presented as part of Symposium on *The Changing English Primary School*, British Eductional Research Association Conference, Liverpool, September.

Osborn, M. and Broadfoot, P. (1992a) 'The impact of current changes in English primary schools on teacher professionalism', *Teachers College Record*, 94, 1, pp. 138–151.

Osborn, M. and Broadfoot, P. (1992b) 'A lesson in progress? Primary classrooms observed in England and France', *Oxford Review of Education*, 18, 1, pp. 3–16.

Osborn, M., Broadfoot, P., Pollard, A., Croll, P. and Abbott, D. (1994) 'Teachers' professional perspectives: Continuity and change', Paper presented as part of Symposium, *Managing Change in the Primary School*, CEDAR International Conference, University of Warwick, April.

Otty, N. (1972) *Learner-teacher*, Harmondsworth, Penguin.

Paul, B.D. (1953) 'Interviewing techniques and field relations' in A.L. Kroeber, (eds.), *Anthropology Today An Encyclopaedic Inventory*, Chicago, University of Chicago Press.

Penney, D. and Evans, J. (1991) 'From policy to provision: The development and "implementation" of the National Curriculum for physical education', paper presented at the St. Hilda's Conference, Warwick, September.

Phillips, E.M. (1980) 'Cognitive development and design education', *Design Education Research Note 4*, Milton Keynes, Open University.

Phillips, R. (1991) 'National Curriculum history and teacher autonomy: The major challenge', *Teaching History*, October, pp. 21–24.

Pinar, W. (1986) 'Autobiography and the architecture of self', paper presented at American Educational Research Association, San Francisco, April.

Plummer, K. (1983) *Documents of Life*, London, Allen & Unwin.

Pollard, A. (1980) 'Teacher interests and changing situations of survival threat in primary school classrooms' in P. Woods, (ed.), *Teacher Strategies*, London, Croom Helm.

Pollard, A. (1982) 'A model of coping strategies', *British Journal of Sociology of Education*, 3, 1, pp. 19–37.

Pollard, A. (1985) *The Social World of the Primary School*, London, Holt, Rinehart and Winston.

Pollard, A. (1987) 'Primary school teachers and their colleagues', in S. Delamont, (ed.), *The Primary School Teacher*, Lewes, Falmer Press.

Pollard, A. (1991) *Learning in Primary Schools*, London, Cassell.

Pollard, A. (1992) 'Teachers' responses to the reshaping of primary education', in M. Arnot, and L. Barton, L. (eds), *Voicing Concerns*, London, Triangle Books.

Pollard, A. (ed.) (1994) *Look Before You Leap? Research evidence for the curriculum at Key Stage 2*, London, Tyrell Press.

Pollard, A., Broadfoot, P., Croll, P., Osborn, M., and Abbott, D. (1994), *Changing English Primary Schools? The Impact of the Education Reform Act at Key Stage One*, London, Cassell.

Powell, M. and Solity, J. (1990) *Teachers in Control*, London, Routledge.

Qvortrup, J. (1990) 'A voice for children in statistical and social accounting: A plea for children's right to be heard' in A. James, and A. Prout, (eds), *Constructing and Reconstructing Childhood*, Basingstoke, Falmer Press.

Revell, R. (1993) 'Do we not bleed? The affective nature of primary headship', paper presented at *British Educational Research Association Conference*, September, Liverpool.

Richards, C. (1987) 'Primary education in England: An analysis of some recent issues and developments' in S. Delamont, (ed.), *The Primary School Teacher*, Lewes, The Falmer Press.

Riley, J. (1992) *The National Curriculum and the Primary School: Springboard or strait-jacket?*, London, Kogan Page.

Rizvi, F. (1989) 'Bureaucratic rationality and the promise of democratic schooling' in W. Carr, (ed.), *Quality in Teaching: Arguments for a reflective profession*, London, Falmer Press.

Rogers, C. (1983) *Freedom to Learn for the 80s*, New York, MacMillan.

Ross, M. (1978) *The Creative Arts*, London, Heinemann.

Rowe, S. and Humphries, S. (1994) *Playing Around: Activities and exercises for social and cooperative learning*, London, Forbes Publications.

Rudduck, J. (1985) 'The improvement of the art of teaching through research', *Cambridge Journal of Education*, 15, 3, pp. 123–127.

Sarason, S. (1982) *The Culture of the School and the Problem of Change* (rev. edn), Boston, Allyn and Bacon.

Savva, H. (1994) 'Bilingual by rights' in A. Pollard, and J. Bourne, (eds), *Teaching and Learning in the Primary School*, London, Routledge.

Schiller, C. (1979) *Christian Schiller: In his own words*, London, Black.

Schön, D.A. (1983) *The Reflective Practitioner: How professionals think in action*, London, Temple Smith.

Schutz, A. (1964) 'The stranger: An essay in social psychology' in A. Brodersen, (ed.), *Collected Papers, II*, The Hague, Martinus Nijhoff, pp. 91–105.

Scriven, M. (1986) 'Evaluation as a paradigm for educational research' in E.R. House, (1986), *New Directions in Educational Evaluation*, Lewes, Falmer Press.

Sharp, R. and Green, A. (1975) *Education and Social Control: A study in progressive primary education*, London, Routledge & Kegan Paul.

Shipman, M.D. (1975) *The Sociology of the School* (2nd edn), London, Longman.

Sikes, P., Measor, L. and Woods, P. (1985) *Teacher Careers: Crises and continuities*, Lewes, Falmer Press.

Simmonds, G. and Nias, J. (1989) 'Russian dolls: An account of teachers' professional learning' in P. Woods, (ed.), *Working for Teacher Development*, London, Peter Francis.

Siraj-Blatchford, I. (1993) 'Ethnicity and conflict in physical education: A critique of Carroll and Hollinshead's case study', *British Educational Research Journal*, 19, 1, pp. 77–82.

Smyth, J. (1991) *Teachers as Collaborative Learners*, Buckingham, Open University Press.

Southgate, V., Arnold, H. and Johnson, S. (1981) *Extending Beginning Reading*, London, Heinemann.

Spender, D. (1982) *Invisible Women: The schooling scandal*, London, Writers and Readers Publishing Cooperative Society Ltd.

Stanislavski, C. (1972) 'Emotional involvement in acting' in J. Hodgson, (ed.), *The Uses of Drama*, London, Eyre Methuen.

Stebbins, R. (1970) 'The meaning of disorderly behaviour: Teacher definitions of a classroom situation', *Sociology of Education*, 44, 2, pp. 217–236.

Stebbins, R. (1975) *Teachers and Meaning: Definitions of classroom situations*, Leiden, E.W. Brill.

Strauss, A.L. (1962) 'Transformations of identity' in A.M. Rose, (ed.), *Human Behaviour and Social Processes: An interactionist approach*, London, Routledge & Kegan Paul.

Symes, C. (1992) 'The aesthetics of titles and other epitextual devices or, you can't judge a book by its cover', *Journal of Aesthetic Education*, Vol. 26, No. 3, pp. 17–26.

Tann, C.S. (1988) 'The practice of topic work' in C.S. Tann, (ed.), *Developing Topic Work in the Primary School*, Lewes, Falmer Press.

Tizard, B., Blatchford, P., Burke, J., Farqhar, C., and Plewis, I. (1988) *Young Children at School in the Inner City*, Brighton, Lawrence Erlbaum.

Tom, A. (1984) *Teaching as a Moral Craft*, New York, Longman.

Tripp, D.H. (1993) *Critical Incidents in Teaching: Developing Professional Judgement*, London, Routledge.

Troman, G. (1993) 'Whatever is happening to teachers?' *The Redland Papers*, Issue No. 2, Bristol, University of the West of England.

Turner, V.W. (1969) *The Ritual Process*, London, Routledge & Kegan Paul.

Turner, V.W. (1974) *The Ritual Process: Structure and anti-structure*, Harmondsworth, Penguin.

Turner, V.W. (1979) *Process: Performance and pilgrimage*, New Delhi, Concept.

Vass, P. (1993) 'Have I got a witness? A consideration of the use of historical witnesses in the primary classroom', *Teaching History*, October, pp. 19–25.

Vulliamy, G. and Webb, R. (1993) 'Progressive education and the National Curriculum: Findings from a global education research project', *Educational Review*, 45, 1, pp. 21–41.

Vygotsky, L.S. (1962) *Thought and Language*, Cambridge, Mass., MIT Press.

Vygotsky, L.S. (1978) *Mind in Society: The development of higher psychological processes*, Cambridge, Mass., Harvard University Press.

Wallace, M. (1993) 'Discourse of derision: The role of the mass media within the education policy process', *Journal of Education Policy*, 8, 4, pp. 321–337.

Waller, W. (1932) *The Sociology of Teaching*, New York, Wiley.

Walmsley, L. (1935) *Foreigners*, London, Jonathan Cape.

Walsh, W. (1966) *The Use of Imagination: Educational Thought and the Literary Mind*, Harmondsworth, Penguin Books.

Webb, R. (1993) 'The National Curriculum and the changing nature of topic work', *The Curriculum Journal*, 4, 2, pp. 239–252.

Weiner, G. (1989) 'Professional self-knowledge versus social justice: A critical analysis of the teacher-researcher movement', *British Educational Research Journal*, 15, 1, pp. 41–51.

Westbury, I. (1973) 'Conventional classrooms, 'open' classrooms and the technology of teaching', *Journal of Curriculum Studies*, 5, 2, pp. 91–121.

Wheatley, D. (1992) 'Environmental education – an instrument of change?' in G. Hall, (ed.), *Themes and Dimensions of the National Curriculum: Implications for policy and practice*, London, Kogan Page.

Whistler, T. (1988) *Rushavenn Time*, Brixworth, Northamptonshire, Brixworth V.C. Primary School.

White, J. (1993) 'What place for values in the National Curriculum', in P. O'Hear, and J. White, (eds), *Assessing the National Curriculum*, London, Paul Chapman.

White, J.J. (1989) 'The power of politeness in the classroom: Cultural codes that create and constrain knowledge construction', *Journal of Curriculum and Supervision*, 4, 4, pp. 298–321.

Wilcock, M. (1994) 'St. Andrew's Church of England Primary School' in A. Pollard, and J. Bourne, (eds), *Teaching and Learning in the Primary School*, London, Routledge.

Wiles, S. (1985) 'Language and learning in multi-ethnic classrooms: Strategies for supporting bilingual students' in G. Wells, and W. Nicholls, (eds), *Language and Learning: An interactional perspective*, Lewes, Falmer Press.

Winkley, D. (1990) 'A view from a primary school' in T. Brighouse and R. Moon (eds), *Managing the National Curriculum: Some Critical Perspectives*, London, Longman.

Woods, P. (1981) 'Strategies, commitment and identity: Making and breaking the teacher role' in L. Barton, and S. Walker, (eds), *Schools, Teachers and Teaching*, Brighton, Falmer Press.

Woods, P. (1986) *Inside Schools: Ethnography in educational research*, London, Routledge and Kegan Paul.

Woods, P. (1990a) *Teacher Skills and Strategies*, Lewes, Falmer Press.

Woods, P. (1990b) *The Happiest Days? How pupils cope with school*, Lewes, Falmer Press.

Woods, P. (1993a) *Critical Events in Teaching and Learning*, London, Falmer Press.

Woods, P. (1993b) 'Managing marginality: Teacher development through grounded life history', *British Educational Research Journal*, 19, 5, pp. 447–465.

Woods, P. (1994) 'Critical students: Breakthroughs in learning', *International Studies in Sociology of Education*, 4, 2, pp. 123–147.

Woods, P. and Pollard, A. (eds) (1988) *Sociology and Teaching*, London, Croom Helm.

Woods, P.J. (1993) 'Keys to the past – and to the future: the empirical author replies', *British Educational Research Journal*, 19, 5, pp. 475–488.

Young, M.F.D. (ed.) (1971) *Knowledge and Control: New directions for the sociology of education*, London, Collier-Macmillan.

Zajano, N.C. and Edelsbert, C.M. (1993) 'Living and writing the researcher–researched relationship', *International Journal of Qualitative Studies in Education*, 6, 2, pp. 143–157.

Name index

Subject index

ORGANIZING FOR LEARNING IN THE PRIMARY CLASSROOM
A BALANCED APPROACH TO CLASSROOM MANAGEMENT

Janet R. Moyles

What is it that underlies classroom organization, routines, rules, structures and daily occurrences? What are the prime objectives and what influences the decisions of teachers and children? What is it useful for teachers to consider when contemplating the issues of classroom management and organization? What do different practices have to offer?

Organizing for Learning in the Primary Classroom explores the whole range of influences and values which underpin *why* teachers do *what* they do in the classroom context and what these mean to children and others. Janet Moyles examines teaching and learning styles, children's independence and autonomy, coping with children's differences, the physical classroom context and resources, time management and ways of involving others in the day-to-day organization. Practical suggestions are given for considering both the functional and aesthetic aspects of the classroom context. Opportunities are provided for teachers to reflect on their own organization and also consider innovative and flexible ways forward to deal with new and ever increasing demands on their time and sanity!

This book is to be highly recommended for all primary school teachers . . .
(Management in Education)

. . . indispensable to courses in initial teacher education and to providers of inset.
(Child Education)

Janet Moyles brings her long experience of the primary school to *Organizing for Learning in the Primary Classroom* . . . I particularly like the attention she gives to the physical environment, giving lots of advice about arrangements of furniture and the role of the teacher's desk . . .
(Times Educational Supplement)

Contents
Introduction: Polarizations and balance – Teachers and teaching: beliefs and values – The learning environment: organizing the classroom context – The children and their learning needs: balancing individual and whole class approaches – Grouping children for teaching and learning: providing equal opportunities and promoting appropriate behaviour – Time for teaching and learning – Deploying adult help effectively in the classroom: delegation and responsibility – Evaluating classroom organization and management – Conclusion: the primary classroom, a place and a time – References – Index.

208pp   0 335 15659 2 (Paperback)   0 335 15660 6 (Hardback)